Contributions to Finance and Accounting

The book series 'Contributions to Finance and Accounting' features the latest research from research areas like financial management, investment, capital markets, financial institutions, FinTech and financial innovation, accounting methods and standards, reporting, and corporate governance, among others. Books published in this series are primarily monographs and edited volumes that present new research results, both theoretical and empirical, on a clearly defined topic. All books are published in print and digital formats and disseminated globally.

More information about this series at https://link.springer.com/bookseries/16616

Ibrahim Mert

Assessment of Accounting Evaluation Practices

A Research-Based Review of Turkey and Romania

Springer

Ibrahim Mert
Istanbul Aydın University
Istanbul, Turkey

ISSN 2730-6038 ISSN 2730-6046 (electronic)
Contributions to Finance and Accounting
ISBN 978-3-030-98485-4 ISBN 978-3-030-98486-1 (eBook)
https://doi.org/10.1007/978-3-030-98486-1

This Springer imprint is published by the registered company Springer Nature Switzerland AG
The registered company address is: Gewerbestrasse 11, 6330 Cham, Switzerland

About this Book

In the current era of industrial and technological advancement, economic entities require financial stability in businesses. The evaluation of the accounting systems is required to ensure that the accounting practices currently employed are capable enough of not only monitoring and recording the financial events and transactions taking place at a faster pace but also forecasting the futuristic worth of the assets in the current era of digitalization. The evaluation of the accounting systems and frameworks can be varied based on the evaluator's perspective. The international financial organizations and multinational firms have different parameters for evaluation, while the governments are more interested in the variables such as GDPs and per capita income. Therefore, it is necessary to have a common ground established, which can provide methodologies for the examination of the different accounting systems working around the globe. The standards presented by IFRS apply to the simple as well as the complex systems of the financial exchange and are used by the banks and international financial firms around the world. It is also necessary to evaluate the nature and framework of the local accounting systems adopted in countries, and how these systems are complying with IFRS standards while keeping in view the national economic goals.

In this book, a detailed overview of the IFRS standards has been provided, and the concepts of valuation in the context of the standards have been discussed. The book also provides details about the historical context of valuation, and the modern valuation parameters such as intellectual capital have also been explained. The important questions related to accounting such as "What are the goals of accounting?" "To what extent do existing accounting practices and standards address the goals of accounting?" "What can be done to improve the ways in which accounting practices and standards address the goals of accounting?" are critical and broad. However, these questions should be answered comprehensively for the understanding, analysis, and improvement of the accounting methods. The main purpose of the research presented in this book is to analyze the responses of the accounting experts and standards developers about these questions. The accounting systems of Turkey and Romania have been evaluated in light of the survey conducted by 56 investors

(28 from each country). The study performed in this book consists of the application of the answers provided by the investors to the empirical study performed on the accounting system of Turkey and Romania. The study also compares the accounting methods of the companies (historic cost and fair value methods) based on the responses of the investors to the stock pricing and transparency.

In the book, the effects or position of fair value evaluation regime have been discussed during financial crisis periods. How fair value methods trigger the chain of the crises have been analyzed. The experiences on this perspective were revealed to illustrate the situation and its disastrous effects.

The elements of the modern economic systems include the digitalization of the operations, especially the financial operations. The use of information technology in the accounting system has changed the pathways of recording the details of the transactions and monitoring the transfer of the resources as well. The use of data science and artificial intelligence in the field of accounting and finance has resulted in the enhancement of the efficiency of the accounting system. The elements and the framework of the modern accounting system have been discussed to provide insights into the modern practices that are being adopted in the accounting sector. Finally, the results of the studies conducted during research and conclusions that have been drawn from the results have been explained.

Contents

List of Figures

List of Tables

Chapter 1
Introduction

The purposes of evaluating accounting systems can be condensed into the set of goals promoted by a particular evaluator. For example, according to the European Central Bank (2006), the purpose of evaluating accounting systems is to ensure that such systems ensure a high degree of financial stability. Goals can be large or small. Financial stability is a large goal, but the European Central Bank (2006) segmented it into ten smaller goals. The nature of goals will vary depending on the interests and philosophies of the evaluator. The European Central Bank (2006) takes a continent-wide and macroscopic approach. On the other hand, national governments might have smaller goals, such as ensuring that a particular accounting system accords with an existing set of national laws or practices (Epstein and Jermakowicz 2008). Thus, it cannot be concluded that there is a commonality of purpose in evaluating accounting systems; the differing scope, character, and aims of the evaluator have been to be taken into account.

Given the prevalence of IFRS, one of the more common purposes of accounting evaluation systems in recent times has been to offer feedback on the IFRS standard. This goal has prompted entities ranging from the European Central Bank (2012) to the large accounting firms to create position papers on evaluation. However, there is also a large body of national-level evaluations of accounting systems. Two of these systems, namely those associated with evaluation in Romania and Turkey, will be the empirical centerpiece of this study. The purpose of national-level evaluations is different from evaluations afforded by transnational accountancies and institutions. At the national level, governments, business consortia, and other key stakeholders are most concerned about issues of compliance and efficiency. They are not primarily concerned with bringing about changes in the letter of IFRS but rather in looking across internal, national, and international standards in a manner that will allow local goals to be realized. Such goals are often colored by a country's geostrategic position and political circumstances. For example, Turkey is a rapidly-liberalizing and growing economy with increasing links to the world of global capital and no obligation to a particular international accounting standard, while Romania is part of the European Union (EU) and, therefore, obliged to live up to IFRS (Mankiw

I. Mert, *Assessment of Accounting Evaluation Practices*, Contributions to Finance and Accounting, https://doi.org/10.1007/978-3-030-98486-1_1

2011). As such, the purposes of evaluating accounting systems are very different in Romania and Turkey. Yet the same basic approach prevails; evaluation takes place from a starting-point in which goals are articulated and defined and then moves to a gap analysis in which the ability of current standards and practices to meet the goals is evaluated.

One of the core functions of accounting is the communication of an organization's financial data to key stakeholders of the organization, especially shareholders. The history of modern stock-based companies, from the British East India Company onwards, can be told through attempts to convey a higher quantity of quality of information to shareholders. As part of this historical trend, one of the key considerations faced by public companies has been the decision between the use of fair value versus historic cost methods.

A company's financial position cannot be fully understood without knowing (a) how much the company has paid for certain assets or services and (b) what a company can expect to receive if it liquidates particular assets. Large companies routinely invest millions and even billions of dollars in purchases of capital assets such as manufacturing and computing equipment. Such purchases present numerous complexities in terms of communicating cost and value. For example, given the presence or absence of thriving secondary marketplaces, it is possible that a $1 million asset purchase could be worth anywhere from 10 to 150% of its purchase price. In the past, the relative weakness of secondary markets made it less likely that companies could resell their assets, but in contemporary times it is more often the case that companies can liquidate the vast majority of what they own. However, the existence of dynamic, global markets means that the historic cost paid for an asset might be less or more than what an asset is worth at a given moment in time.

The value of a company that is able to liquidate its capital assets for a high percentage of purchase price is, ceteris paribus, higher than the value of a company that lacks the ability to liquidate its assets at close to purchase price. This scenario illustrates one of the reasons that fair value accounting has come to be an important tool. By eschewing historic costs in favor of current market value, fair value approaches make it possible, at least, in theory, for companies to present a more accurate accounting of their worth.

Dynamic considerations in secondary markets are not the only reasons that fair value might be a more accurate approach to accounting. Companies also do a great deal of cross-border business, and fluctuations in currency prices can also result in significant shifts in value that are less likely to be captured in the historic cost method.

Because of these and other reasons, the use of fair value accounting has become increasingly popular, especially after this method was embedded in international financial reporting standards (IFRS). Nonetheless, there continues to be significant controversy over the use of fair value accounting. One of the outstanding questions pertaining to fair value accounting is how to value assets that have not been placed on a secondary market. In this context, the advantage of the historic cost method is that there is a single, unambiguous cost or value structure based on an actual transaction. The utilization of fair value accounting requires companies to engage in some form of speculation (admittedly, based on considerations of similar transactions and other legitimate data sources) about what their assets are really worth. However, IFRS also contains fairly detailed guidance about how such speculation can be grounded in market realities.

Accounting assessment is only possible if three difficult questions are answered: (1) What are the goals of accounting? (2) To what extent do existing accounting practices and standards address the goals of accounting? (3) What can be done to improve the ways in which accounting practices and standards address the goals of accounting? These questions are asked and answered, in different ways depending on who is doing the questioning. Historically, these questions have been asked by scholars, governments, accounting companies, banks, and transnational standards boards, leading to a multiplicity of approaches to measurement and valuation within the discipline of accounting.

The purpose of this study is not to attempt to answer these questions but rather to examine how accounting scholars and standards boards have attempted to answer them, apply some of the suggested answers to an empirical study of accounting in Romania and Turkey, and identify the strengths and weaknesses of the proposed answers. In order to do so, it is first necessary to offer a general overview of the concepts of value and evaluation, accounting measurement, and accounting evaluation.

The purpose of writing the book is to determine whether variation in a company's main accounting method (choosing between historic cost and fair value approaches) was associated with variation in answers to the following investor sentiment questions:

- The first question to be answered; (1) Are you generally optimistic about the company's stock price increasing?
- The second issue to be analyzed; (2) Are you likely to buy more stock in the company?
- And the third object to be researched; (3) Do you find the company to be transparent concerning the information it discloses to you via prospectus?

These questions were answered by surveying investors in 28 Romanian and 28 Turkish companies, half of which were fair value users and half of which were historical cost users.

1.1 Current State of Knowledge

The current state of knowledge about the use of fair value and historic cost can be approached from a number of perspectives. To begin with, there is a theoretical perspective (explored at length in the literature review of this study) in which fair value is held to possess numerous accuracy-related advantages over historic cost. However, there is also an empirical perspective pertaining to how investors respond to the usage of fair value accounting among public companies. The literature on the theoretical advantages of fair value usages far outweighs, in both volume and quality, the literature on the empirical advantages of fair value as inferable from investor sentiment or behavior. The focus of this study is empirical, so particular attention should be paid to the state of empirical knowledge on fair value accounting.

With this delimitation in mind, the empirical literature on fair value accounting suggests that this method of accounting requires shareholders to have a good understanding and appreciation of how markets work. The signals sent by fair value accounting are likely to be more useful to investors who understand how the use of fair value methods can result in a more accurate and information-rich balance sheet. Investors of lower sophistication levels are less likely to be able to read these signals and respond to them in the form of investor sentiment. However, these conclusions have been drawn by scholars who have studied the formation of company-investor communication and investor sentiment in experimental settings, not in the context of real investor-company interactions.

With these background points in mind, the current state of knowledge on fair value use in accounting can be summed up as follows. First, there is an agreement that, especially in contemporary times, assets have the potential to be sold, resold, and otherwise used to generate revenue in a manner that might or might not be consonant with the prices paid for assets (Williams 2003). The same observation can be made not only for assets but also for debts and other kinds of entries on accounting ledgers (Williams 2003). In an age of globalization, highly liquid markets, and the monetization of any and every asset, debt, or entry on an organization's ledgers, historic cost is no longer necessarily the only viable option for capturing value, as it was when Dicksee (1898) explained value in the context of auditing.

Although there is a consensus opinion that historic cost account is likely to be less relevant to current market and business conditions, there is also a consensus opinion that fair value accounting cannot be understood as a single, simple approach to representing value (Demski et al. 2002; Magnan 2009). As Magnan stated, the purpose of fair value accounting is to capture "true and fair...business reality" (p. 191), but establishing this reality can be contentious. As Magnan stated, definitions of fair value can vary depending on stakeholder interests and market perceptions.

In addition to the kinds of conceptual objectives to fair value accounting offered by Demski et al. (2002) and Magnan (2009), there are also numerous practical objectives to this approach. As Power (2010) argued, there can be extensive ambiguity and confusion in trying to assign values to assets or debts that are not on a market. If fair value is determined by scanning the market for examples of similar assets having sold at particular prices, then the challenge is to ensure that the comparison assets are genuinely similar to the asset that is being assigned a fair value (Power 2010). Ultimately, unless an asset is placed on the market and attracts an offer, there is no foolproof method of assigning it a fair value (Magnan 2009; Power 2010).

The critiques of fair value offered by scholars such as Demski et al. (2002), Magnan (2009), and Power (2010) were not intended to promote historic cost accounting, but rather to make accounting practitioners, scholars, and standard-makers available of various problems that had to be solved in order to achieve fair value accounting's potential. In this regard, IFRS has created a large and detailed body of guidance for fair value utilization. Matis and Mustata (2004) have argued that, in fact, fair value should not be considered the sole alternative and that historic cost accounting should be retained in cases in which there is good reason to believe that there is no great discrepancy between historic cost and actual. This approach has also been championed by the IFRS itself. Thus, there is a consensus that, while fair value is likely to have numerous advantages and can be improved through critique, there is also leeway for companies to continue using historic cost accounting in appropriate scenarios (Matis and Mustata 2004). This consensus has resulted in supporters of fair value acknowledging the usefulness of historic cost in certain respects, and in supporters of historic cost recognizing the value of the fair value approach as well. For example, while Yuii Ijiri (2005) supported the use of historic cost accounting, his recommendation of a price adjustment owes something to the market-based spirit of fair value accounting.

Ijiri's (2005) position reflects what is perhaps the ultimate consensus on the topic of historic cost and fair value accounting, which is that the market is important. Even strong proponents of historic cost, such as Ijiri, have suggested adjustments to historic cost accounting that are designed to take the verdict of the market into account. Meanwhile, proponents of fair value have also recognized situations in which historic cost could be a better or at least simpler determinant of market value (Matis and Mustata 2004). What has changed from the nineteenth century to the present is the insistence on the primacy of the market, not merely as a source for original prices but also as a determinant of actual, current prices. This insistence has permeated the field of accounting research and, while tipping the balance of power towards fair value accounting, has also led to important structural changes in the approaches of historic cost theorists such as Ijiri.

1.2 Case Study: A Research Based Design

In order to practically understand the theroatical concepts a case study was fomrulated keeping in view the concepts and the practical utility of these concepts in understanding the dynamics of the financial marketing, a reseaerch based case-study has been designed. Through observation, national and international bibliographic sources such as articles, books, legislations and regulations, statistics, analysis, studies, and reports have been analyzed. Documentary sources have been studied, evaluated and classified methodologically in terms of the need for knowledge of literature, empirical facts, assumptions, and ideas according to the pros and cons, strengths and weaknesses. Frequent benchmarking and SWOT analysis have been applied to identify similarities, differences, advantages and disadvantages between Fair Value and Historical Cost on financial statements. On the other hand, some statistical analysis (factor analysis and cluster analysis have been utilized to analyze the collected data. Additionally, tables, figures and appendices were used to exposure and support opinions expressed in the research results.

The *Description* is to collect and centralize information from the past into the present developments, including duplication on evolutionary stages.

The *Classification* has some descriptive influences, helps the process of centralization and highlighting the similarities and differences by group and selection based on certain criteria.

The *Explanation* lies in an attempt to highlight the meaning of comments by highlighting relations and establishing causal relationships based on some theories.

The *Prediction* involves overcoming the stages of description and explanation, by showing some views on possible future developments of the event, based on credible arguments.

Two coexist methodology, inductive research (from practice to theory) and deductive research (from theory to practice), have been utilized where necessary. The theory was based on reviewing classification and generalization of accounting. The inductive approach starts from the particular (knowledge of accounting practice) to general (development or improvement principles and rules). Deductive research starts from theory and aims at the implementation of that prediction. Researching deductive accounting theory dominates the last decades, it based on logical constructions covering the needs of all users, without taking into account only certain specific practical situations.

The fundamental aim of the methodology is to help us understand in categorical terms as much as possible, not as the product of science as knowledge itself. To be able to fulfill its mission, scientific research methodology includes appropriate definition of the field of study, principles and rules of conducted investigation, establishing working tools for collecting and interpreting data and theoretical construction or reconstruction strategies. Research methodology used in this paper respects the principle of combining qualitative research with quantitative to enhance the obtained results.

The research methodology for the study was quantitative, co-relational, and cross-sectional. The study was designed so as to measure the relationship between the independent value of accounting method (a dichotomous variable including either fair value or historic cost methods) and the dependent variables of

(a) Higher mean investor optimism,
(b) Higher likelihood of buying more stock in the company, and
(c) Higher evaluations of company transparency, controlling for the variables of revenue, profitability, month-over-month stock growth, and year-over-year stock growth.

Controlling for these key variables, and delimiting the study to companies in two relatively small and homogeneous markets, made it possible to isolate the contributions of fair value usage to investor sentiment.

The study was conducted on 56 publicly-listed companies in Turkey and Romania. The following data were gathered (Table 1.1).

Table 1.1 Variables in empirical study

Variable name	Description and coding
Company	There were 56 companies in the study; each was assigned a number from 1 to 56
Country	1 = Turkey; 2 = Romania
Fair value	0 = Does Not Use Fair Value; 1 = Uses Fair Value
Revenue	Annual revenue in millions of USD
Profit margin	Profit margin over most recent fiscal year
MOM share growth	Month-over-month increase in stock price
YOY share growth	Year-over-year increase in stock price
Industry	1 = Manufacturing, 2 = Holding Company, 3 = Telecommunications, 4 = Agriculture, 5 = Technology, 6 = Financial Services, 7 = Logistics, 8 = Construction
Optimism	A measure of investors' optimism about the company, with 1 = not at all, 2 = no, 3 = not really, 4 = neutral, 5 = a little bit, 6 = yes, 7 = absolutely
Likely to buy	A measure of investors' likelihood of buying further stock in the company, with 1 = not at all, 2 = no, 3 = not really, 4 = neutral, 5 = a little bit, 6 = yes, 7 = absolutely
Company transparent	A measure of how transparent investors find the company to be, with 1 = not at all, 2 = no, 3 = not really, 4 = neutral, 5 = a little bit, 6 = yes, 7 = absolutely

Data on the country, fair value use, revenue, profit margin, share growth, and industry were drawn from publicly-available databases of listed companies in Turkey and Romania. Data on optimism, likeliness to buy, and company transparency were gathered from a survey of 56 investors, 28 from Turkish markets and 28 from Romanian markets. Each investor held stock in exactly one of the companies evaluated in the study.

The population of the study consisted of investors in Turkish and Romanian companies. It is unknown how many people (or institutions) are investors in such companies, so a power analysis could not be conducted to calculate the generalizability of the sample to the population. The sample was obtained by the following means. First, the social media sites Facebook and LinkedIn were used to identify both individuals and organizations who were involved in investing in both Turkish and Romanian companies. Next, messages were sent to the identified organizations and individuals to solicit participation in the research study; these messages were sent in the Turkish and Romanian languages in order to increase the response rate. A total of 79 messages were sent, yielding the final sample of 56 individuals (response rate = 70.88%).

In order to be recruited into the study, respondents had to electronically complete and return an informed consent form disclosing the nature of the research, the conditions of participation, and their rights to refuse or withdraw participation at any time and without penalty. In accord with the principles of ethical data collection (Creswell 2009), no data collection or analysis took place until each member of the sample returned the informed consent form. These forms did not subjects' names or other identifying information and were stored on an encrypted laptop.

After obtaining consent from subjects, the next step in the empirical study was to direct participants to an electronic survey. This survey was structured as follows. First, the subjects were directed to frame their responses based on their investment in only one company of their choice; this company had to be publicly listed in either Turkey or Romania. Since many subjects doubtlessly had investment holdings in several companies, they were asked to choose the one public Turkish or Romanian company in which they had the largest degree of investment.

Next, the subjects were asked three questions about the company they had chosen, as follows:

1. Are you generally optimistic about the company's stock price increasing?
2. Are you likely to buy more stock in the company?
3. Do you find the company to be transparent concerning the information it discloses to you via prospectus?

No effort was made to define the variables of optimism or transparency. Since optimism and belief in a company's transparency are both subjective, the decision was made to allow subjects to define these concepts in whichever ways made sense to them.

After subjects nominated their 1 allotted company and disclosed their degrees of optimism, likelihood of buying, and evaluation of transparency, additional research took place in order to identify the following variables as they pertained to each company: (1) Did the company use fair value accounting? (2) What was the annual revenue of the company for the most recently-concluded fiscal year? (3) What was the month-over-month increase in stock price for the company, with the starting point being July 1, 2012, and the ending point being July 31, 2012? (4) What was the year-over-year share growth for the company, with the starting point being January 1, 2011 and the ending point being December 31, 2011? (5) What industry is the business in? These questions were answered through a combination of public company database analysis and follow-up emails to each of the companies in the survey.

Once these data were collected, it was possible to answer the research questions posed by the study in the appropriate manner.

References

Creswell JW (2009) Research design: qualitative, and mixed methods approaches, 3rd edn. Sage, Thousands Oaks, CA

Demski JS, Fellingham JC, Ijiri Y, Sunder S, Glover JC, Jinghong P (2002) Some thoughts on the intellectual foundations of accounting. Account Horiz 16(2):157–168. https://doi.org/10.2139/ssrn.305904. Accessed Aug 2012

Dicksee LR (1898) Auditing: a practical manual for auditors, eBook, 8th ed., rev. and enl. Gee, London. Accessed Aug 2013

Epstein BJ, Jermakowicz EK (2008) Integration and application of international accounting and financial reporting standards. Wiley, New York, NY

European Central Bank (2006) Assessment of accounting standards from a financial stability perspective. Retrieved from http://www.ecb.int/pub/pdf/other/assessmentaccountingstandards2006en.pdf

European Central Bank (2012) Annual accounts management report for the year ending 31 Dec 2012. https://www.ecb.europa.eu/pub/pdf/annrep/ecb.annualaccounts2012.en.pdf

Ijiri Y (2005) US accounting standards and their environment: a dualistic study of their 75-years of transition. J Account Public Policy 24(4):255–279

Magnan ML (2009) Fair value accounting and the financial crisis: messenger or contributor? Account Perspect 8(3):189–213

Mankiw NG (2011) Principles of economics. Cengage, New York, NY

Matis D, Mustata, R (2004) From historical cost to fair value. Audit si Convergenta Contabila, Editura Sincron, pp. 619–633. ISBN 973-9234-53-4, Cluj Napoca

Power M (2010) Fair value accounting, financial economics and the transformation of reliability. Account Bus Res 40(3):197–210. https://doi.org/10.1080/00014788.2010.9663394

Williams HA (2003) A mediated hierarchical regression analysis of factors related to research productivity of human resource development postsecondary faculty. Doctoral Dissertation, Louisiana State University. http://etd01.lnx390.lsu.edu:885/docs/available/etd.-0326103-212409/. Accessed Aug 2013

Chapter 2
Theoretical Approaches of Value and Valuation

Financial information is the heart of economic life in market systems. In neoclassical economic theory, rational economic decisions can only be made on the basis of such information (Krugman and Wells 2009). Buyers and sellers must have a fairly precise empirical basis for understanding value in order for a cumulative economic activity to be efficient. Historically, some form of information regulation has always accompanied commerce (Mankiw 2011). In contemporary times, financial information as generated by corporate entities is typically subject to some combination of internal, national, and international accounting regime, depending on variables such as where the company is listed (Norton et al. 2006).

Accounting practices continue to vary widely and for a number of reasons. To begin with, some aspects of accounting—for example, the choice of certain methods of book-keeping-remain altogether unregulated and, therefore, fall to the choice of the company, even though accounting standards might provide guidance or recommendations for such practices (Pounder 2009). Additionally, there is latitude for a wide variety of approaches even within standardized accounting regimes. For example, the International Financial Reporting Standards (IFRS) is a principles- rather than rules-based accounting regime, which means that IFRS allows companies some leeway in their accounting practices (Nandakumar et al. 2010). Even U.-S. Generally Accepted Accounting Practices (GAAP), which are rule-based and are ten times as long as IFRS, contain some leeway in that, in Saudagaran's (2009) estimation, GAAP allows for "more aggressive accounting practices" (p. 206) that open the door for multiple approaches to compliance with the standard.

The existence of multiple accounting practices and regimes, and the presence of latitude in the world of accounting decision-making creates many potential problems for accounting scholars and policy-makers. One of these problems is the difficulty of assessing accounting practices. This problem is created not just by the multiplicity of accounting standards but also by the conceptual difficulty of determining the fit between the standards and more specific criteria of information quality and other desiderata within accounting (Needles and Powers 2010). A specific aspect of the

I. Mert, *Assessment of Accounting Evaluation Practices*, Contributions to Finance and Accounting, https://doi.org/10.1007/978-3-030-98486-1_2

problem is how to assess the two different kinds of valuation that are current in accounting theory and practice, namely the historical cost and fair value approaches.

2.1 Discussions for Development of Accounting as a Science

There were only a few attempts to create an accounting theory to define instructions of accounting up to the twentieth century. In the twentieth century, accounting had effort to produce theoretical approaches of accounting from which proper practice could be gained. These efforts collected data from practical applications and tried to convert them discussable forms. This part is trying to analyze some of these discussions. We will also try to understand how the created theories help us to be able to analyze today's practical approaches.

2.1.1 Early Periods

Accounting is a double entry bookkeeping registration system. Accounting is applied all over the world in any kinds of industries or non-profit organizations and government or local authorities. There is no clarity about when the way of double-entry was first applied but it is accepted that first time Fra Luca Bartolomeo de Pacioli, Italian mathematician (1445–1517), published the definition of book-keeping system regarding double entry bookkeeping system and he is called as the "father of accounting". On the other hand, A.C. Littleton (1886–1974) described the basics of accounting with his book, An Introduction to Elementary Accounting (Littleton 1920). During the past years, accounting has been improved and adopted to the needs of new complicated situations of economical movements.

2.1.2 Modern Economy Period

It is mostly accepted that Industrial Revolution in England was the beginning point of the accumulation of high capitals. From there on, the specifications of the modern economy period can be described as high technology, complicated industrial organizations, multinational entities, on line commerce and non-profit organizations. This much complicated economic world needs to have more organized follow-up the system as far as cost, price and profit are concerned in order to help the decision makers to reach the correct conclusions.

It is a gradually spread argument point that the extraordinary growing of the industrial development assisted the double entry bookkeeping or double entry bookkeeping accounting system pushed up the industrial development.

After the growth of the industrial economy world, firms had more capital accumulation against costs. The other main perspective was the separation of management from the ownership. That means management skills were accepted as a valuable assets.

2.1.3 *First Discussions*

Up to the starting of the twentieth century, there were the first theoretical discussions. Charles E. Sprague's book, The Philosophy of Accounts, was trying to add theoretical accuracy and consistency for teaching accounting to the students through logically structured terminologies.

He identified the algebraic sigh of the accounting equation ($A = L + P$). Even though some of his points had been already defined by the previous writers, he discussed in his book the rationalization of accounting. It was a referring to the ownership theory meaning the owner is the center of accounting interest. His book was a very effective in the academic world and took man references especially up to 1940s.

Since economical life existing with individual entities, the mission of accounting needs to catch the benefits of the company, not the interests of the owner as the ownership theorizers are claiming. As entity theorizers support that the owner is only one of the interests groups of the company that provide capital to the company and that will be appreciated by dividend distribution. On the other hand, William Andrew Paton supported the entity theory but it took time for accepting his thoughts.

2.1.4 *Effects of Economical Movements, Depressions*

Accounting theory and new implementations have been mostly developed in the US.

Consolidation of Financial Reports

Free capitalism meaning minimizing government effects in the economy was an accepted economic ideology. Financial statements were prepared according with the Company Acts, and they were not consolidated up to 1930s.

Economic Depression

1920s business optimism ended with the winds of Great Depression in 1929. This worldwide economic crisis brought some regulations in the accounting world such as establishing regulations of the accounting profession meaning the personal qualifications for applying the profession, establishing rules for defining activities for accountants, and establishing theoretical structures for the purpose of having homogenous and constant accounting applications. Later on, all these establishments became the starting point for Generally Accepted Accounting Principles.

Researching Principles

After the Great Depression of 1929, The Securities and Exchange Commission (SEC) was formed, and it ruled to the listed companies to providing appropriate full disclosures of financial statements for the information of the shareholders. Performing the accounting results according with the said disclosures made the financial statements reliable. On the other hand, in 1959 Accounting Research Studies (ARS) was established to have standard applications in accounting, the accumulated data was called Opinions.

For practitioners, theoretical associations were not sounding interesting because there was always conflict possibility with the clients if the said theoretical approaches would be applied. For this reason, accountant environment established the American Accounting Associations (AAA).

2.1.5 Bases of Theories

A lot of efforts were performed in order to establish accounting principles that would be accepted in the eyes of most people as significant and fundamental point. The word of principle composes different kinds of meanings such as a regulation, rule, structure or belief that defines our activities. Another word, we live according with our principles. At the same time, the principles are considered as concrete truths that have many detailed subtitles.

Conceptual Definition

In order to understand accounting theory, the meanings of terminologies and definitions of accounting literature should be known clearly. These terminologies are defined in the Accounting Research Studies 1, as advance principles and 3, extended accounting principles.

Accounting applicants were studying for GAAP and in the end GAAP would define the field of the theoretical structure of accounting. By the fail of APB and ARD, the accounting applicants started defining the structural points of financial reporting standards.

The accounting scientists separated between conditions of exploration and conditions of explanation. They thought that it was impossible to restructure and explain how theorizers concluded with their first thoughts. For this reason, modernists' explanation says that scientific system has focused on how theories are valid to overcome the accounting problems by explaining them. Day-to-day practicing of the accounting profession will concrete the meanings of the principles clearly in the minds of the professions. Finally, the knowledge has been accumulated by application of day-to-day practices, meaning experience. The opposite of this thought is knowledge is not depending on day-to-day practice or experience because we already have the ideas, but they can be exploring by utilizing through experiences.

Fake Discussion

The unique conclusion is that theories will be settled by the deduction of ideas gained from using of knowledge and accumulating the experiences through day-to-day experience.

2.1.6 Assessment for Theory Foundation

Sterling claims "accounting ought to measure something and then communicate that measurement" (Sterling 1970, p. 454).

Accounting reports are showing the economic activities of a company through numerical numbers. Assessment scope of these economic activities should be clearly defined. According to Sterling, the scope should assess values. On the other hand, Christensen and Demski think that the scope should assess informative activities. Thus, the further thoughts say that the targets are not the same, another word while one focuses on the end of the activities; the other considers value as bringing information about the activities.

While the time passes, the accounting profession in the world goes to international financial standards (IFRS). In this aspect, measuring the economical activities is firmly regulated by the authorities.

Defining the hypotheses is a beginning step, and they need to be examined by applying the day-to-day activities. The obtained results should be compared by considering the similarity of the field.

2.1.7 Developing Accounting

In the twentieth century, several accounting writers gave significant values to the accounting field. In this century accounting was a very close partner of the economics discipline. With this close relation, accounting was taught in the universities. These two disciplines were considered with as related concepts. In the beginning, doctoral studies of accounting were followed by the professors of economics department (Paton's Accounting Theory). For example, Canning was a professor of the economics department at Stanford University but he wrote a book with the name of The Economics of Accountancy (Canning 1929). In this book, he illustrated accounting with words of economics.

2.2 Principle of Theoretical Discussions

The purpose of this dissertation is to compare and contrast investor response to two distinct accounting approaches to measuring and reporting value. Accordingly, it is appropriate to begin by discussing the concept of value as it has evolved in accounting during classical, neoclassical, and contemporary times. This introductory section will offer a description and critique of different theoretical and technical approaches to value as they have been employed in the history of accounting.

2.2.1 The Classical Period

To begin with, it is important to determine a historical starting point for the theory and practice of accounting. According to Hopwood and Miller (1994), the first two accounting documents to have survived are dated from C.E. 1157 and 1221, respectively. The so-called Farolfi ledger, dating from 1300, is the first complex example of an accounting document (Hopwood and Miller 1994). Thus, the classical period of accounting can be said to date from the twelveth or thirteenth centuries onwards.

During this time, the concept of value was not treated in a complex way, at least in Farolfi ledger and related documents. In the Farolfi ledger, a value was delimited to the recording of debits and credits (Hopwood and Miller 1994). Even when double-entry bookkeeping spread in the fourteenth century, the concept of value remained constrained to the recording of credits and debts (Hopwood and Miller 1994). There are two main reasons for this trend in accounting practices of the classical period. First, the accumulation of capital and capital assets was far more limited in comparison to what transpired during and after the Industrial Revolution (Mankiw 2011). Businesses were smaller and had more limited capital assets. Additionally, there was a limited secondary market for such assets. Organizations tended to use assets to the end of their useful life; the concept of leasing had not yet become popular (Krugman and Wells 2009). As such, there was not a pronounced need to record the value of assets owned by an organization.

The second reason for the relatively simplistic treatment of value during the classical period had to do with the nature of business itself. The word *accounting* has its primary meaning the dispensation of knowledge to a party with some authority over, and interest in, this knowledge (Nikolai et al. 2009); the application of accounting, then, infers some responsibilities between the company executing the accounting and the company to which the accounting is made.

In the context of modern business, ownership of capital was popularized through the concept of stock. The first widely-recognized stock-based company was the British East India Company, which obtained its charter in 1600—over three centuries after the classical period of accounting began (Mankiw 2011). Before stock-based companies became popular, companies simply had fewer stakeholders to report to. In addition, accounting was not as thoroughly governed by law and regulation as it would later become. Inevitably, when the number of stock-based companies proliferated in the seventeenth and eighteenth centuries, both courts and legislatures faced the challenge of protecting the rights of stockholders, a goal that was partly accomplished by creating detailed accounting requirements, including requirements pertaining to the disclosure of asset value (Krugman and Wells 2009).

Thus, it is a mistake to assume that the simplistic treatment of the concept of value during the classical era of accounting was a function of macroeconomic conditions such as low inflation. Inflation has been historically documented as dating back to the first use of metal coins. Rather, the appropriate conclusion is that businesses in the era of classical accounting (1) did not own many capital assets, (2) had a smaller number of stakeholders, (3) did not face onerous legal or regulatory standards pertaining to the disclosure of asset value, and (4) did not operate in an environment in which capital assets were fungible or leasable. Given all of these conditions, it is not surprising that neither theories nor techniques of accounting during the classical period paid attention to the question of recording and reporting all but the simplest kinds of value, *viz.*, credit and debit.

2.2.2 The Neoclassical Period

The neoclassical period of economics began with the work of Adam Smith. It is, therefore, appropriate to examine Smith's theory of value and explore how value became a more complex and integral component of accounting theory and practice during this time. The concepts of value and evaluation are at the heart of this study and, therefore, require careful definition and examination. In The Wealth of Nations, Adam Smith (1801) wrote that "*The word value, it is to be observed, has two different meanings, and sometimes express the utility of some particular object, and sometimes the power of purchasing other goods...*" (p. 251). Smith termed these two kinds of value as a value in use and value in exchange, respectively. When applying the concepts of values and evaluation to accounting systems, these two different kinds of value ought to be kept in mind.

A discussion of value, as applied to accounting, is necessarily complex because accounting both has value in itself and is also a means of recording the value of goods and services. The subsequent discussion will, therefore, be divided into two sections, with the first section touching on the value of accounting itself and the second session examining how accounting can assign values to goods and services.

Moral thinking was not the only overtly philosophical intrusion into economics. Before Smith (and after him, though to a lesser extent), a number of thinkers offered abstract, immeasurable definitions of economic ideas such as value, cost, and labor. While Smith's work is still rooted in the political philosophy of the eighteenth century, its use of scientific methods shows traces of the economic revolution to come. There are several convenient examples of Smith's concrete contributions to analytical economics, beginning with a theory of price:

> The market price of every particular commodity is regulated by the proportion between the quantity which is actually brought to market, and the demand of those who are willing to pay the natural price of the commodity, or the whole value of the rent, labour, and profit which must be paid in order to bring it thither. (Smith 1801, p. 56)

As such, there are prices that could clear the market and prices that could result in no sales. The study of this spectrum of possible outcomes is also known as equilibrium economics. Samuelson refers to "The genius of Smith's formation of a general equilibrium model" (Samuelson 2002, p. 5) because, complemented by other passages in The Wealth of Nations, Smith was pointing the way towards a mathematical model of supply and demand that was worked out more fully after his death, starting with Smith disciple David Ricardo and continuing all the way until Paul Samuelson, whose economic analysis is grounded in Smith's concepts.

Smith was not an econometrician, much less a formal mathematician, but The Wealth of Nations pays minute attention to facts and figures in ways that influenced the subsequent development of accounting thought and practice. It demonstrates, for the first time in the history of economic thought, a purely quantitative frame of mind, as when Smith traces the historical prices of wheat prices from 1202 to 1756 (Smith 1801, p. 259). Klein discusses one of the most interesting uses that Smith got out of this data and placed the achievement in context:

> Smith analyzed price movements in relation to each other, to silver prices, and unusual supply factors.... [his] way of decomposing price into factor rewards....is the forerunner of the present attachment to full-cost pricing in which all the factor costs are covered. (Klein 1999, p. 18)

Smith's attitude to, and specific use of, data both anticipated and contributed to the paths that analytic economists would take over the next two centuries. For example, Smith's repeated use of the time-series, a snapshot of change in particular statistics over time, would come to be a staple of econometrics.

Perhaps Smith's most important contribution to analytical economics was his influence on the formation of a marginal theory, which resulted in the marginal revolution of the late nineteenth century. Consider Spiegel's succinct description of the marginal revolution:

> The unifying principle...was the marginal one....it pointed the way toward the establishment of theoretical optimum positions, or equilibrium, at which consumers and producers would maximize such magnitudes as satisfaction or net revenue. (Stiglitz et al. 2006, p. 505)

The idea of economic equilibrium, which is one of the foundations of the marginal revolutions, originates with Smith. Marginal economists shared Smith's interests in attempting to discover market-clearing prices, relating factor costs to pricing, and accounting for the utility itself. However, the marginal revolution clarified a point that had long confused economists, including Smith himself: how to account for the high cost of apparently inutile goods such as diamonds and the low cost of absolute necessities such as water. While scarcity had been advanced as part of the explanation, it was clearly insufficient; consider that a mediocre artist could create a terrible sculpture that was the only one of its kind in the world and yet fail to sell it.

Smith thought that the value of precious metals and other scarce, unnecessary substances originated in both utility and beauty (Smith 1801, p. 176). This was the germ of an idea that marginal economists would develop into a full theory. If beauty was part of a good's value, then it stood to reason that value was somehow in the eye of a beholder, not just an outcome of the cost of labor that had gone into the production or discovery of a good. This insight is directly applicable to the idea of fair market value accounting.

Scarcity, while no longer a governing theory, played a role in the calculation of marginal utility, and, together with other concepts, helped to explain the water-versus-diamonds problem that plagued Smith and other economists. Water, because of its high availability, has a low marginal utility. Imagine that gallons 1–10 are used for drinking, gallons 11–20 for bathing, and 21–30 for household cleaning. Gallons 31 and up have a very low marginal utility because consumers had little use for them. Diamonds, because they are scarce, have a high marginal utility. If a consumer could only afford to buy two diamonds, he or she would put them on only their most valuable resources—for example, giving a spouse a ring. If a consumer had 100,000 diamonds, many other uses would be found for them—such as paperweights, toys, etc. In a society like that of the Incas before the Spanish conquest, gold must have been like this—so abundant that it could be used as a toy, household decoration, etc. So, technically, it is the combination of scarcity and marginal utility on the one hand, plus costs of acquisition and production (including labor) on the other, that help to determine price, and interacts with the market (the 'invisible hand') bring this price to an equilibrium.

In all fairness, Smith neither described nor envisioned anything like a full theory of marginal economics that truly ushered in the revolution of analytical economics. But, based on Tribe's statement that, in the marginal paradigm, "Each agent sought to maximize its own welfare through a calculus of choice; economics became a logic of optimizing decisions capable of mathematical representation" (Tribe 1991, p. 154), it is clear that Smith's notion of equilibrium pricing, an invisible hand regulating the sum of transactions, and use of time-series to track the "calculus of choice" through the ages, were all inspiring forces behind the marginal revolution. The marginal economists simply made the 'invisible hand' visible by rigorously quantifying the forces and inputs that defined prices, value and other economic phenomena.

Adam Smith's displacement of moral man with economic man, his use of data, and his theories of equilibrium, cost, price, and value, all contribute to the revolutionary of his work and, through it, to the revolutionary nature of marginal economics in the late nineteenth century. While some of Smith's theoretical contributions—notably his commitment to labor's contribution to value, and his theories of national

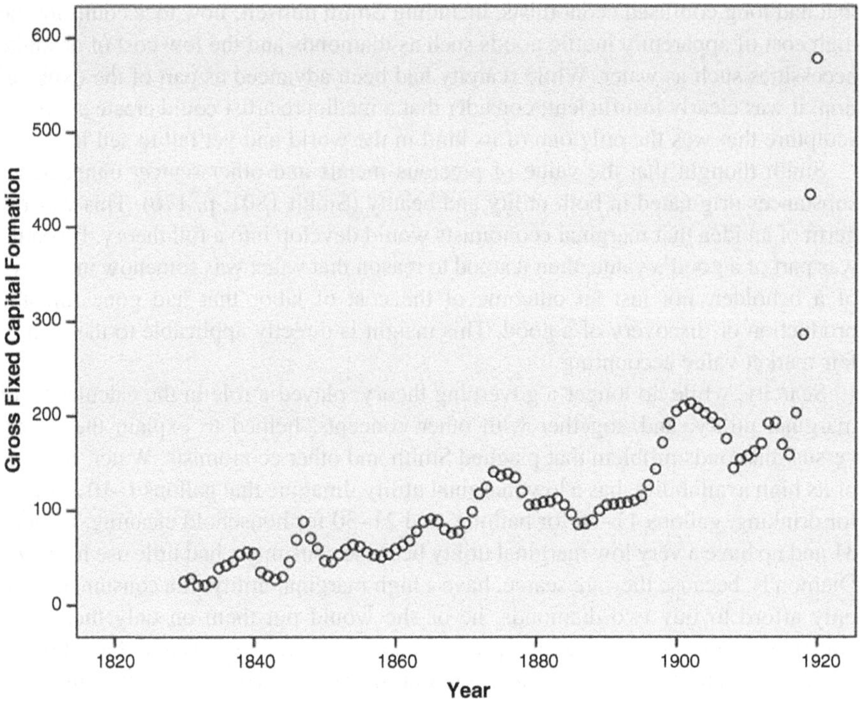

Fig. 2.1 Scatter plot, English gross capital formation (1830–1920). Note: Original graphic based on data from Bank of England Annual Report (2012)

wealth accumulation—have been rejected by mainstream economics, The Wealth of Nations is nonetheless the great work of modern economics.

Again, while The Wealth of Nations was not conceived as a treatise on accounting theory or practice, many of the bedrock economic principles on which accounting would subsequently rely were first or most forcefully articulated by Smith. It is, therefore, appropriate to have a fairly thorough understood of what Smith thought about value, cost, and economic transactions.

By Smith's time, capital asset accumulation had increased in scope and intensity, giving rise to a basis for factoring cost into accounting practices and theory in more complex ways (Mankiw 2011). It is important to offer an overview of this macroeconomic change because it was ultimately responsible for creating the conditions that required the discipline of accounting to change during the neoclassical period. One way of appreciating the change is to track gross capital formation in England over the years 1830–1924. Figure 2.1 illustrates the extent to which England—subsequently to be followed by many other countries, soon to be collectively called the developed world—moved away from an agricultural economy to an industrial economy based on both capital formation and stock ownership.

Notable in Fig. 2.1 is how quickly gross capital formation accelerated after the middle of the nineteenth century, coinciding with the Industrial Revolution. As gross capital formation grew, companies grew larger and required the kind of large-scale financing that was only possible with participation in the capital markets. Stockholders and regulators alike began to demand a fuller accounting from companies, including a disclosure of asset values. As Previts et al. (2011) concluded,

> At the end of the nineteenth century, businesses were often large and widely held, with capital from a vast network of stakeholders. Thus, demand for financial reports continually increased and the ledger was no longer the end product of accounting. Investors craved summaries that were concise, succinct, uniform in arrangement, and understandable. (p. 109)

The theory of accounting changed in tandem with its practice because, as Previts et al. noted, accounting professors and writers were almost always practitioners as well.

While it is important to note the role of stockholders as drivers of the demand for asset value disclosure that began to be common among publicly-listed companies in the United States and England during the late nineteenth century, another important motivator of change was taxes (Mankiw 2011). The United States, in particular, began to adopt an aggressive policy of taxation of capital assets, which in turn required disclosure of such assets. For publicly-listed companies, then, asset value disclosure served two purposes, a capital markets function and a regulatory or legislative one.

Smith (1801) and the pioneers of neoclassical economics were neither accounting theorists nor practitioners, and as such it is not surprising that the basic neoclassical framework does not include insights or guidance that is specific to accounting. However, there are some general neoclassical principles that do constitute an explanatory foundation for asset disclosure, and that deserve to be explained in more detail.

Perhaps the most famous explanatory metaphor invoked by Smith (1801) was that of the so-called invisible hand. The theory of the invisible hand stipulated that, if buyers and sellers were offered maximum freedom to treat with each other in fair ways, the sum of these uncoordinated actions was an orderly and efficient market. The fairness requirement of the invisible hand theory is that a basic amount of commercial information should be available to all interested parties. When information is withheld or distributed selectively, the efficiency of the entire market suffers, even though a few market participants might benefit. The entire subsequent history of valuation in accounting can be understood from this neoclassical perspective. Valuation disclosures exist in order to bolster an efficient market, which is what both companies and investors require to prosper.

The theory of valuation in accounting was developed more extensively in the early twentieth century, well after the introduction of neoclassical ideas in economic thought. However, there are aspects of Smith's (1801) neoclassical theory, particularly the theory of value, that apply conceptually to value, and that ought to be discussed before examining the modern approach to valuation.

The concept of accounting's innate value can be explored by asking the following question: What kinds of value can a service have? Following Smith's (1801) taxonomy, a service can have utility in use and utility in exchange. The exact nature of these two kinds of utility will depend on the nature of service. Assuming that the service is what economists call an information good, the analysis becomes easier. If the information good is, for example, a reliable stock market tip, utility in exchange is high. Someone in possession of a reliable stock market tip can exchange this information for money—e.g., by reselling this information to others or by buying stock on the strength of the information (Mankiw 2011). A stock market tip has low utility in use, however because the information in itself is not necessarily useful to have. On the other hand, knowledge of calculus can be considered information good that has a high utility in use, because the mere possession of this information can allow a person to solve various problems and, in so doing, generate innate intellectual satisfaction. Smith (1801) believed that utility in use and utility in exchange were typically opposed to each other, such that goods with a high utility in use (like water) had much lower utility in exchange and vice versa. This theoretical insight applies to valuation considered as an information good; when accounting is used to present a record of asset value, such information has high utility in use but little use in exchange, because the information is available to all who read the relevant accounting disclosure.

One promising foundation for the discussion of value and valuation theory as applicable to information goods came from the work of F.A. Hayek (1968) and his description of information goods as part of the so-called discovery procedure of capitalism. Hayek argued that, in capitalism, it cannot be predicted "which particular individuals will benefit. . .and which will not" (p. 14). By contrast, in centrally-planned economic systems, winners and losers are designated in advance. Thus, assuming the existence of market conditions, the value in exchange of an information good can be said to lie in Hayek's discovery procedure. In a free market, information is valuable insofar as it offers free economic actors some competitive edge that can then be converted into economic value. Accounting appears to be this kind of information good, with (a) a high utility in exchange for market consumers of accounting information who will base stock purchase decisions on the information gleaned from accounting data and (b) high utility in use for companies that obtain information about their own operations from accounting or for other actors.

So far, the economic and political bases for the reporting of asset value have been explored. However, attention must also be paid to the actual theory of asset value, especially as this theory developed within the framework of historical cost accounting. Because the theory developed towards the close of the nineteenth century, well after the zenith of the Industrial Revolution and over a century after Adam Smith introduced neoclassical principles, the theory should be discussed under the heading of modern approaches to valuation in accounting.

2.2.3 Academical Concepts

Companies published financial reports are the most visible accounting product. These financial statements summarize the resources and debts on the balance sheet and where the sources and debts flowed in the income statement. The reporting entity is not a defined firm as its relationships are likely to be wider than identified by its formal reporting. For instance, some arrangements are usually eliminated in these reports. "*Entity's control of resources would be incompletely and inaccurately measured. Some assets, such as proprietary knowledge or capital assets received through lease arrangements, would not be included* (Demski 2005)."

Equality is commonly based on what customers have paid and which resources were consumed for satisfying those customers. Such wide-ranging points as product warranties and potential product liabilities, uncollectible accounts, pension plans, advertising, research and development and employee training deliver precise identification of what customers have paid or what resources were consumed.

Apparently, financial reports should be prepared to accord with the Generally Accepted Accounting Principles (GAAP). The financial reports need to be audited, where the auditor certifies to claim the reports are according with GAAP. One reason for regulations is the measurement concepts. The second reason based on investor protection concerns and related to the complexity is the potential for opportunism. Absent auditing, the financial report, is simply management's self-report of its financial results, and the unverified claims were measured according to GAAP. The auditor's studies can surely be discussed and judged.

There are two principal responsible standard definers in the world for financial reports; in the US, the Financial Accounting Standards Board (FASB), and the exterior of the US, International Accounting Standards Board (IASB). Because of having different priorities of these boards, having a common standard rule has delayed. For example, leases and compensation of employees have not defined in the balance sheet and income statement according with the GAAP.

There are two concepts appear in time, measurement school concept and informative school concept.

The Measurement School Concept

The measurement school's ideas are based on classical economic theories. According with the ideal conditions for the perfect economy theory, value and income are defined as perfectly as assets and sources of the firms. The measurement school focuses on this ideal support all its ideas in order to reach this perfect market situation to be settled.

The measurement school points out the importance of the definitions of income, revenue, expense, asset, and liability. Historical background of accounting is created by measurement school.

Certainty and clarity of the concept definitions such as depreciation and exchange rates are the advantages of the measurement school. Even though in some applications it is not purely respected to the measures of GAAP, some of these applications are reported with the principles of the measurement school. Another word, in measurement school, the concept of the measure is known clearly by the issuer.

There are some negative points of the measurement school. For example, while it is focusing on defining the ideal concepts, it does not consider the cost to reach the application of the said ideal concepts.

The Informative School Concept

In contrarily, the idea of the information school is coming from economic uncertainty. It does not follow strictly the reports of accounting, but it aims at information. That means that accounting is turning the activities of the company to the numbers. Another word, accounting is just one of the sources to identify the company. For example, government, commerce offices, municipalities, newspapers, tax offices, statistical institutions, and even public have some information about the companies. Additionally, companies often declare its situation by itself to the different addresses.

There are positive aspects of information school. For example, it directs us on thinking when we face with the limitless economic and analyze the economic sources what create the differences, variations or imbalances. It is intentionally formed and regulated for the reason of not to be speculated. On these aspects, it refers to historical cost practices since it excludes the speculative and subjective points.

As negativity of information school, it does not have the clarity to define which ones have prior effects on the company among so many information points.

2.3 Modern Approaches to Valuation in Accounting

Historical cost accounting was the first dense and systematic approach to valuation in accounting. It developed as a response to the increase in the number of stock-based firms and reporting requirements imposed on such firms by stockholder demand and regulatory activities in the late nineteenth and early twentieth centuries. In this section, the main techniques and theories of the historical cost approach will be discussed and contrasted with the fair value approach.

To begin with, the definition of historical cost is the cost paid to acquire an asset (typically, a capital asset that falls into the category of property, equipment, or factory) and to bring that asset to the appropriate condition and location for operational use (Nikolai et al. 2009). Over time, accounting standards have become extraordinarily specific in explaining what counts as a cost (for example, by distinguishing acquisition, exploration, development, and restoration costs) and how costs are classified. Accounting standards have also developed means of differentiating between tangible and intangible assets and associating costs with each of these asset categories (Nikolai et al. 2009).

Bringing this kind of rigor and thoroughness to the reporting of costs is part of the market theory. Along with the increased reporting requirements that began to apply to listed firms in the late nineteenth and early twentieth centuries came many new measures of corporate efficiency. Such measures were rendered possible by all the new data that were available and were also necessary in order to help investors identify appropriate firms in which to invest.

One of these measures was known as return on assets (ROA). ROA was a measure that allowed firms to be compared to each other despite variations in revenue, the cost of goods sold, and other variables. To take a simple example, a firm with $1 million worth of assets and $2 million of net income would have an ROA of 2, given that ROA is defined as net income/total assets. Another firm with $1078 million in revenue and $1110 million of net income would have an ROA of 1.029. Thus, even though these two companies are highly different from each other in terms of both net income and total assets, the use of the ROA calculation would allow an investor to compare the efficiency of both companies.

Initially, the theory of historical cost valuation as articulated by American scholars arose out of two conditions widely prevalent in the nineteenth century: (1) A relative lack of inflation in the United States (which, with the exception of a brief spike in inflation associated with the Panic of 1857, experienced lower levels of inflation during the nineteenth century than at any time in its previous history, either as an independent nation or as a colony; and (2) the immaturity of secondary markets for assets. In an environment of slow price changes, general stability, and the lack of practical or theoretical mechanisms for pricing assets in secondary markets, it was natural for the pioneers of applied accounting theory to choose a historical cost model.

However, the two background conditions that informed the development of historical cost valuation theory and practice changed rapidly. In the United States, inflation spiked numerous times in the early twentieth century. In addition, the industrial economy matured and resulted in the creation of ample secondary markets for capital assets. Thus, the historical approach became vulnerable to two criticisms: (1) volatility in asset prices and (2) an increased disconnection from the market reality of asset prices. It was in response to these trends that the theory of fair value accounting was advanced as an alternative to historical cost valuation.

For the ROA calculation to be possible, it is necessary for asset value to be reported. There are two approaches to such reporting. One is to list the cost of the asset when it was purchased and taking into account the additional costs needed to bring the asset to usable status. Another approach, often known as the fair value approach, is to use the current cost of the asset. Each of these approaches has its theoretical justifications, which become clearer when the historical development of the concept of assets is better understood.

Assets are the centerpiece of accounting; no theory of value, or specific practice of accounting for value, can be understood without first examining the concept of assets. The accounting literature began to use the concept of assets in the nineteenth century. At that time, the word *asset* had already acquired a specific meaning in commercial and legal contexts, a meaning that informed how accounting theorists came to conceive of assets. Understanding the evolution of the meaning of *assets* is a way of understanding how this concept began to take on specific meanings within accounting.

According to the Oxford English Dictionary (2013), the word *asset* derives from the Old French word (c. 1000 CE) for sufficiency. By around the year 1300, after the Norman conquest of England, the Anglo-Norman language contained the word *asez*, referring to an amount of property sufficient to repay a debt or to meet certain claims. By the early sixteenth century, English law understood the word *asset* to refer to any effect, good, or estate that could be used to pay off a debt. It was not until much later that the word *asset* acquired the meaning of "an item on a balance sheet representing the value of a resource, right, item of property, etc." (Oxford English Dictionary 2013, para. 3). In fact, the first such usage of the word *asset* did not appear until 1825 when it was used to refer to the amount of revenue generated by the English colonial enterprise in India.

In 1898, accounting theorist Dicksee, writing in a general textbook named Auditing, used the following phrase: "It would have seemed more natural to have placed Plant before Stock-in-trade, as being, properly speaking, a 'fixed asset'" (p. 276). Dicksee defended that idea of the asset as a representation of what was owned. The idea of costs and cost allocation was largely absent from how accounting theorists understood both assets and value during this period of accounting history. However, as Williams (2003) noted, there were dissenting theorists who laid the foundation for what would become the fair value approach to accounting: "*Continued support for the simple notion of assets as exchangeable things or property can be found in the 20th century accounting literature. However, during the latter part of the 19th century, the emphasis moved away from property rights, to cost and cost allocation. A new school of thought emerged which challenged the conventional notion of assets and the function of the balance sheet... The accounting literature examined revealed the use of, and strong support for, market values over several centuries. However, conventional accounting is firmly rooted in the historical cost-based record, despite its widely acknowledged inconsistencies. (Williams 2003, p. 140).*"

Williams argues that, in essence, accounting theorists and practitioners were well aware of the problems associated with recording transactions at historical cost, but that there was no widely-accepted framework for moving beyond this convention. Until fairly late in the Industrial Revolution, there was no practical reason for abandoning the historical cost approach to valuation. As mentioned earlier in this chapter, the Industrial Revolution helped to lead to a spike in gross capital formation, which in turn meant that more long-lived investments were being made. Before the Industrial Revolution, even large companies had had relatively short-lived investment cycles. For example, the British East India Company, one of the largest companies of early modern times, had raised capital to fund merchant expeditions to India, paying investors back with British ships sold their goods in India or brought back Indian goods to be sold in the British market. What changed during the Industrial Revolution was that, with the advent of large-scale manufacturing and industry, more companies were making long-lived investments. An example of this transformation was the rise of railway companies in the U.S. and U.K. These railway companies made expensive investments in rail infrastructure that lasted a great deal of time. At the same time, manufacturing companies were investing in factories and other assets of an equally long-lived nature.

Recording these kinds of transactions at historical cost led to numerous theoretical and practical problems with valuation. For example, companies that paid dividends out of their profit had to find some way of accounting for the change in the value of their long-lived investments over time. A railway companying paying $1 million for a railroad in 1840 could either represent the $1 million expense at historical cost, no matter how many years went by, or it could try to account for the change in the asset through depreciation. The practice of depreciation began with railroads and gradually spread to companies in all major industries by the end of the nineteenth century, by which time it was common for yearly depreciation costs of 5–10% to be assessed on physical assets.

The popularization of depreciation can be understood as an important evolutionary change in how accounting theory had treated value. For the first time, there was a move to recognize the change in value brought about over time and in a manner that attempted to reflect the genuine value of an asset (regardless of the possibility of actually selling the asset). However, the popularization of depreciation did not in itself undo the basis for historical cost accounting. Historical cost accounting remained fairly strong throughout the nineteenth and much of the twentieth century, partly drawing its strength from the somewhat ambiguous distinction between fixed and floating assets.

The distinction between fixed and floating assets was a major topic of discussion in the accounting literature in the late nineteenth century and early twentieth century and contributed to the longevity of the historical cost model. Defenders of the distinction argued that fluctuations in asset value while real enough, ought not to be taken into consideration, for reasons discussed by Dicksee: *…these assets have been acquired, and are being permanently retained, not with a view to their being eventually realized at a profit in the ordinary course of business, but with a view to their being used for the purpose of enabling trading profits to be made in other ways. … For practical purposes, therefore, these fluctuations may fairly be said to be of no account. (Dicksee 1898, p. 5).*

The argument, therefore, was that any asset that was not actually intended to be sold should be treated as a fixed asset, with its value recorded at historical cost regardless of what the market value of the asset might be. Theorists—such as Dicksee—who defended this idea argued that fluctuations in market value ought to be recognized only insofar as they applied to floating assets. However, in practice, accounting theorists who defended the fixed/floating distinction tended to argue that most of the businesses' assets should be classified as fixed, thus removing market value fluctuations from consideration.

There were some obvious vulnerabilities in the argument made by Dicksee. To begin with, it was not necessarily the case that changes in the value of an asset would not impact profit or loss. Dicksee argued that any changes in the real market value of a so-called fixed asset should not be recognized because companies did not intend to realize appreciation in asset value, presumably by reselling the assets. However, there are other ways in which companies could realize the benefits from an appreciation in the value of fixed assets, even without reselling those assets. For example, if the price of iron ore appreciated by 300%, then the stock market valuation of a publicly-listed railroad company would likely go up, since investors would realize that the assets of the railroad company could be acquired and resold at great profit. This example illustrates one of the problems with Dicksee's proposed dichotomy between fixed and floating assets since the change in the value of a fixed asset can clearly affect the public valuation of a company.

Another, more conceptual problem with Dickssee's argument was the claim that a company's actual behavior should count for more than the actual value of its assets when trying to account for a change in asset value. In the example of iron ore appreciation given above, it can be argued that the intention of the company to resell the ore is immaterial to the question of whether the company is more or less valuable as a result of the price appreciation. There is an argument to be made that investors need to understand the changed value of the company regardless of whether or not the company tries to realize its changed value by selling an asset. It should also be noted that, in the 1970sn and 1980s, so-called corporate raiders made a great deal of money by acquiring companies with underpriced or unrecognized assets on their books, then breaking down a company and selling its assets. This example demonstrates how the market inefficiency created by undervaluing the assets of a company can lead to negative results. In theory, it would be more efficient to value assets at their fair value.

At the same time that accounting theorists resisted the inclusion of market value fluctuations because of their reliance on the fixed/floating assets dichotomy, the concept of depreciation was co-opted by the historical cost approach rather than leading to an adoption of fair value. Initially, the idea of depreciation gained currency as a way of recognizing and accounting for an actual market value phenomenon, the chance in the value of long-lived assets. Understood in this way, depreciation could have served as a means of adjusting asset value based on market value. However, what took place instead was that depreciation gave way to formulas, such as 5% annual depreciation, which were not necessarily in accordance with market value. Thus, the opportunity for depreciation to insert more emphasis on fair value in asset valuation was lost, replaced by possibly unrealistic and rote formulas.

Rather, according to Williams, the strongest basis for fair value accounting in the accounting literature and practice of the early twentieth century was the redefinition of assets as a deferred or unallocated cost: "*A move away from the view of assets as property and the growing emphasis on costs enabled costs per se to be considered as assets. The idea was introduced that an asset was something of value because it would provide a benefit in the future*" (Williams 2003, p. 146). It was this idea that would grow into what is known as fair value accounting, but not for some time to come.

In understanding the development of fair value accounting, it is necessary to bear in mind that the concept of fair value long preceded the execution. According to Williams (2003), the concept of assets at unallocated or deferred costs—a concept that was already in circulation by the end of the nineteenth century—was the root of fair value accounting. However, what seems to have delayed the development of this concept into a complete system of accounting comparable in scope and rigor to historical cost accounting appears to have been issues of implementation. In 1957, the American Accounting Association (AAA) issued the following comment on the use of historical cost: "*The value of an asset is the money equivalent of its service potentials. Conceptually this is the sum of the future market prices of all streams of service to be derived, discounted to their present worth. However, this conception of value is an abstraction which yields but limited practical basis for quantification. Consequently, the measurement of assets is commonly made by other more feasible means non-monetary assets are typically stated at acquisition cost or some derivative thereof. (AAA 1957, p. 4).*"

The AAA's complaint against fair value accounting was thus not conceptual but practical. Historical cost accounting was, by comparison to fair value approaches, relatively simple, and had also been adopted wholeheartedly by numerous companies and accounting standards boards. The evolution of modern accounting can, therefore, be understood as the struggle to balance the admitted simplicity and acceptance of historical accounting while the evolving consensus those aspects of the fair value approach were more accurate and thorough.

Accounting is the framework through which value is expressed and assigned (Saudagaran 2009). Thus, having understood the roots of value in economic theory and having introduced the role of accounting as an arbiter of value, it remains to offer a more precise examination of how measurement and valuation function within the discipline of accounting, as will be done in the remainder of the study.

2.3.1 Equity Asset Valuation

For equity asset valuation, the concept of equity security is critical in understanding this method of valuation. The ownership claims of a company's net asset represent equity security (Pinto et al. 2020). Equity security is a relevant and suitable parameter for the analysis of the investment of a firm it provides helpful information about the portfolio as well, as it represents a significant wealth portion of a company's investment profile. Many other reasons make the study of equity security a vital parameter, such as the evaluation of the amount of wealth of a company allocated to the equities gives valuable insight into the risk and return attributes of the complete profile of the company (Pinto et al. 2020). Moreover, different equity securities have various ownership claims over the total assets of a company. All the equity securities usually do not belong to the same ownership. This aspect affects the risk and return attributes in various ways (Pinto et al. 2020).

2.3.2 The Evaluation of Equity Security and the Value of the Company

Equity securities are released by the companies in the main markets to increase capital and liquidity (Pinto et al. 2020). The additional value of liquidity created in this way also provides the company with an extra 'currency' that can be used to acquire directly and can also be used to provide benefit to the employees in the form of stock shares as well (Pinto et al. 2020). The method used by one of the fastest-growing companies listed on the fortune 500 lists. The main objective of increasing the capital of the company is to enhance the magnitude of the company's revenue creation ventures and provide benefits to shareholders, as well as for improving the total income of a company (Pinto et al. 2020). In most of the scenarios, the capital raise is done as a part of the long-term growth of a company, purchasing long-term assets, making investments, acquiring the shares or a franchise of new growth companies, as well as for expansion of business in the new geographical region. All the measures are mentioned above ultimately raise the book value of the company.

2.3.3 Return on Equity (ROE) and Accounting Parameters

ROE is the main parameter that investors of the equity utilize for the evaluation that the higher management of the company is appropriately using the capital wealth that was provided for the generation of profit. ROE evaluates the total amount of the income available for the shareholders generated by the net equity capital invested in the company. The return on equity is calculated as the total amount of the income that is available to common shareholders divided by the average total book value of equity (BVE) (Pinto et al. 2020).

$$ROE_t = \frac{NI_t}{Average\ BVE_t}$$

The above equation, 'NI_t' represents the net income earned in the year 't', and 'BVE' is the book value of the equity.

Return on equity is based on the assumption that total income produced in the current year has been generated with the help of the existence of the equity at the start of the year and any new equity that has been invested in the time frame of the year.

2.3.4 *Intellectual Capital: A Modern Valuation Tool*

This section relates the fusion of modern technologies, opportunities, and accounting practices to explore the new pathways that have changed the framework of accounting, such as big data analytics, blockchains, and current accounting practices that are ultimately helping in the creation as well as increasing the value of intellectual capital aid the value creation of the companies and ultimately supporting the goals of sustainable development (Al-Htaybat et al. 2019).

Since the establishment of the accounting system, various technological and digital changes have taken place. Since the advent of the fourth industrial revolution, there are changes established in the way of doing businesses, increasing values, and every aspect of the industry has been digitized. The number of followers and the views that a company's social media account gets has turned into an asset and an opportunity for the future economic growth of the company. Keeping in view these changes, the modern accounting practices and evaluation parameters come into existence for managing modern businesses as well as to monitor them.

As mentioned previously, the concept of value creation is also viewed from a different perspective. Dumay has mentioned three types of values (Dumay 2016). The first type of value mentioned by Dumay is the monetary value that is the primary value, representing the capital of the company, the utility value: this provides the transmission about the effectiveness and usefulness of the products, services, and goods for the information of stakeholders and the ability to generate the monetary value. Social value is based on the evaluating the benefit a company provides to society (Dumay 2016). The final form of the modern value is sustainability value, a measure of the company's operation and commitment to the goals of sustainable development (Dumay 2016). The last two forms of the values have shown more impact in recent years. The investors and the lending institutes tend to invest in the companies and firms working directly or indirectly to the cause of sustainability, green energy, and the environment. Sustainability should not be reviewed from the environmental perspective. It also includes the development of sustainable human resources.

In simpler terms, intellectual capital can be referred to as the combined knowledge of a firm and its resources that can contribute to the economic benefit to the company. The advent and rise of the knowledge economy is the new concept that emphasizes intellectual capital and involves this at different levels (Loyarte et al. 2018).

The value of the intellectual capital of a company can be based on the difference between market valuation and the book value that represents the net assets of the company (Dumay et al. 2020). The start of the 1990s, the people and the associations responsible for setting the accounting standards were not so much eager or interested in measuring economic value because the traditional and conservative approach of accounting didn't allow for accounting the future value (Dumay et al. 2020). The companies such as Skandia Group, Dow chemicals, and Hughes aircraft are the ones

Table 2.1 Measured parameters of intellectual capital included in the Skandia accounting model

FINANCIAL FOCUS 1994		CUSTOMER FOCUS 1994	
Fund assets (MSEK)	3666	Market share	2.3%
Fund assets/employee (MSEK)	228	Number of accounts	14,524
Income/employee (SEK 000)	50	Customers lost	1.1%
Income/managed assets	0.027%	Fund assets, excl. Skandia Link, per customer (SEK 000)	78
		Satisfied customer index (scale 1–5)	3.95
PROCESS FOCUS 1994		**RENEWAL & DEVELOPMENT FOCUS 1994**	
Adm. expense/managed assets	0.455	Competence development expense/employee (SEK 000)	7
Adm. expense/total revenues	75%	Satisfied employee index (scale 1–5)	3.08
Cost for admin error/management revenues	1.5%	Marketing expense/managed assets	0.12%
Average volatility, shares	0%	Marketing expense/customer (SEK)	308
Average volatility, interest rates	0%		
Total yield compared with index	+3.2%		
HUMAN FOCUS	**1994**		
Number of employees	143		
Employee turnover	5%		
Average years of service with company	10.8		

Source: Dumay et al. (2020)

who started to measure the intellectual capital and started adding it to the system (Dumay et al. 2020).

Skandia group was the first company to add intellectual capital reporting to the annual report issued by the company (Dumay et al. 2020). Table 2.1 shows the measured parameters of intellectual capital included in the Skandia accounting model (Dumay et al. 2020).

From the evaluation perspective, accounting specialists evaluate the accounting performance of different firms to evaluate the potential of growth in terms of market value, book value, and currently the value of intellectual capital. Even the evaluation standards have changed. The reviewer critically analyzes the tax information of the company. The social and sustainability value of the company is as significant as market value. For the evaluation of the organizational performance, the management should be able to recognize the importance of the accounting practices in the economic system. For decision making in monetary units, the financial reports are considered to serve as an index for making important decisions to either invest or not of the investment companies or parties (Gogan et al. 2016). However, in the current era of information, where the intellectual capital constitutes a significant portion of the product's value, the traditional financial statements that are released on an annual basis report and describe the partial value of the assets of the intangible company. Intellectual capital generation and reporting is an effective strategy that companies can adopt to gain good advantage on the market and will ultimately result in increasing the market value of the company.

2.4 The Concept of Value and Valuation in Financial Accounting

Financial accounting as it is carried out by public companies can be understood not just as a set of techniques and practices pertaining to a system of accounting, but also as part of a field of communication between a company and its investors. Scholars have always recognized this kind of communication as one of the basic functions of accounting (Crandal 1969). However, it has not been until relatively recently in the history of the discipline that this relationship has been frequently examined with the assistance of other research advances, particularly advances in the field of communication theory or information theory. The scholarly literature on accounting has often focused internally, with accounting theory focused on the three basic precepts discussed in Hendriksen and Breda's (1991) seminal work on accounting theory: (a) providing improved understanding of current practices as used by accountants, (b) evaluating the robustness and completeness of accounting practices, and (c) developing new practices and approaches to accounting.

When accounting is understood not only in internal terms but external terms—that is, part of a system of information exchange between a reporting entity and the stakeholders of that reporting entity—then it becomes necessary to ask questions about the relationship between the use of accounting and the subsequent response of stakeholders. Such questions have typically been asked from the perspective of qualitative research and have only more recently been incorporated into quantitative research paradigms (Rogers et al. 2011).

Financial accounting consists of a great many techniques, tools and approaches. There are numerous ways of distinguishing between these approaches—for example, the use of U.S. Generally Accepted Accounting Principles (GAAP) versus non-GAAP methods. There is thus no one way in which to operationalize the concept of economic event disclosure. The specific variable of interest in the context of this study is the use of fair value accounting. Fair value accounting is of interest partly because of gaps in the literature, which in turn relate to practical problems. For example, it is known that many companies in emerging economies do not use fair value accounting (Peng and Bewley 2010), which creates a dilemma for investors who want to be able to benefit from the high returns of companies in emerging markets but who might also be wary of the accounting signals sent out by such companies. On the other hand, it might also be the case that the lure of high returns outweighs a wariness about accounting methods. Because this question is both unanswered and of high relevance given the present state of emerging markets and global investor sentiment, fair value accounting can be considered an appropriate operationalization of the concept of financial disclosure of economic events.

2.5 The Object of Financial Accounting Valuation

The objects of financial accounting valuation can be understood through a review of some literature related to fair value use in financial accounting.

The first article to be analyzed is that of Magnan (2009). Magnan's article was important for a number of reasons, theoretical as well as practical. First, Magnan made a point about fair value accounting (and, by extension, other kinds of accounting) that thought-provokingly disputed the trend in the accounting literature (see for example Demski et al. 2002) to place fair value accounting within the framework of information and communication theory. Magnan supported this point with various compelling arguments, including the following: (a) Fair value accounting, although intended to be a unifying variable, actually consists of several variant approaches and therefore cannot be considered as a signal with a stable identity; (b) fair value accounting is not merely a messenger of financial information but might also be a factor in real-world business outcomes. While Magnan did not mount a direct attack on information theory as a foundation for fair value accounting, or any other accounting system, these points were nonetheless helpful in adding much-needed complexity to the application of information theory to accounting.

Even if is accepted that information theory is at the base of accounting as a system of signals designed for consumption, Magnan (2009) raised the point that the communication system is far more complex than the binary sender-receiver paradigm of information theory. In particular, Magnan suggested that an exclusive focus on investors' information needs might not be consistent with either overall market efficiency or fairness, and that there is a potential tension between investors' and companies definitions of "true and fair. . .business reality" (p. 191). Thus, even if information theory is applied to fair value accounting research and practice, Magnan suggested that the process of signal generation and exchange was far more complicated than it has been acknowledged to be by supporters of fair value accounting.

These aspects of Magnan's (2009) article had important implications for regulatory leadership as it pertains to accounting and deserves to be discussed further in that context. First, Magnan argued that "regulators' objectives. . .include the stability of the banking system and the well-being of society as a whole" (p. 191). Such objectives are clearly difficult, and perhaps impossible, to achieve; however, if regulators take such a broad approach to their job function and mandate, they are required to exercise a form of leadership that goes beyond enjoining or forbidding specific accounting standards and approaches. Magnan critiqued both regulators and accounting policy-makers for being slow to issue fair value guidance and for incomplete and unhelpful guidance. Potentially, then, there is a leadership role to be played by regulators and accounting experts in generating more rapid and comprehensive guidance for the use of fair value accounting. Such leadership, Magnan suggested, would not only take the form of better-informing companies who intend to use this method but also balance the interests of investors, companies, and markets in a fairer fashion.

There is a complementary leadership role to be played by CEOs, CFOs, and other organizational leaders considering the adoption of fair value accounting. As Magnan (2009) stated, *Fair Value Accounting provides relevant and useful information to investors as they attempt to value firms. However, the move toward Fair Value Accounting constitutes a major shift in the basic tenets of financial reporting and raises many implementation issues because it changes how management and other stakeholders view the firm. Such changes are likely to affect the decisions and actions of managers and stakeholders. (p. 195).*

Setting aside the question of incomplete or slow guidance from policy boards, there are still important leadership steps that can be taken by organizational leaders in the implementation of fair value accounting. The goal of such leadership steps would not only be to achieve compliance with fair value accounting in a manner that would benefit investors but also to align corporate practices with fair value accounting in a strategic manner. For example, a company that adopts the kind of market- and model-based measurements required by fair value accounting can apply those orientations to activities outside accounting as well.

Magnan also suggested that the advent of fair value accounting creates modest leadership opportunities for accountants, given that "Fair Value Accounting requires accountants to have a better understanding of markets: how they work and when they do not work" (p. 199). This point was also made by Power (2010), who suggested that fair value account was leading accountants to become more integrated into more explicitly economic ways of thinking about what they do. While these impacts of fair value accounting might not count as leadership per se, they do indicate how the roles of ordinary accountants are changing.

The practical usefulness of Magnan's (2009) work in the context of the proposed research lies in the suggestion of possible open-ended questions that can be posed to study participants once they have completed the quantitative portion of the study. In particular, it would be enlightening to ask investors in fair value accounting companies how exactly they benefit from fair value investing. In addition, Magnan's discussion of the theory of fair value accounting would improve the literature review associated with the proposed study since Magnan summarizes numerous perspectives on fair value accounting in a thorough and critical fashion.

Given that fair value accounting has been adopted by a large number of companies, it is important to understand how and why regulatory and business leaders came to prefer the fair value approach to the transactional approach. Such an overview is provided by Power's (2010) seminal overview of fair value accounting and its relationship to what Power called the transformation of reliability. Power stated, first of all, that the widespread adoption of fair value accounting has been more than just an accounting decision; rather, fair value accounting has served as a catalyst for both a form of globalization as well as a form of standardization: "*Fair value could be said to be much more than just a technical measurement convention; for its proponents it came to represent a change process that was global in aspiration and was increasingly intolerant of the apparent incoherence of mixed measurement systems* (p. 197)." Thus, the decision to adopt fair value accounting can be understood as highly strategic in scope; while the practical outcome of such a decision might seem to be merely the adoption of a technical measurement, the context of the adoption decision is intertwined with new strategic perceptions of value, disclosure, and global reach.

Power (2010) used the theme of reliability to discuss the usefulness of fair value accounting. Fair value accounting is said to be reliable because of its emphasis on "*markets and the value they produce* (p. 200)". Given that traditional transaction-based accounting has not been integrated into markets in this way, many leaders and managers in companies that have adopted fair value accounting have had to change their conceptions about what accounting does, what accounting is for, and how and why accounting sends particular signals to investors. The use of fair value accounting has, in this sense, prompted leaders to try to integrate their traditional concepts of accounting with market-based models of value, which, according to Power, has resulted in greater sophistication among corporate leaders who are active in defining and implementing accounting policy.

Power's (2010) article, while constituting an important discussion of how fair value accounting has transformed the notion of reliability and in the process made new and productive demands on corporate leaders, furnishes background information and arguments for a literature review, but is not as directly relevant to the question of how and why shareholders respond to fair value-using companies in particular ways. Accordingly, the last three studies discussed in this portion of the response will all be pertinent to the question of shareholder sentiment, which is the direct focus of the research question.

Investors are not typically thought of as leaders. Yet, as Lucey and Dowling (2005) observed, investors make sovereign decisions about their investments that can have leadership implications, especially when the investing entity is not an individual but a mutual fund or other collective. However, even when the investor is an individual, the decision to buy, sell, or hold a stock on the basis of some kind of information about a company is highly comparable to the leadership actions made by corporate officers who act on incoming data.

2.5.1 Elements of Financial Accounting Valuation

One of the gaps in the literature on fair value accounting is that it is not well-known how or why the use of fair value accounting prompts investors, whether individual or corporate, to make investment decisions. However, there are seminal papers on investor decision-making theory that can be used to provide some necessary background information. If it is accepted that investors make leadership decisions when they decide how to spend their money, then these studies can furnish an appropriate background for a study of investor behavior related to fair value-using companies and, in so doing, cast light on elements of valuation in financial accounting.

Pitre (2012) conducted a particularly relevant study on this topic. Although the study was delimited to non-professional investors, it still cast light on how the use of fair value accounting could not only assist investors (which, as Magnan 2009 pointed out, are a nearly-universal assumption in the literature) but also hurt them. The theoretical starting point of Pitre's discussion was that of rationality, specifically a form of rationality based on Bayesian approaches to data analysis. Pitre observed that "*If investors behaved in a perfect Bayesian manner, they would extract and use all available information from the fundamental data in the same way, resulting in both high accuracy and low dispersion*" (Pitre 2012, p. 94). Of course, investors do not behave in this way, a fact to which Pitre's experiment called attention in a particularly interesting way.

Pitre (2012) asked research participants to make investment decisions based on two kinds of reporting structures, a frequent versus a less-frequent approach. Pitre found that, although in theory the disclosure of more information might have been expected to improve investor performance, what actually happened in the experiment was that investors exposed to more frequent data failed to see key patterns in the data and, as a result, did not outperform those who were exposed to more limited reporting frequencies. While this study did not compare traditional versus fair value accounting, there is something of an analog between the fair value accounting system and the use of more frequent reporting periods. Both more frequent reporting and fair value accounting are intended to improve investors' bases for making decisions. Fair value accounting adds a layer of market-based evaluation, giving investors information that they did not possess before. More frequent reporting serves the same function since investors obtain earlier access to data for which they would otherwise have to wait. However, Pitre found that raising the level of information available did not predict improved performance, at least by nonprofessional investors. This result raises the possibility that fair value accounting might not in fact be any more beneficial for investors than the traditional transactional method of accounting.

Methodologically, the Pitre (2012) study raises the possibility of expanding the proposed research question. For example, in addition to asking investors in fair value-using companies about their confidence in a stock and their likelihood of buying, holding, or selling a stock, it might be useful to ask such investors about what, in their opinion, the use of fair value accounting adds to their decision-making processes. Such a question could be asked in an open-ended manner and could be posed after subjects completed their responses to the quantitative questions associated with the study.

While Pitre's (2012) study applied to individual and nonprofessional investors, Chen et al. (2013) conducted a study that was applicable to the kinds of leadership exercised by managers who use fair value accounting. Fair value accounting is not merely a form of disclosure to investors but also a means of supporting decision-making within the organization itself. Chen et al. found that fair value can alter managers' decision-making behavior in a manner comparable to how the most frequent disclosure of financial information altered nonprofessional investors' decision-making processes in Pitre's study.

Chen et al.'s (2013) study was fairly complex. The core of the study was an effort to test the following hypotheses (pp. 75–77), each of which casts some light on how the use of fair value accounting might influence the decision-making of managers:

H1: Managers are more likely to hedge risk exposure with derivatives when only the economic impact information is presented than when both the economic impact and the fair value accounting impact information is presented; this effect is more likely when the price volatility of the hedged asset is higher but less likely when it is lower.

H2: The joint effect of hedging impact and price volatility on managers' hedging decisions is mediated by their relative considerations of economic versus accounting factors.

H3: Managers are more likely to hedge risk exposure with derivatives when historical cost accounting is applied than when fair value accounting is applied.

Each of these hypotheses rested on the common assumption that presenting fair value accounting information would curtail the riskiness of managers' decision-making because of the role played by volatility.

Chen et al.'s (2013) hypotheses were confirmed in an experiment. Interestingly, the use of fair value accounting created a disadvantage rather than an advantage for managers who were deciding whether to engage in appropriate hedging activities. This result indicates that, because of managerial aversion to reporting volatility, fair value accounting would be a suboptimal managerial decision tool in some contexts. Consequently, leaders who hold decision-making power ought to be aware of the limitations of fair value accounting. Chen et al.'s results are not directly applicable to the methodology of the proposed research question but, taken together with Pitre's (2012) results, they help to explain some of the possible risks associated with using fair value accounting to make investment decisions, regardless of whether these decisions are made by stockholders deliberating the purchase of securities or by corporate leaders executing financial strategies.

While Chen et al.'s (2013) and Pitre's (2012) studies suggested some of the risks that reliance on fair value accounting can pose to both investors and managers, Abdel-Khalik (2010) proposed a bold solution to address the needs of investors, corporate leaders, and regulators alike—the combination of fair value and historical cost approaches. Abdel-Khalik's work represented a particular challenge to regulators and policy-makers to whom the choice is between either fair value accounting or historical cost accounting. As important as it is to challenge accounting standards in this way, there is a tension between Abdel-Khalik's argument that the market will benefit from more information and Chen et al.'s and Pitre's arguments that the market might benefit from less. Abdel-Khalik's article was chosen for inclusion in this literature review because it underlines the need for further analysis. Because so few studies on the topic of the usefulness of fair value investing as a decision support tool have been carried out, there is a lack of consensus in the literature about how and why fair value accounting is important in financial decision-making processes.

2.5.2 The Concepts of Value, Cost, and Price in Management Accounting

One of the most fascinating aspects of Collier and Agyei-Ampomah's (2008) argument is the association of the "risk culture" (p. 1) in general with management accounting in particular. For those who are accustomed to thinking of accounting as a dry and quotidian exercise in balancing the books, an activity carried out in some realm remote from strategy and business relevance, this claim should serve as a stimulating counterargument. Moreover, if one takes a step back, it is possible to argue that the open systems of the organization align closely with management accounting theory. One way in which to understand this alignment is through the open systems theory of organizations, which helps to explain the object of management accounting valuation.

The Object of Management Accounting Valuation

Rabin (2003) offered the following visual model of the open systems model and its role in organizational science (Fig. 2.2).

The open organization is one that acts on inputs, via a transformative process, to create outputs. For example, a tire company might take the input of rubber and place it into the transformative process of a factory to produce the output of a tire. This process is a loop. The tire company might discover that it costs $1 to produce a tire that sells for $1.25 and decide to lower the costs of production so as to gain more profit. In the open systems theory of organization, obtaining data about the costs of production and deciding to lower them counts as an example of feedback. The organization constantly monitors its production loop in order to identify and

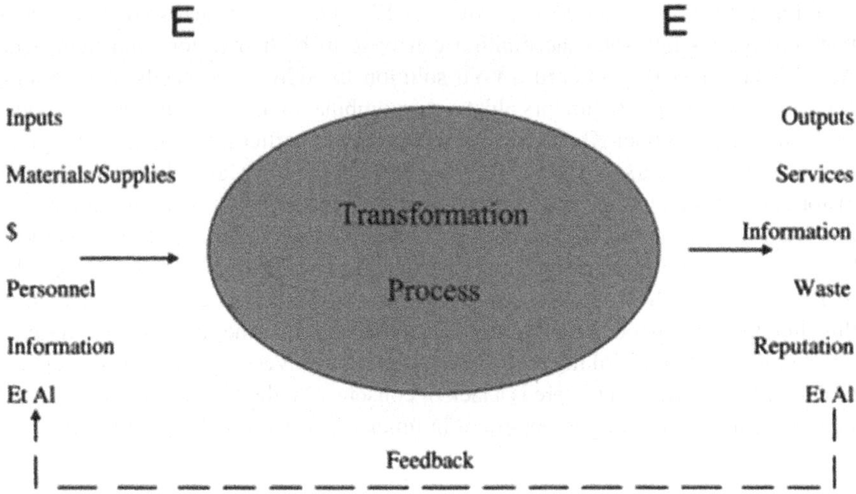

Fig. 2.2 The open systems theory of organizations [Source: Rabin (2003)]

eliminate waste and add other efficiencies. In order to do, the company must be able to understand its processes, wring data out of them, and be disciplined enough to alter its productive cycle (in this hypothetical case, with the purpose of lowering the cost of per-tire production). The work of Bell (1984) suggests that accounting is perhaps the key component of the open systems cycle, as accounting is the function that determines budgetary commitment, monitors processes for costs and margins, and otherwise determines if any particular strategic move of the company is profitable or not.

Money is the lifeblood an organization—the one key factor that determines whether an organization can act or not, depending on strategic circumstances (Johnson et al. 2005). Thus, accounting—and, in particular, management accounting, is tremendously strategic and sits right on the foundation of the organizational theory of open systems, as Hoque (2005) has pointed out: "Managers in an organization make decisions to achieve their organization's objectives. These decisions are about how to make their organizations translate their strategic goals or objectives into action. To do so, they need information, and accounting provides financial and cost information to managers to assist them in making decisions" (p. 4).

In other words, without management accounting, there is no empirical standard for feedback in Rabin's (2003) model of open organizations; the corporation that functions without this sort of accounting foundation will, according to this theory, not be able to refine continually its productive cycle in order to add efficiency, eliminate waste, and lower costs. Indeed, given that these three functions are very important for the functioning of a company, it is likely that a company of sufficient size without adequate management accounting at its foundation would probably collapse (Morgan et al. 2008).

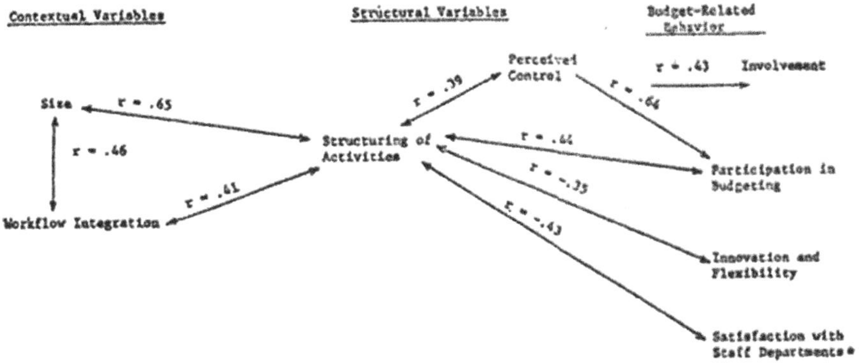

Fig. 2.3 The role of accounting in open systems [Source: Bell (1984, p. 158)]

The point is not just that management accounting is important and allows the perpetual re-looping of production processes based on feedback, a la the open systems model of Rabin (2003). The point is a larger one, namely that accounting is at the heart of a control-based approach to the organization. All strategy feeds through accounting (i.e., the various branches of accounting); without accounting, there is no financial strategy as all. Macintosh and Quattrone (2010) have expressed this point in the following way: "[Controls]. . .go beyond the traditional job of providing financial information after the fact to monitor operational performance towards predetermined plans. And they can be explicitly designed and used to focus on strategic variables" (p. 23). According to Macintosh and Quattrone, controls play a role in each and every stage of the product lifecycle; they are ubiquitous, and they can be structured in such a way as to guide processes. Thus, the control is not necessary an after-the-fact event, a post mortem of a particular process, but a strategic trigger.

Figure 2.3 illustrates how controls exist at the levels of building, differentiating, holding, harvesting, and divesting. The focus of controls is, respectively, prospects, sales, profits, efficiency, and cash flows as a business moves through the product lifecycle from birth to maturation. Surely, a product or service can go through these stages without being governed by controls, but, in such a circumstance, Macintosh and Quattrone (2010) suggest that the chance of success is diminished (Fig. 2.4).

If a project has to be funded internally and money is tight, accounting and analysis can indulge in certain initiatives—such as the restructuring of payments that are due to vendors—to obtain the funds. By the same token, accounting and analysis serve as a check on rash decisions. Just as the heart might cause a rush in circulation to create a blush and dissuade someone from asking out a person very likely to reject them, accounting and analysis is the group that will raise the alarms in case it is faced with a proposition of great risk and little chance of success. Thus, accounting and analysis can check the energy of an organization as well as abet it.

Accounting is an instrument that can be used across a broad spectrum. On one end of the spectrum, accounting can be used as an instrument to perform certain financial

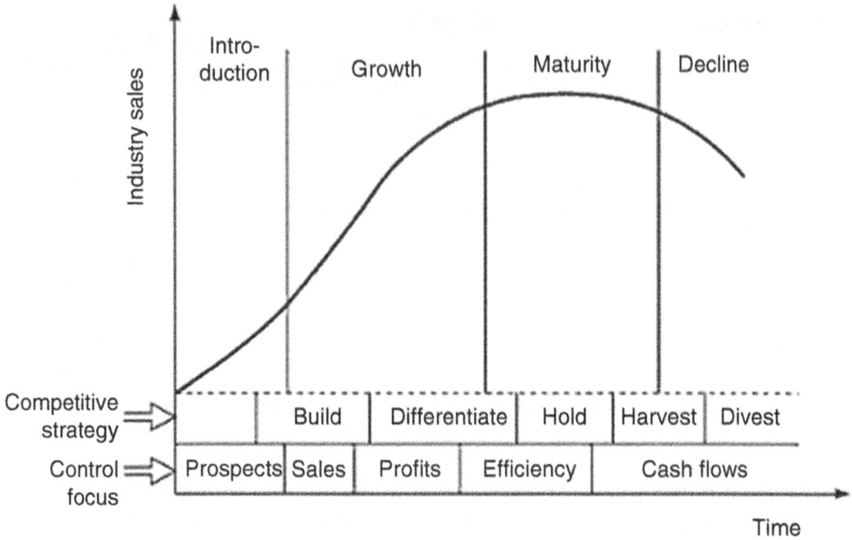

Fig. 2.4 The controls-driven organization [Source: Macintosh and Quattrone (2010, p. 152)]

tasks and cut off from a truly strategic and participative role in the organization. On the other end of the group, accounting can sit right at the very heart of an organization, integrating every major task under a single control- and risk-oriented structure. Understanding how and why things get done in an accounting group is dependent on the role of the group within the organization. Assuming that an accounting group is an ethical, interconnected, and strategic contributor to the organization, then things get done because accounting understands its central role. Accounting understands how the rest of the organization is relying on it, and how important its role is, and therefore works more quickly and efficiently than an accounting group that is in ignorance of how its contributions impact the organization, or that is actually disconnected from strategic significance. Research suggests that both employees and organizations who understand where they fit in and why they are useful will be more motivated and productive; at the group level, there will be a sense of self-directedness lacked by groups that do not enjoy strategic centrality (Aguayo 1991; Bandura 1997).

Based on these theories and principles, the object of valuation in management accounting is to make decisions that provide useful data to run the business, which in effect means understanding assets, debits, and controls at the high level.

The Elements of Management Accounting Valuation

In practical terms, perhaps the most element of management accounting valuation pertains to the choice of the accounting standard. Given that IFRS is closely associated with fair value valuation, it makes sense that, from a management accounting perspective, companies are concerned with the costs of switching to IFRS.

The management literature suggests that there are two reasons that motivate businesses to make sweeping changes to their processes: Coercion or profit. According to Krugman and Wells (2009), coercion typically consists of the framework of laws and penalties that are brought to bear on businesses, whereas profit consists of the surplus value that a business can create by taking some action. A third consideration, just as important as coercion and profit, is a risk. For example, if there is little risk of a business being either caught or penalized for not adhering to a specific law, then the management literature (to say nothing of the case study literature) suggests that companies might decide to break the law. Various factors that fall under the rubrics of coercion, profit, and risk can be sorted into the larger categories of costs and benefits (Dompere 2010).

One of the risks associated with adopting fair value accounting is that, especially if fair value is adopted as part of IFRS, there is an associated cost of switching to this accounting system. If the cost of switching is counterbalanced by benefits (such as entering into compliance with national or international law, or winning more investor confidence), then the costs can be justified.

As Bruggemann et al. (2013) pointed out, mandatory IFRS came into effect into the European Union on January 1, 2005, 3 years after it had first been publicized via an IAS Regulation. According to Bruggemann et al. (2013), cost-benefit theory is particularly helpful in explaining European companies' responses to mandatory IFRS: *Firms that expect net benefits of IFRS adoption will adjust their contractual setup within the IFRS regime. In contrast, firms that expect net costs of IFRS adoption have incentives to self-select out of the group of firms for which IFRS application is made mandatory. Some firms, while adopting IFRS overall, may attempt to avoid certain individual IFRS rules that are anticipated to be particularly costly (p. 31).*

With this point in mind, it is possible to discuss the theoretical costs and benefits of IFRS adoption. As discussed by Wiecek and Young (2009), the benefits fall into positive and negative categories. The main positive benefit is that adopting IFRS will stimulate capital inflow into a particular company. The main negative benefit is that, by adopting IFRS, a company will evade legal and regulatory penalties; this benefit can be described as negative because it does not represent the attainment of an actual good, but rather the avoidance of a non-good. According to Stickney et al. (2009), the main costs of IFRS adoption are the physical costs of making the change, which can include process costs, information technology (IT) costs, and general accounting costs.

If IFRS were a single, easily-implemented and easily-monitored business change, than the cost-benefit analysis might be more straightforward. However, as Bruggemann et al. (2013) pointed out, there are several IFRS options. Companies can, for example, delay adoption or adopt selectively. Because of the flexibility of options, there is no one single cost-benefit analysis that applies in general to IFRS adopters. However, there are some recurring cost-benefit themes in the empirical literature, which is discussed at greater length in the next section of the literature review.

Understanding the theoretical basis for the costs and benefits of IFRS adoption can be made more complicated by the fact that IFRS is itself a standard under constant revision. Take for example IFRS 1, which is the short name for the guide to First-Time Adoption of International Reporting Standards. IFRS 1 was thoroughly rewritten in 2008 so as to be clearer to first-time IFRS adopters; mere months after the rewriting, IFRS was altered to create certain exemptions pertaining to transfers of assets from customers, lease arrangements, and oil and gas assets (Nandakumar et al. 2010). Thus, a thorough cost-benefit will probably depend on the exact state of the IFRS at the time of adoption.

Another difficulty in reaching conclusions about the theoretical basis of IFRS adoption costs and benefits. Is that (a) the move towards making IFRS mandatory has been delayed by some national accounting boards/regulatory bodies and (b) it remains possible that judicial challenge or popular protest will allow dissenters to keep from implementing IFRS, either in whole or in part. In situations having to do with the adoption of business processes, costs and benefits are more easily modeled if the repercussions of non-adoption are more easily understood. Because of the absence of a firm timetable, a penalty structure, or hard incentives for or against adoption, the theoretical basis for understanding the costs and benefits of IFRS adoption in the U.S. remains murky. It is all the more necessary to turn to empirical methods to learn more about how real companies perceive the costs and benefits of adoption.

One of the problems that have surfaced, in terms of the cost of convergence to IFRS to individual companies, is that the precise magnitude of the cost is not well-known or agreed upon. Johnson's (2009) work suggested that, according to accounting firms themselves, the cost of the convergence was expected to be between 0.5 and 1% of annual revenue. According to the Securities and Exchange Commission, the costs of adopting IFRS are expected to be in the range of 0.125–0.13% of annual revenue (Johnson 2009). Finally, according to a survey of large public companies themselves, the expected costs of transition are expected to be in the range of 0.1 and 0.7% of their revenue (Johnson 2009). Clearly, then, there is a lot of variabilities in what the costs of adhering to IFRS are expected to be. According to Johnson (2009), many larger companies in already dire economic straits (given the ongoing fallout from the Great Recession of 2008) lacked the revenue to make a full-fledged transition to IFRS, while other companies found that such a transition would distract them from more strategic initiatives. The diversity of background conditions makes it necessary to examine IFRS implementation on a case-by-case basis to determine what can be learned about large companies' attitudes.

When IFRS adoption took place across the European Union, there was already a fairly robust framework in place to accommodate and accept IFRS in several spheres of business and bureaucratic life (see for example Epstein and Jermakowicz 2010). If IFRS is seen as a part of a constellation of changes, then it will be easier for adoption to take place; on the other hand, if IFRS adoption is a form of one-off compliance that does not dovetail with the other reporting, bureaucratic, or administrative responsibilities of an organization, then the motivation to adopt is lower (Benston 2006).

Another detailed case study of a SEC registrant's adoption of IFRS was provided by Gornik-Tomaszewski and Sellhorn (2010) in a recent issue of the Review of Business. Despite the depth and breadth of information in this case study, it was limited by the fact that the identity of the IFRS adopter was concealed. Gornik-Tomaszewski and Sellhorn (2010) created the fictitious Tomsel Corp. as a pseudonym for a large European SEC registrant that planned to switch from U.S. GAAP to IFRS in 2011. The issue of privacy loomed large in the current study as well. Because information about internal accounting policies, strategies, and procedures is considered to be highly sensitive information, it is often difficult to build real-world case studies. One method of circumventing this limitation, as in Gornik-Tomaszewski and Sellhorn (2010) work, is to create a pseudonym for the profiled company. The case study carried out by Gornik-Tomaszewski and Sellhorn (2010) called attention to the pure accounting expenses related to the transition to IFRS. For a large SEC registrant that operates globally, and particularly given the retrospective nature of IFRS reporting responsibilities, the project of IFRS adoption is fraught with difficulties imposed by the sheer volume of data. Thus, Gornik-Tomaszewski and Sellhorn (2010) research can be seen as a re-assertion of the various costs faced by SEC registrants transitioning to IFRS.

2.5.3 Accounting Principles in Valuation

This section contains a brief definition of four important valuation principles, namely the historical cost principle, prudence principles, going concern principle, and consistency principle.

The historical cost principle; The historical cost principle is that fixed assets are shown at cost price.

The prudence principle; The prudence principle is based on neither overstating nor understanding profits, assets, liabilities, and loss, and also on not recognizing profits or gains until they materialize.

The going concern principle; The going concern principle operates under the assumption that the business will not be closed in the near future.

The consistency principle; The consistency principle requires an application of the same methods/standards to accounting.

2.5.4 *Valuation Bases for Accounting: Historical Cost and Fair Value*

This section of the chapter contains a brief summary of valuation as it functions in both the historical cost and fair value paradigms.

- *The Financial Statements should represent the current situation of the company, correctly.*

There are many factors come from internal or external of a company and these factors might create differences between the registered value in accounting and the market value of assets and liabilities (Fig. 2.5).

Usage/deformation, inflation, interest rates, interest maturities, exchange rate movements, technology, tax rates, stock prices/manipulations, fashion, economic crisis have effects on financial statements.

- *The values of assets and liabilities on a company's financial statements need to be reliable.*

The correctness of Financial Statements is very significant because there are interest groups, and these interest groups have expectations from the companies and these interest groups want to know what their expectations should be from the company. And, in order to know what the expectations should be from the company, the interest groups need to have correct outcomes from accounting of a company.

Shareholders, stake holders, financial authorities, financial institutions, managers, suppliers, clients, worker unions have expectations from the company.

Correctness of financial statements is significant!

Interest groups	→	**Expectations from the company**
Expectations	→	?
?	→	**Correct outcomes from accounting**

As Matis and Mustata (2004) argued, all transactions from ancient times onwards have relied on, whether implicitly or explicitly, on the concept of value. For a long time, there was no theoretical apparatus applicable to values and valuation; value was treated as whatever cost was paid for a specific good or service, with little formal thought devoted to how and why value is established in the first place.

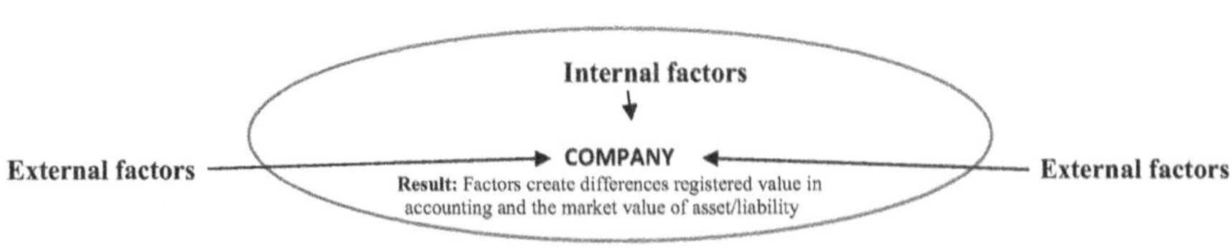

Fig. 2.5 Effective factors on creating differences on historical cost and Fair Value

Matis and Mustata (2004) traced the evolution of valuation theory to the nineteenth century. One of the characteristics of valuation theory during this formative stage was the emerging consensus among economists that the value of a good or service was distinct from the ultimate basis for that value, be it marginal utility, replacement cost, or any other concept. Consensus on this aspect of valuation theory was remarkably broad, uniting such otherwise opposed economists as Adam Smith and Karl Marx; economists were essentially in universal agreement that market value transcended what might be cased base value (represented by production costs, replacement costs, marginal utility, &c.).

Understood in this manner, the problem of value was no longer to find the root of value (since the market defined value), but rather to find accurate ways to calculate the value. Matis and Mustata (2004) argued that the problem of value calculation was segmented into three subordinate problems, namely the calculation of (a) value of use, (b) market value as a price reference, and (c) the role of time.

This valuation problem, although identified in the nineteenth century, has never been conclusively solved. In particular, the role of time remains irresolvable because of the uncertainty of future returns associated with an asset. As such, it does not appear to be an a priori way to solve issues related to the choice of appropriate discounting rates and other quantifications of future value. Rather, accounting theory and practice have generated various alternative approaches to incorporating time into valuation calculations, and standards such as IFRS also offer some guidance on this topic.

One way in which to avoid dealing with the potential complexities of fair value is to employ historic cost. However, as Matis and Mustata (2004) pointed out, the historic cost has various limitations that can render it inappropriate for modern accounting. While historic cost has the benefit of being verifiable and fixed, the main shortcoming of this approach is that there can be a significant disparity between the historic cost of an asset and its actual market value. This disparity was not necessarily much of a problem when markets were less active and sophisticated; however, over time, markets have grown steadily in importance, and the expanded ability for buyers and sellers to enter into transactions over nearly any good or service, at any time, means that there is almost always going to be a meaningful disparity between market (that is, fair) value and historic cost.

In practice, the use of the historic cost approach has led to two kinds of distortions, over-valuation, and under-valuation. These distortions and other problems associated with the historical cost approach have led to the steady adoption of fair value throughout Europe, including Romania.

Matis and Mustata (2004) argued for the position championed by the IFRS, which is that there is room for historical cost approaches alongside the use of fair value. However, whereas IFRS suggested that individual companies find ways to combine historical cost with fair value accounting (as is the case when revaluating financial assets), Matis and Mustafa suggested that individual companies of lower complexity adopt historic cost approaches while group companies adopt the more complex fair value approach. However, this recommendation was not based on empirical research such as a cost-benefit analysis of the use of historic cost accounting in smaller companies.

Valuation at Historical Cost

In accounting theory, fair value is the price of an asset, good, or service that most accurately reflects current and realistic conditions (Previts et al. 2011). Fair value can be distinct from other kinds of value, such as market value and historical value. The market value of a manufacturing plant might be $1 billion, but fair value might be considerably lower—perhaps because of the small number of potential number of buyers of such a plant, combined with the fact that potential buyers might already have plants of their own. Thus, the fair value of the manufacturing plant would be lower than its market price. The same kind of reasoning applies to the historic price. For example, the historic price of a parcel of land might be $10 million, but appreciation in real estate might mean that the land can easily be sold at $50 million. The fair value principle would, in such a scenario, require the value of the land to be recorded at $50 million rather than at $10 million.

Valuation at Fair Value Cost

In accounting theory, fair value is the price of an asset, good, or service that most accurately reflects current and realistic conditions (Previts et al. 2011). Fair value can be distinct from other kinds of value, such as market value and historical value. The market value of a manufacturing plant might be $1 billion, but fair value might be considerably lower—perhaps because of the small number of potential number of buyers of such a plant, combined with the fact that potential buyers might already have plants of their own. Thus, the fair value of the manufacturing plant would be lower than its market price. The same kind of reasoning applies to the historic price. For example, the historic price of a parcel of land might be $10 million, but appreciation in real estate might mean that the land can easily be sold at $50 million. The fair value principle would, in such a scenario, require the value of the land to be recorded at $50 million rather than at $10 million.

These examples demonstrate that value is a floating concept rather than a fixed one. Accounting is the framework through which value is expressed and assigned (Saudagaran 2009). Thus, having understood the roots of value in economic theory and having introduced the role of accounting as an arbiter of value, it remains to offer a more precise examination of how measurement and evaluation function within the discipline of accounting.

Accounting began in an effort to standardize and bring order to organizational life. However, scholars have focused extensive critical attention on how accounting policies, decisions, and techniques have various consequences, both intended and unintended, that defy the desire for a single best way of doing things. Fair value accounting is mired in its own set of controversies that, in this section of the study, have been explored via critical analysis of five important scholarly articles. The works of Magnan (2009) and Power (2010) were important theoretical explorations of fair value accounting, with Magnan making important critiques about fair value's effects on the market ecosystem and relationship to information theory and Power explaining how fair value has transformed accounting-related leadership by bringing it into line with market values and models. Both of these works would be indispensable additions to any literature review on fair value accounting. However, both Magnan and Power addressed fair value accounting more from the perspective of companies and regulators than from the perspective of investors. The work of Chen et al. (2013) and Pitre (2012) cast some light on how the use of fair value can prejudice investment decision-making, both of stockholders seeking securities and of corporate leaders seeking to make business decisions, but Abdel-Khalik (2013) suggested that investors, as well as corporate leaders, could benefit from a system in which historical cost and fair value accounting systems were used alongside each other. There appears to be little consensus in the literature, but many fruitful suggestions as to how fair value accounting can be studied further.

If I can repeat that, actually, a lot of people think that Fair Value is the market price but sometimes it is not. We can repeat by using the definition of FASB that: "*Fair value is the price that would be received to sell an asset or paid to transfer a liability in an "orderly" transaction between market participants at the evaluation date. SFAS No. 157 (ASC Topic 820).*"

So, there is an important term in this definition as you realized. So, the word "orderly" is very significant here. What FASB indicates (FASB is the institution that regulate the accounting rules in the US). By saying "orderly", FASB is proposing 3-level Fair Value Hierarchy and said that if possible, first use level-1 Fair Values, if level-1 Fair Values is not available, use level-2, if not level-2 then level-3.

The 3-Level Fair Value Processing Hierarchy

Level 1 (Quoted prices)—Evaluation based on "quoted prices" in the market for identical assets and liabilities exist in the market (*sufficient frequency*) (Fig. 2.6).

Quoted prices are the recent prices in the market at which assets or liabilities have been traded. Quoted prices represent the most recent bid and ask prices at which buyers and seller agree on.

On the other hand, the bid price indicates the maximum price that a buyer wishes to pay for an asset. The asking price indicates the minimum price that a seller wishes to receive. A trade or transaction occurs when the buyer and seller agree on a price.

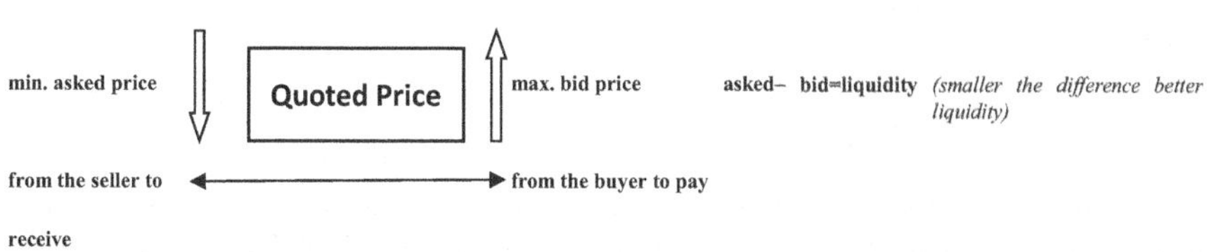

Fig. 2.6 Price realization between seller and buyer

The difference or spread between the bid price and asking prices, is a key indicator of the liquidity of the asset, generally speaking, the smaller the difference, the better the liquidity or the higher the liquidity value.

Level 2 (Observable)—Evaluation based on "similar" assets and liabilities exist in a market *(qt. prices for similar a/l in active markets, qt. prices for similar or identical a/l in inactive markets, inputs other than quoted prices that are observable for a/l such as interest rates, credit risks and so on).*

no quoted prices? → **market observables**

So, there might not be quoted prices in the market. In that case, what we do is we just go down the hierarchy, and we find Level-2 Fair Value. What Level-2 Fair Value is that this Fair Value is based on market observables. What does that mean? That means that there might not be an active market for a specific asset, but there might be an active market for the similar asset to our original asset. So, we consider the price of the similar asset and we adjust that price to our original asset.

Level 3 (Unobservable)—Evaluation based on "internal assumptions/ guesswork".

And finally, the last one is Level-3 Fair Value. So, there are lots of discussions and critiques about Level-3 Fair Value. According to the Level-3 Fair Value, there is no any quoted price for our original asset and there is no any similar asset to our original asset in the market. Then what we should do? According to the Level-3 Fair Value, what we should do is, we should apply to our own evaluation methods to finalize the evaluation process.

no quoted prices, no market observables?

→ **company's own evaluation method**

Why to Use Fair Value?

Now this question is raising, why should we use Fair Value? There are plus and minus, advantage and disadvantage, pros and cons by using of Fair Value Accounting. So, there are three main important advantages to state what can be the reasons to use Fair Value Accounting.

One of the reasons why we should use Fair Value is that what the supporters or proponents of Fair Value claim that;

- *Fair Value provides timely and more relevant more accurate information in the financial statements information that allows interest groups to exercise better decisions about the company*
- *Over the years, multiple standards have been issued by the regulators to increase the usage of Fair Value in financial reporting*

So, actually the regulators, either IFRS or FASB, have issued lots of standards and what they want is to have a big pressure towards using Fair Values in financial reports more and more.

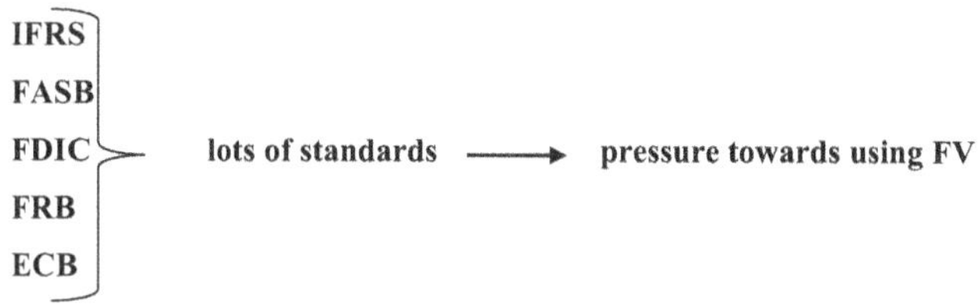

- *The long-term targets of financial regulator institutions such as FASB and IFRS are all financial reports to be prepared by using Fair Value*

So, instead of using Historical Cost for evaluation of assets and liabilities what regulators want is to prepare and report all financial instruments at Fair Value.

Fair Value has become very popular over the years. Fair Value has been in force, in an application for many years. Fair Value was one of the first standards regulated. If we go as back as 1980s, if we go back to the period of Savings and Loans Crises, we can see that the financial statements have been started reporting through Fair Value oriented regime.

So, if we can look at 1980s what we can see that all the assets and liabilities of total bank holding companies in the US have been started reporting at Fair Value. So, we can see from the chart that the usage of Fair Value has been increased over the years. So, if we can go back into 1980s, the usage of Fair Value was not considerable much. But after FASB regulated the ordinance of 115 by regulating forms of discloses, the usage of Fair Value started increasing. So, over the years FASB has issued other different standards, and it seems that, if we look at the years past, it seems that, the use of Fair Value has actually increased dramatically comparing 1980s.

So, as a future target, it seems that, all financial instruments, all financial statements, forms of the Balance Sheets, Income Statements and disclosures of the financial statements are going to be prepared at Fair Value oriented accounting regime (Fig. 2.7).

Fair Value's Position in Financial Crisis

Fair Value is an interesting phenomenon.

- *Fair Value has the potential of exacerbating contagion among banks potentially leading to a breakdown of the entire banking system.* (Khan 2010)

What can be the problems of using Fair Value? If we go back to 2008, when the financial crisis on its top level, during the financial earthquake in all over the world, there were lots of discussions regarding the causes of the financial crisis and there were different addresses to blame or to accuse as the source of the crisis. So, one of the addresses to accuse was accounting. In this perspective, accounting means was Fair Value. That means the eyes of the critiques focused on Fair Value. So, these critiques of Fair Value have claimed that Fair Value makes the contagion worse in financial sectors, specifically in banking sectors and Fair Value based reporting

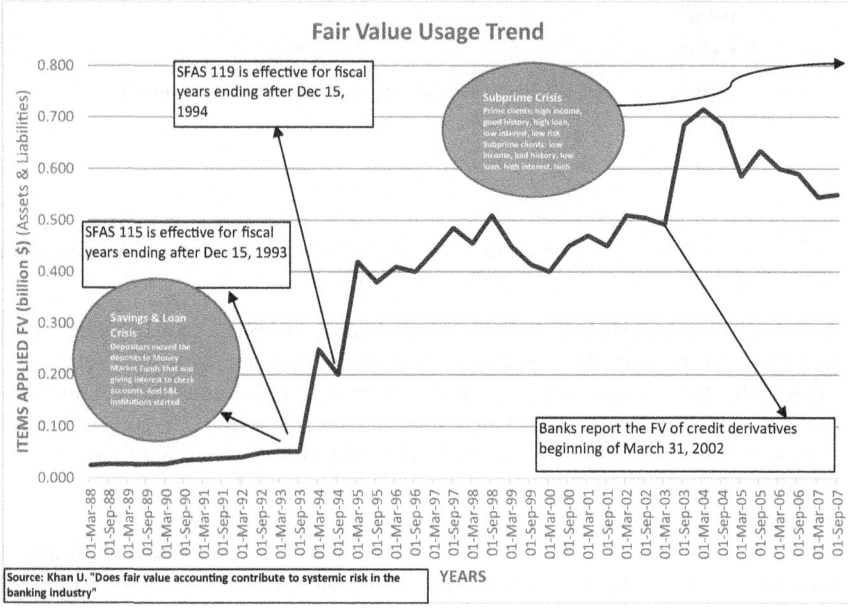

Fig. 2.7 Fair Value usage trend (Khan 2010)

regime causes a systemic risk in financial sectors and, of course, that affects in the end the real sectors.

reasons of the subprime crisis in 2008? → ?accounting?!! → worse contagion → financial sector crisis ▶ reel sect. crisis → Economic Crisis

Contagion refers to the spread of either economic boom or economic crisis throughout the economical region. A famous example is the "Asian Contagion", which occurred in 1997 and started in Thailand. The economic crisis in Thailand spread to bordering Southeast Asian countries and then eventually spilled over to Latin America.

- *Investment decisions based on Fair Value outcomes could lead to self-fulfilling forced sales and falling prices.* (IMF 2008)

IMF had a definition at this point. Now, let's look at little bit what IMF said regarding this issue that investment decisions based on financial reports produced at Fair Value, might lead to forced sales of company's assets and the result of the forced sells would cause to down more the prices of company's assets.

- *Fair Value caused the financial meltdown that followed the subprime crisis. The fair-value rules have destroyed hundreds of billions of dollars of capital in our financial system.* (Isaac 2006)

And, there was another criticism came from FDIC. And, the chairman of FDIC, William Isaac, William Isaac was the chairman of FDIC from 1978 to 85, and what he said was in his speech in front of the members of the Congress, actually what he said took a lot of attention because what he said might be one of the toughest critiques to Fair Value Accounting. He directly accused that Fair Value Accounting was the cause of the Subprime Crisis. Anyway, even though it was a very extreme critique but there were such critiques to Fair Value.

FDIC (Federal Deposit Insurance Corporation): It's an independent federal agency of the United States federal government that keeps public confidence to the financial system by insuring deposits against failure of financial institution.

Subprime market: There are two types of borrowers: Prime borrowers: have a high income, good history, big loan, low interest. Subprime borrowers have low income, bad history, low loan, high interest. SP contracts have grown tremendously too much around at the end of 2006.

Subprime crisis: In the beginning of 2007, there was a tremendous increase in high-risk mortgages that went out of control at the end of the year, and contributed to one of the most severe recessions. The housing mortgages increased extremely in the mid-2000s and together with low-interest rates at the same period encouraged the lenders to make home loan contracts with individuals with poor credit. When the borrowers got into difficulty of payment, which gave the start up to the subprime crisis or subprime meltdown.

How Fair Value Might Push Up the Negatives in a Financial Crisis?

In Fair Value oriented accounting regime, the users of Fair Value, and the Fair Value user companies actually have been connected to market meaning there is an interconnection among each other.

- *Interaction of Fair Value and externally imposed solvency requirements may create a vicious circle of falling prices, leading to an increase in systemic risk.* (Cifuentes et al. 2005)

So, now let's ask this question: Can Fair Value play a role in the financial crisis? So, to answer this question, we should focus on the days of the financial crisis. During the financial crisis, all the prices are under a shock, and that shock depresses the prices of assets, and depressed prices of the assets are falling down. So, in order to go further, we need to remember that the companies that prepare their financial reports at Fair Value have a connection to the price movements in the markets. So, because of this tide connection all the price movements in the market, it doesn't matter up or down would have a reflection in the financial instruments of the company through the application of Fair Value. In the end, falling price of the assets might force the banks to dispose of, to sell some of their assets in order to catch the required ratios. They are obliged to reach some ratios that are regulated by national banks or other regulator institutions.

- *Starting point of an economic crisis "depresses" the market value of assets, and that depress may lead to "forced sales decisions" to avoid from violation of economic crisis. And the "forced sales" may lead to "further fallings in prices"* (Fig. 2.8).

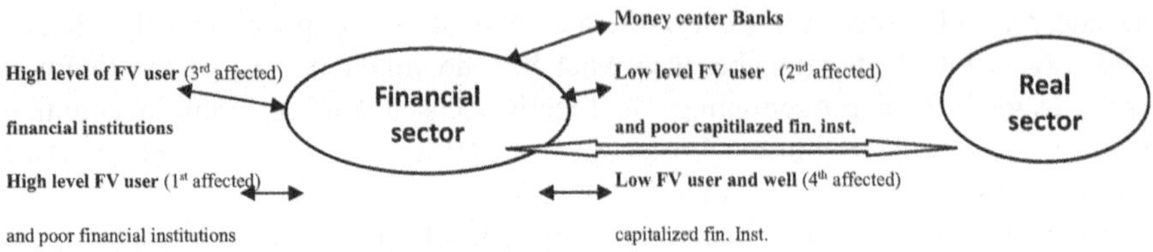

Fig. 2.8 Financial crisis steps on companies

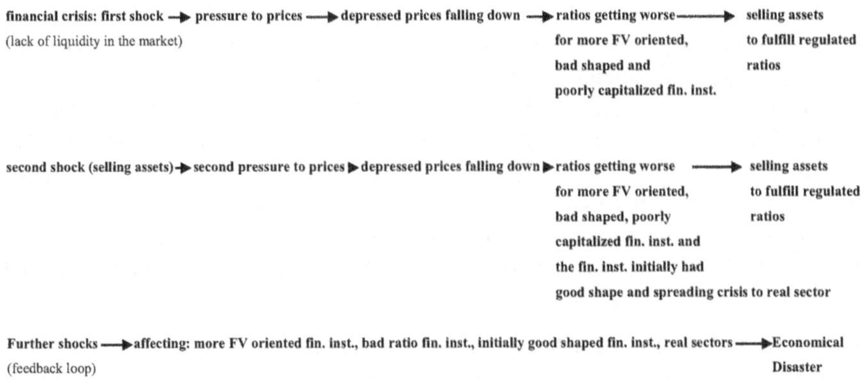

So, this huge pressure on the prices that comes from the market which is under financial depression, under financial crisis, is falling the prices of assets and forcing the financial institutions, principally the banks, the banks which have more Fair Value orientation or poorly capitalized to dispose to sell some of their assets because they are obliged to fulfill the regulated ratios. In order to comply with the regulated ratios, they might be forced to sell some of their assets. And, so, starting this point, if the banks start selling their assets to catch the ratios, there might be a push on the prices level and that would further fall in the prices of the said assets. Following this step, the other banks that were not affected initially from the first shock of the crisis, now they would be under a pressure to sell their assets in order to catch the obliged ratios and this would create another fall in the prices. So, during this financial earthquake, this is a kind of vicious circle, and this is called as the feedback loop of Fair Value.

In economics, Feedback Loop refers to a situation where part of the output of a situation is used for new input. An example of a positive feedback loop would be one where success feeds

- *Forced disposals can lead to further falling in prices*

So, as we can estimate, the next steps of the financial crisis, this vicious circle might continue and might push for further disposals and further lowering the prices of interconnected assets. So, this interconnected effect of Fair Value Accounting can create such a vicious circle, so falling prices might require new ratios to comply with, and new ratios might require new sells of assets and so on. So, this is an ongoing action up to having new balance in the market. That means Fair Value Accounting might have an interconnected risk during the financial crisis, in financial institutions. And, this risk in the financial sectors will destroy the real sectors, and that would create another vicious circle and, in the end, economy would be destroyed.

Fair Value's Interaction Effect

During the financial crisis, actually the pressure of the crisis shock does not affect the fundamental values of the assets. The pressure of the shock, during the financial crisis, can only affect the amount of the liquidity that is available during the depressive period of the crisis. That during the shock of the financial crisis, the liquidity in the market is extremely low. For this reason, if the liquidity is extremely low, the asset's liquidity value becomes extremely low, so the Fair Value of the asset becomes extremely low. So, if there is an extreme drop in the prices of the assets of a financial institution during the financial crisis, that financial institution has to regulate its ratios which are imposed by the regulators such as FDIC and National Banks. If the financial institution does not catch the imposed ratios, it may be considered by the regulators as insolvent. At the end, when the markets have liquidity, meaning there is no financial crisis, markets can absorb the additional sells of assets without having a considerable impact on prices.

high liquidity = no crisis = many buyers = absorbing additional sales = no impact on prices and no necessity adjustment for ratios ⇨ liquidity value =~ fundamental value

low liquidity = fin. crisis = few buyers = rejecting additional sales = prices are low necessary adjustment for ratios other wise=Insolvent!! ⇨ liquidity value lower than fundamental value

Because of Fair Value, these financial institutions would be forced to sell their assets in order to provide the regulated ratios. On the other hand, in the same period, in the same period of the depressive financial crisis, the other banks which are based their financial instruments under Historical Cost Accounting, would not face the same situation. That means they would not need to sell their assets to avoid the severe of the financial crisis because severe of the financial crisis would not violate their fundamental ratios.

HCA users=low liquidity = fin. crisis = few buyers = rejecting additional sales = prices are low no necessity adjustment for ratios=NO insolvency situation!! ⇨ liquidity value lower than fundamental value

As a kind of summary, we can summary that the extending of usage of Fair Value based reporting regime has a direct correlation with the increase of potential of the financial crisis. What I wanted to say that as far as a country or as far as a sector or as far as a unique company is concerned, the risk to be affected from financial crisis has a connection with the usage rate of Fair Value in financial reports. If I can simplify, if a company has more Fair Value considerations in its reports, it would have been exposed more to the effects of the violations of the financial crisis, comparing the other company that has not, or that has less Fair Value consideration in its financial reports.

On the other hand, as I explained, extending of usage of more Fair Value oriented reporting within financial institutions might increase the possibility of interconnected risk and this risk has contagion among the financial institutions. The contagion means transmitting or spreading their economical performances to each other in a positive way or negative way to each other. If there is more Fair Value usage, there is more contagion in the companies, financial institutions, banks, money center banks and so on.

Liquid markets have high liquidity with many buyers and sellers, and there is no big difference or spread between the ask and bid prices. In a liquid market, execution of a trade quickly and with a desirable price is possible because of existing of lots of buyers and sellers. There is no big impact in the difference or spread of the bid and ask price.

Illiquid markets have low liquidity and the asset cannot easily be traded for cash without a considerable loss in value. These assets can be named as illiquid assets and these assets cannot be sold quickly because of a lack of ready buyers to buy these assets. The lack of ready buyers leads to larger differences between the ask price (from the seller) and the bid price (from a buyer), comparing the difference in the liquid periods.

In finance, fundamental value refers to the value of a company, asset, liability, stock, currency or product defined by fundamental analysis without reference to market values. Fundamental value may not be the same as the current market value.

Money center banks have the same structure as common banks, but they borrow and lend with governments, large corporations, and common banks. These financial institutions do not have borrowing-lending activity with consumers.

Investors' Opinion on Usage of Evaluation Methodologies

The main finding of the event study is that FVA is "recognized" and "appreciated" by the investors (Table 2.2).

Table 2.2 Investors' opinion on evaluation methodologies

	Use FVA	Use HCA
Mean investor optimism Are you generally optimistic about the company's stock price increasing?	5.04	3.64
Mean investor likelihood to buy company stocks Are you likely to buy more shares in the company?	5.25	3.75
Mean investor evaluation of company transparency Do you find the company to be transparent regarding the information disclosed to financial statements?	4.61	4.07

2.5.5 Conclusion

Value of the assets and liabilities are in a continuous motion and it needs to be adjusted because it is very important how to support the interest groups in order to enable them to take a correct decision about company.

The debate over the utilization of Fair Value and Historical Cost is ongoing. Although Fair Value has been accepted by FASB and IFRS and becomes a global standard, there are many companies that continue to use Historical Cost.

We can have a summary that it seems that there is a strong connection between a more usage of Fair Value and more risk especially during a financial crisis period, during a low liquidity period in the markets.

- *Since Fair Value's appearance, Fair Value has continued to spread throughout the world, and it is clearly observable that Fair Value will continue to grow in usage and importance.*
- *A more usage of Fair Value Accounting has a parallel connection with a more interconnected risk level within the companies. That means that "More usage" of FVA means "more interconnection to market"*
- *The increase in company interaction to the market with a more Fair Value usage is more severe in crisis periods because it would be easier to spread the contagion. That means that "More interconnection to market" means to be "more exposed to severe in economic crisis"*

Another word, the companies might be affected more which have more Fair Value oriented assets, reports during the economic crisis in low liquidity.

- *Investors recognized and appreciated the usage benefits of Fair Value Accounting by having more relevant market information.*

That means that investors recognize and appreciate Fair Value Accounting because of having more timely and correct information regarding companies' financial statements.

References

AAA (1957) Accounting and reporting standards for corporate financial statements and preceding statements and supplements. American Accounting Association, Chicago

Abdel-Khalik AR (2010) Fair value accounting and stewardship. Account Perspect 9(4):253–269. https://doi.org/10.1111/j.1911-3838.2010.00013.x

Abdel-Khalik AR (2013) Accounting for risk, hedging and complex contracts. Taylor and Francis Publishing, New York. https://doi.org/10.4324/9780203137536. ISBN9780203137536

Aguayo R (1991) Dr. Deming: The American who taught the Japanese about quality. New York, NY: Touchstone Management Books 2000 Ltd. ISBN-10: 1852510854, ISBN-13: 978-1852510855

Al-Htaybat K, Hutaibat K, Alberti-Alhtaybat LV (2019) Global brain-reflective accounting practices: forms of intellectual capital contributing to value creation and sustainable development. J

Intellect Cap 20(6):733–762. https://doi.org/10.1108/JIC-01-2019-0016. Emerald Publishing. ISSN:1469-1930
Bandura A (1997) Self-efficacy: the exercise of control. W.H. Freeman and Company, New York. ISBN-10: 0716728508, ISBN-13: 978-0716728504
Bank of England Annual Report (2012) Presented to Parliament by the Chief Secretary to the Treaury by Command of Her Majesty
Bell J (1984) The effect of presentation form on the use of information in annual reports. Manag Sci 30(2):137–262. https://doi.org/10.1287/mnsc.30.2.169
Benston GJ (2006) Fair-value accounting: a cautionary tale from Enron. J Account Public Policy 25 (4):465–484
Brüggemann U, Hitz JM, Sellhorn T (2013) Intended and unintended consequences of mandatory IFRS adoption: a review of extant evidence and suggestions for future research. Eur Account Rev 22(1):1–37
Canning JB (1929) The economics of accountancy; a critical analysis of accounting theory. The Ronald Press Company, New York
Chen F, Hope OK, Li Q, Wang X (2013) Financial reporting quality and investment efficiency of private firms in emerging markets. Account Rev 86(4):1255–1288. https://doi.org/10.2308/accr-10040
Cifuentes R, Ferruci G, Shin HS (2005) Liquidity risk and contagion. J Eur Econ Assoc 3(2–3):556–566
Collier PM, Agyei-Ampomah S (2008) Management accounting risk and control strategy (CIMA Official Learning System). Elsevier, p 566. ISBN:978-0-7506-8713-3
Crandal RH (1969) Information economics and its implications for the further development of accounting theory. Account Rev 44(3):457–466
Demski JS (2005) Accounting and economics. University of Florida, Aug 2005. http://fisher.osu.edu/~young.53/Demski_Accounting_and_Economics.pdf
Demski JS, Fellingham JC, Ijiri Y, Sunder S, Glover JC, Jinghong P (2002) Some thoughts on the intellectual foundations of accounting. Account Horiz 16(2):157–168. https://doi.org/10.2139/ssrn.305904
Dicksee LR (1898) Auditing: a practical manual for auditors, eBook, 8th ed., rev. and enl. Gee, London. Accessed Aug 2013
Dompere KK (2010) Cost-benefit analysis and the theory of fuzzy decisions: identification and measurement theory (Studies in Fuzziness and Soft Computing). Springer Publishing. ISBN-13: 978-3642060564, ISBN-10: 3642060560
Dumay J (2016) A critical reflection on the future of intellectual capital: from reporting to disclosure. J Intellect Cap 17(1):168–184. https://doi.org/10.1108/JIC-08-2015-0072. Emerald Publishing. ISSN:1469-1930
Dumay J, Guthrie J, Rooney J (2020) Being critical about intellectual capital accounting in 2020: an overview. Crit Perspect Account 70(10285):1–9. https://doi.org/10.1016/j.cpa.2020.102185
Epstein BJ, Jermakowicz EK (2010) Interpretation and application of International Financial Reporting Standards. Wiley Publishing. ISBN: 978-0470-45322-3
Gogan LM, Artene A, Sarca I, Draghici A (2016) The impact of intellectual capital on organizational performance. Procedia Soc Behav Sci 221(7):194–202. https://doi.org/10.1016/j.sbspro.2016.05.106
Hayek FA (1968) Competition as a discovery procedure. Q J Austrian Econ 5(3):9–23
Hendriksen ES, Breda MFV (1991) Accounting theory, 5th edn. Irwin Professional Publishing
Hopwood AG, Miller P (1994) Accounting as social and institutional practice. Cambridge University Pres, Cambridge, pp 1–39
Hoque Z (2005) Linking environmental uncertainty to non-financial performance measures and performance: a research note. Br Account Rev 37(4):471–481. https://doi.org/10.1016/j.bar.2005.08.003
International Monetary Fund (IMF) (2008) Global financial stability report: Financial stress and deleveraging—macro-financial implications and policy (Washington, DC, October). https://

www.imf.org/en/Publications/GFSR/Issues/2016/12/31/Global-Financial-Stability-Report-October-2008-Financial-Stress-and-Deleveraging-Macrofi-22027
Isaac W (2006) Speech of William Isaac, former FDIC Chief, in Congress on March 12, 2006. https://www.govinfo.gov/content/pkg/CHRG-111hhrg48865/html/CHRG-111hhrg48865.htm
Johnson S (2009) Mary Schapiro vows to be tough enforcer. http://www3.cfo.com/article.cfm/12958299?currpag=0
Johnson G, Scholes K, Whittington R (2005) Exploring corporate strategy: text and cases, 7th edn, Harlow, Pearson Education Limited
Khan U (2010) Does fair value accounting contribute to systemic risk in the banking industry? SSRN Electron J: https://doi.org/10.2139/ssrn.1911895. Columbia Business School Research Paper Series. Available at SSRN https://ssrn.com/abstract=1327596 or https://doi.org/10.2139/ssrn.1327596
Klein GA (1999) Sources of power: how people make decisions. MIT Press, Cambridge, MA
Krugman P, Wells R (2009) Economics. Worth Publishers, New York, NY
Littleton AC (1920) An introduction to Elementary Accounting. Isha Books (January 1, 2013), ISBN 10-9332853746, ISBN 13-978-9332853744
Loyarte E, Garcia-Olaizola I, Marcos G, Moral M, Gurrutxaga N (2018) Model for calculating the intellectual capital of research centres. J Intellect Cap 19(4):787–813. https://doi.org/10.1108/JIC-01-2017-0021
Lucey BM, Dowling M (2005) The role of feelings in investor decision making. J Econ Surv 19 (2):211–237. https://doi.org/10.1111/j.0950-0804.2005.00245.x
Macintosh NB, Quattrone P (2010) Management accounting and control systems: an organizational and sociological approach. Wiley Publication. ISBN 978-0-470-71447-8(pbk)
Magnan ML (2009) Fair value accounting and the financial crisis: messenger or contributor? Account Perspect 8(3):189–213
Mankiw NG (2011) Principles of economics. Cengage, New York, NY
Matis D, Mustata R (2004) From historical cost to fair value. Audit si Convergenta Contabila, Editura Sincron, 619–633. ISBN 973-9234-53-4, Cluj Napoca
Morgan DL, Fellows C, Guevara H (2008) Emergent approaches to focus group research. In: Hesse-Biber SN, Leavy P (eds) Handbook of emergent methods. Guilford, New York, pp 189–205
Nandakumar A, Mehta KJ, Ghosh TP (2010) Understanding IFRS fundamentals. Wiley, New York, NY
Needles BE, Powers M (2010) International financial reporting standards: an introduction. Cengage, New York, NY
Nikolai LA, Bazley JD, Jones JP (2009) Intermediate accounting. Cengage Learning, New York, NY
Norton CL, Diamond MA, Pagach DP (2006) Intermediate accounting: financial reporting and analysis. Cengage, New York, NY
Oxford English Dictionary (2013) Oxford English Dictionary. 11th ed. (9 May 2013). OUP Oxford. ISBN-10: 0199666156, ISBN-13: 978-0199666157
Peng S, Bewley K (2010) Adaptability to fair value accounting in an emerging economy: a case study of China's IFRS convergence. Account Audit Account J 23(8):982–1011. https://doi.org/10.1108/09513571011092529
Pitre JP (2012) Effects of increased reporting frequency on nonprofessional investors' earnings predictions. Behav Res Account 24(1):91–107. https://doi.org/10.2308/bria-50039
Pinto J, Henry E, Robinson T, Stowe J, Wilcox S, Pinto J, Henry E, Robinson T, Stowe J, Wilcox S (2020) Equity asset valuation, 4th edn. Wiley
Pounder B (2009) Convergence guidebook for corporate financial reporting. Wiley, New York, NY
Power M (2010) Fair value accounting, financial economics and the transformation of reliability. Account Bus Res 40(3):197–210. https://doi.org/10.1080/00014788.2010.9663394
Previts GJ, Walton P, Wolnizer P (2011) A global history of accounting, financial reporting, and republic policy. Emerald Group Publishing, New York, NY

Rabin J (2003) Encyclopaedia of public administration and public policy. Marcel Dekker, Inc. New York. Print/Online: 0-8247-4240-0, Online: 0-8247-0945-4

Rogers JL, Buskirk AV, Zechman SLC (2011) Disclosure tone and shareholder litigation. Account Rev 86(6):2155–2183. https://doi.org/10.2308/accr-10137

Samuelson L (2002) Evolution and game theory. J Econ Perspect 16(2):47–66

Saudagaran SM (2009) International accounting: a user perspective. CCH, New Delhi

Sellhorn T, Gornik-Tomaszewski S (2010) Implications of the 'IAS Regulation' for research into the international differences in accounting systems. Account Eur 3(1):187–217. https://doi.org/10.1080/09638180600920392

Smith A (1801) The wealth of nations. N. Kelly, Dublin

Sterling RR (1970) On theory construction and verification. Account Rev 45(3):444–457

Stickney CP, Weil RL, Schipper K, Francis J (2009) Financial accounting: an introduction to concepts, methods, and uses. Cengage Learning, New York, NY

Stiglitz J, Ocampo JA, Spiegel S, Ffrench-Davis R, Nayyar D (2006) Stability with growth: macroeconomics, liberalization and development (initiative for policy dialogue series) 1st ed. ISBN-13: 978-0199288144, ISBN-10: 9780199288137

Tribe K (1991) The economic journal and British economics, 1891–1940. Unpublished dissertation, Keele University

Wiecek IM, Young NM (2009) IFRS Primer international GAAP basics. Wiley Publishing. ISBN 10: 0470483172, ISBN 13: 9780470483176

Williams HA (2003) A mediated hierarchical regression analysis of factors related to research productivity of human resource development postsecondary faculty. Doctoral Dissertation, Louisiana State University, 2003. http://etd01.lnx390.lsu.edu:885/docs/available/etd.-0326103-212409/. Accessed Aug 2013

Chapter 3
Normalization, Harmonization and Convergence of Accounting Evaluation

The purpose of this chapter is to discuss the broad framework for accounting valuation in IFRS, as well as the frameworks for accounting valuation in Turkey and Romania. An analysis of these frameworks is a means of providing a discussion of accounting theories and practices that is more specific than that offered in the first chapter of the study, and that prepares the way for the even more specific discussion of historical cost and fair value approaches that follows in the third chapter of the study.

The purposes of evaluating accounting systems can be condensed into the set of goals promoted by a particular evaluator. For example, according to the European Central Bank (2006), the purpose of evaluating accounting systems is to ensure that such systems ensure a high degree of financial stability. Goals can be large or small. Financial stability is a large goal, but the European Central Bank (2006) segmented it into ten smaller goals. The nature of goals will vary depending on the interests and philosophies of the evaluator. The European Central Bank takes a continent-wide and macroscopic approach. On the other hand, national governments might have smaller goals, such as ensuring that a particular accounting system accords with an existing set of national laws or practices (Epstein and Jermakowicz 2008). Thus, it cannot be concluded that there is a commonality of purpose in evaluating accounting systems; the differing scope, character, and aims of the evaluator have been to be taken into account.

Given the prevalence of IFRS, one of the more common purposes of accounting evaluation systems in recent times has been to offer feedback on the IFRS standard. This goal has prompted entities ranging from the European Central Bank (2006) to the large accounting firms to create position papers on evaluation. However, there is also a large body of national-level evaluations of accounting systems. Two of these systems, namely those associated with evaluation in Romania and Turkey, will be the empirical centerpiece of this study. The purpose of national-level evaluations is different from evaluations afforded by transnational accountancies and institutions. At the national level, governments, business consortia, and other key stakeholders are most concerned about issues of compliance and efficiency. They are not

I. Mert, *Assessment of Accounting Evaluation Practices*, Contributions to Finance and Accounting, https://doi.org/10.1007/978-3-030-98486-1_3

primarily concerned with bringing about changes in the letter of IFRS but rather in looking across internal, national, and international standards in a manner that will allow local goals to be realized. Such goals are often colored by a country's geostrategic position and political circumstances. For example, Turkey is a rapidly-liberalizing and growing economy with increasing links to the world of global capital and no obligation to a particular international accounting standard, while Romania is part of the European Union (EU) and, therefore, obliged to live up to IFRS (Mankiw 2011). As such, the purposes of evaluating accounting systems are very different in Romania and Turkey. Yet the same basic approach prevails; evaluation takes place from a starting-point in which goals are articulated and defined and then moves to a gap analysis in which the ability of current standards and practices to meet the goals is evaluated.

3.1 Historical Overview of the Development and Convergence of Accounting Standards

The concept of valuation can only be properly understood as part of the larger context of accounting standards. Accordingly, the purpose of this section of the study is to furnish an overview of the development of GAAP and IFRS and to discuss the convergence between these standards. This overview will furnish a background for the most specific discussion of valuation concepts to be provided later in the study.

In the United States, the development of generally-accepted accounting standards (GAAP) can be dated to 1934 (Bogui 2009), the year in which the Committee on Accounting Procedure (addressing GAAP in the private sector) and the National Committee on Municipal Accounting met (addressing GAAP in the public sector). Since then, GAAP has proven to be an enormously influential method of accounting, one that has influenced many countries, including Turkey and Romania, in the decades since its introduction.

The early–to-mid 1930s were a time of heavy financial regulation in the United States, driven by the popular perception that the Great Depression of 1929 was partly caused by a lack of transparency and honesty in the accounting principles of large American companies (Schroeder et al. 2010). After its introduction in the 1930s, U.S. GAAP underwent a series of changes (Reda et al. 2007). As Previts, Walton, and Volnizer (2011, p. 137) pointed out, U.S. GAAP was determined by many different inputs until 2009, a situation that rendered an assessment of GAAP practices more complex.

As Table 3.1 demonstrates, there were four levels of inputs into GAAP (in order of descending importance, from Level A to Level D) and a dozen discrete inputs. However, in 2009, the FASB Accounting Standard Codification became accepted as the only official input into non-governmental U.S. GAAP (Gibson 2010). This way of analyzing the evolution of GAAP is not just of historical value; in the fourth

Table 3.1 Pre-2009 Inputs into U.S. GAAP

Level	Inputs
Level A	FASB standards, FASB Interpretations, FASB Staff Positions, APB Opinions, AICPA ARBs.
Level B	FASB Technical Bulletins, AICPA Industry Audit and Accounting Guides, AICPA Statements of Position.
Level C	EITF pronouncements, AICPA Accounting Standards Executive Committee Practice Bulletins, widely recognized and prevalent industry practices.
Level D	AICPA Accounting Interpretations and FASB Implementation Guides.

chapter of the study, a similar approach will be used to determine how the Turkish and Romanian accounting systems came to adopt IFRS, and what the inputs (including the legal and business inputs) into IFRS have been.

Financial Accounting Standards Board, or the FASB, emerged in 1973, as the successor to both the Committee on Accounting Procedure created in 1934 and the Accounting Principles Board (APB) that was constituted from the American Institute of Certified Public Accountants (AICPA) as a means of ensuring greater independence in the determination of GAAP (West 2003). During the earlier part of its existence, the FASB mandate was limited to the improvement of U.S. GAAP (Braiotta Jr. and Gazzaway 2010). However, during the 1990s, the FASB began to take on a more global role. According to Thomas and Gup (2010), discussing developments in the 2000s, "As part of its role in providing guidelines for U.-S. accounting, FASB participates in a convergence project with the International Accounting Standards Board (IASB). The project's goal is to move toward intercontinental uniformity in financial statements" (p. 392).

The question of the convergence of accounting standards is actually quite fascinating, given the history of trans-Atlantic economic cooperation in the wake of the Second World War (an overview of which is provided by Spero and Hart 2009). The Bretton Woods Conference created an international financial regime united by a great many conventions, including the reserve nature of the U.S. dollar, free trade and the common adoption of tariff protocols, and shared institutions such as the World Bank (Krugman and Wells 2009). The Bretton Woods agreements and institutions eventually led to a shared global neoliberal system (Mankiw 2011). Given the extensive nature of this sharing and cooperation, it is natural to wonder why accounting convergence did not take place earlier.

There are a number of possible answers to this question. Godfrey and Chalmers (2007) argued that, for example, "China, Japan, and India have significant economies that have been insulated in their financial reporting and capital market activities..." (p. 6). Thus, some of the world's largest and most important economies were fairly late to join globalization, having been left out of the Bretton Woods agreements and the initial push towards globalization (Andrews 2008 also favored this position). Another answer was furnished by Clark et al. (2007), who argued that accounting standards convergence has been driven by the globalization of stock markets and capital flow in general. Bird and Rajan (2002) argued that, in general, trade globalization preceded financial globalization; in other words, there was a tradition of free trade, tariff reduction, and global trade agreements long before there was a robust tradition of international capital flows based on speculation, stock market investment and foreign exchange (see also Cline 2010 for a defense of this position). The interconnection of financial systems has driven the adoption of international financial accounting standards precisely because the same investors might now be distributing capital to companies in several different geographies (Kose et al. 2007). In other words, the emergence of global investing has led inexorably to the necessity for global standards of information presentation (Prasad et al. 2007). There are, however, competing explanations of the convergence of accounting standards. Clarke (2009) argued that the sheer weight of international bureaucracy has created a sort of false momentum for convergence. In other words, regardless of whether or not convergence might be beneficial in an era of financial globalization, Clarke raised the possibility that convergence has resulted because transnational institutions and organizations like to justify themselves; Kaufman (2003) argued more generally in support of the proposition that "Bureaucracies have a tendency to be self-perpetuating, to set up systems of rules even when there is no one, in particular, who supports them" (p. 241).

Standards convergence was, from the beginning, the mandate of the International Accounting Standards Board (IASB), founded in 2001 (Bragg 2005). While Clarke (2009) and others have argued that the IASB is an example of a bureaucracy with little popular mandate and bottom-up demand, Roehl-Anderson (2010) argued that IASB emerged organically from the converging interests of accounting standards boards in various countries and reflected a genuine need for common practices. Long-sighted policy-makers and businesspeople might have understood the benefits from IASB-FASB convergence as early as 2001. However, at that point, the main barrier to convergence—at least from an American perspective—was that U.S. GAAP had so many inputs (Collins 2011), as depicted in Table 3.1 (a point that will also be explored when examining how Turkish and Romanian GAAP transitioned to IFRS adoption). In 2009, when FASB became the sole source for U.S. GAAP, and the previous four levels of input collapsed into one, the task of convergence became methodologically and conceptually easier (Pounder 2009).

Having understood the context of both U.S. GAAP as expressed through FASB and the emergence of IFRS through IASB, it would be helpful to compare and contrast the two standards. Such a task is not easy, given that (a) there are dozens of individual differences, some on very technical topics and (b) many of the differences have been closed by specific acts of IASB-FASB cooperation (Warren et al. 2011). One major difference between the two standards is that IFRS is more principle-based than U.S. GAAP, which is more rules-based (Brice 2008). Thus, U.S. GAAP is roughly ten times longer than IFRS (Needles and Powers 2010).

Another method of comparing and contrast the standards are in terms of the spirit rather than the letter of the standards. Along these lines, the claim made by Norton et al. (2006) is that U.S. GAAP, as expressed by FASB, has been more business— than investor-friendly. Saudagaran (2009) claimed that U.S. GAAP enabled "more aggressive accounting practices" (p. 206) than international standards. Of course, this claim has to be taken in context. In the 1930s, when U.S. GAAP began, American accounting standards were actually more stringent and less aggressive than accounting standards elsewhere in the world; even in contemporary times, Niskanen (2007) has argued that U.S. GAAP is fairly conservative and that the onus for so-called creative accounting lies on companies that circumvent and cheat U.S. GAAP. Additionally, Camfferman and Zeff (2007) argued that, even in countries in which the letter of GAAP appears to be more stringent than in America, the letter of GAAP counts for little given the various formal and informal means for circumventing GAAP that exist in those countries. Thus, there is some contention on the issue of whether IFRS are really more stringent than U.S. GAAP, and whether the differences truly mean a great deal given that the emphasis of both systems is on fairness, documentation, transparency, lawfulness, and efficiency (Kimmel et al. 2010). One point of consensus in the literature is that U.S. GAAP and IFRS have certainly moved closer and closer, especially since 2008–2009 (Walton 2011). There are also several theorists who make arguments dramatically opposed to those of Saudagaran (2009) and Norton et al. (2006). For example, Hughes and Sander (2007) argued that IFRS is more aggressive than U.S. GAAP in terms of upward revaluation of intangible assets and in terms of accounting for inventory (see also Brice 2008).

On a purely technical perspective, the IFRS has several instruments that promote reporting quality in ways that outshine GAAP. For example, Lamoureux (2010) has called attention to the way in which IFRS would have detected the kind of fraudulent accounting practices in which Tyco and other U.S. companies indulged in the late 1990s and early 2000s (Nikolai et al. 2009).

It is no secret that accounting and finance are thoroughly global activities. That said, the regulatory environment in the U.S. has been willfully blind to the popularity of global accounting languages and has taken a deliberately parochial approach to the solution of accounting problems. Part of the problem is that U.S. authorities have structured accounting law in order to drive business for U.S. companies, regardless of the impact on accounting quality and the portrayal of financial situations. Wolf (2004) has made the point that, under the accounting and controls standards imposed by the U.S. Sarbanes-Oxley Act (SOX), the U.S. government retains the right to regulate foreign auditors. Guzman and Sykes (2007) made the same point in no uncertain terms: SOX gives "PCAOB [*op. cit.*] oversight over foreign audit firms" (p. 381).

When considering a solution to the various accounting scandals that plagued U.S. public companies in the 1990s and 2000s, U.S. accounting policy refused to recognize that IFRS already had a framework in place to address a number of the most egregious practices. In examining the case of Tyco, Lamoureux (2010) has called attention to three separate incidents of accounting fraud that could be camouflaged in GAAP but not in IFRS, to wit: (1) The illegal use of goodwill from acquired companies (Lamoureux argue that IFRS standards recognize goodwill in more rigid and standardized ways than GAAP, making it far easier to tell if a company is employing illegal goodwill recognition practices); (2) reporting earnings estimates, which is more strictly regulated in IFRS; and (3) disguising personal loans

Table 3.2 Selected differences between IFRS and GAAP

IFRS	GAAP
Comprehensive guidance on the presentation of financial statements provided.	No comprehensive guide to statement presentation is offered.
Identical introduction on offsetting of assets and liabilities; classified balance sheet required (except when a liquidity presentation is used).	Limited introduction on offsetting of assets and liabilities; classified balance sheet not required, but the definition of current/noncurrent differs from IFRS somewhat.
Expenses classified according to function (e.g., cost of sales) or by nature (e.g., salaries).	Expenses classified according to function (e.g., cost of sales) only.
'True and fair' override of IFRS permitted.	Justification for GAAP departure found in auditing literature but very rarely invoked.
Restructuring costs recognized earlier.	Restructuring costs recognized later.

Note: Adapted from Epstein and Jermakowicz (2008, *p. 1128)*

as charity funds. Lamoureux's point is that, if these various Tyco scams had been perpetrated in IFRS, they would have been instantly visible as a fraud.

GAAP's rules for the portrayal of financial situations occur within the context of American politics. The Sarbanes-Oxley Act (SOX) created what is known as the Public Company Accounting Oversight Board (PCAOB) in 2002. PCAOB members are not elected. They are appointed by the Securities and Exchange Commission, based on input from the Secretary of the Treasury and the Federal Reserve. PCAOB members are exclusively Americans, despite the fact that the board's decisions impact numerous foreign companies that are listed on the U.S. stock markets. PCAOB, taking SOX as its statutory basis, is in the business of deciding what auditors can and cannot do, and otherwise turning the often complex and amorphous letter of SOX into American business practice (Tracy 2004).

It is worth noting that PCAOB sits at the nexus of a number of political and economic interests, all of which benefit from the existence of a separate accounting system in the U.S. After all, SOX and PCAOB are (1) mechanisms of exerting executive power over publicly listed companies and (2) a money-generating scheme for consultants and accounting companies, all of who have enjoyed a multi-year bonanza of revenues generated by SOX compliance activity (Gomez and Moore 2009). Epstein and Jermakowicz (2008, p. 1128) offered an excellent high-level overview of some of the differences between IFRS and GAAP in terms of guidance vis-à-vis the financial portrayals of companies. The differences between IRFS and GAAP have been presented below in the Table 3.2 (Epstein and Jermakowicz 2008, p.1128).

There are a number of IFRS quality advantages invoked in this excerpt. The advantages deserve to be reviewed individually in order to make the point that, cumulatively, they constitute a higher-quality system in terms of promoting a more comprehensive and useful portrayal of a company's financial situation.

1. IFRS provides a comprehensive guidance on financial statement presentation whereas GAAP does not. Thus, a U.S. financial statement is, to a foreign investor, bound to be somewhat idiosyncratic, because of the lack of standardization.

2. IFRS also provides guidance on the offsetting of assets and liabilities. This factor offers some built-in fraud protection, as there is reduced leeway for an IFRS-compliant company to fudge its assets and liabilities numbers. This theme is amplified in explanation (5) below.
3. In IFRS, expense classification is more granular. Considering how GAAP has allowed some companies to disguise all manner of fraudulent payouts as expenses, this feature should also be of interest to policy-makers, auditors, and others interested in a higher threshold of fraud prevention at the level of the accounting language itself.
4. IFRS contains a clause explaining how and why it can be over-ridden in the interests of fairness. GAAP has no such structured clause; while there is literature explaining GAAP departures, such literature is not routinely called upon to justify or explain GAAP departures in practice.
5. IFRS recognizes restructuring costs earlier and, in fact, has reduced leeway for a company to delay disclosures that can materially impact it stock price. Overall, then, IFRS is less friendly to the notion of accounting being strategically used to hide a company's weaknesses, or to camouflage events that should be of concern to investors and/or regulators (Zack 2009).

In short, IFRS is designed for information quality, whereas GAAP is a language of convenience for auditors and preparers. This distinction between the two systems can be adopted as a general means of evaluating accounting systems that are not strictly GAAP or IFRS. The key question that assessors need to ask is: In creating standards for the portrayal of financial information, is the system more oriented to information quality or the convenience of businesses and government stakeholders?

On the surface, it seems as if a rule-based rather than principles-based approach would be a superior means of accounting. However, Palepu et al. (2007) argued that rules-based accounting systems allow "managers to circumvent the intention of the standard, even though they may technically comply with it" (p. 90). The problem is that principles-based standards require more thoroughness and professionalism from auditors, since more of the burden of determining whether the reporter is in compliance is shifted to the auditor; by contrast, a rule-based accounting system is easier to examine for compliance (Palepu et al. 2007). Palepu et al. thus raised an interesting point about accounting assessment; what is being assessed is not merely the letter of the standard, but rather the entire ecosystem in which the standard is interpreted and enforced. Thus, at a minimum, any assessment of accounting systems should go beyond the written standard and pay attention to the role of the auditor and the regulatory system within which either rules or principles are enforced.

The U.S. accounting system is often described as more rules-based than principles-based, although the convergence with IFRS is changing this aspect of GAAP (Pounder 2009). According to Porter and Norton (2012), the innate weakness of the rule-based approach—namely the ability of managers to circumvent the intent of a rule while superficially complying with it—is mitigated in the United States by the existence of a self-correcting, loophole-closing accounting standard, coupled with a robust mechanism for detecting and punishing accounting fraud. In this sense, GAAP cannot be assessed negatively solely because of its reliance on rules rather than principles; as Palepu et al. (2007) and Porter and Norton pointed out, the potential weakness of the rule-based approach has to be taken in the context of the larger accounting system, which in the case of the United States is robust.

In 2008, the U.S. Securities and Exchange Commission (2008) released its "*Roadmap for the Potential Use of Financial Statements Prepared in Accordance with International Financial Reporting Standards by U.S. Issuers*", in which the following noteworthy passage appeared: *"This Roadmap sets forth several milestones that, if achieved, could lead to the required use of IFRS by U.S. issuers in 2014 if the Commission believes it to be in the public interest and for the protection of investors (p. 1)."* This statement made convergence between U.S. GAAP and IFRS all but inevitable and cemented the growing integration between IASB and FASB. Thus, by 2008–2009, the convergence of accounting standards had achieved a certain inevitability. In future, convergence will likely mean that assessing accounting practices will be easier since national differences in accounting practices will be elided. For now, though, there are both substantial and subtle differences between common accounting standards; in the case of Turkey and Romania, these differences express themselves partly in divergent approaches to valuation, as will be discussed in this chapter of the study.

3.2 Recognition and Valuation in Accounting According to IAS/IFRS

International Accounting Standards (IAS) were implemented by the International Accounting Standards Committee (IASC) between 1973 and 2001, after which IFRS superseded IAS. For that reason, the remainder of this discussion will focus on IFRS, given that IFRS already includes a great many of the older IAS directives and is now held to supersede other material in IAS.

General information about IFRS can be provided through an overview of IFRS sections 1–13. Key excerpts from each of these sections of IFRS is provided in Tables 3.3, 3.4, 3.5, 3.6, 3.7, 3.8, 3.9, 3.10, 3.11, 3.12, 3.13, 3.14 and 3.15 below, with the information in each case obtained from the IFRS Board (2012). It will become apparent that, despite the fact that only one of the IFRS Sections (Section 13) specifically addresses the question of valuation, many of the other IFRS Sections touch upon the concept of valuation in some way and therefore ought to be presented as part of the analysis.

Fair value measurement is an important component of IFRS and touches upon the European Central Bank's (2006) criteria, as follows:

- Criterion 1: Reliance on principles-based standards: The principle of fair value is one of the core principles of accounting, as it is the bedrock of transparency and fairness.

Table 3.3 Overview of IFRS 1

Section	Details
IFRS 1	IFRS 1 pertains to the first-time adoption of reporting standards. According to the IFRS Board, IFRS 1 consists of four directives, as follows: (a) recognize all assets and liabilities whose recognition is required by IFRSs; (b) not recognize items as assets or liabilities if IFRSs do not permit such recognition; (c) reclassify items that it recognized accordance to previous GAAP as one type of asset, liability or component of equity, but there are a different type of asset, liability or component of equity accordance to IFRSs; and (d) applying IFRSs in measuring all recognized assets and liabilities. The IFRS grants limited exemptions from these requirements in specified areas where the cost of complying with them would be likely to exceed the benefits to users of financial statements. The IFRS also prohibits retrospective application of IFRSs in some areas, particularly where retrospective application would require judgments by management about past conditions after the outcome of a particular transaction is already known. The IFRS requires disclosures that explain how the transition from previous GAAP to IFRSs affected the entity's reported financial position, financial performance and cash flows (pp. 1–2).

Table 3.4 Overview of IFRS 2

Section	Details
IFRS 2	IFRS 2 pertains to share-based payment, whose goals have been described by the IFRS Board (2012) as follows: The IFRS prescribes various disclosure requirements to enable users of financial statements to understand: (a) the nature and extent of share-based payment arrangements that existed during the period; (b) how the fair value of the goods or services received, or the fair value of the equity instruments granted, during the period was determined; and (c) the effect of share-based payment transactions on the entity's profit or loss for the period and on its financial position (p. 1).

Table 3.5 Overview of IFRS 3

Section	Details
IFRS 3	IFRS 3 addresses business combinations. As the IFRS Board (2012) disclosed, The objective of the IFRS is to enhance the relevance, reliability and comparability of the information that a reporting entity provides in its financial statements about a business combination and its effects. It does that by establishing principles and requirements for how an acquirer: (a) recognizes and measures in its financial statements the identifiable assets acquired, the liabilities assumed and any non-controlling interest in the acquire; (b) recognizes and measures the goodwill acquired in the business combination or a gain from a bargain purchase; and (c) determines what information to disclose to enable users of the financial statements to evaluate the nature and financial effects of the business combination (p. 1).

Table 3.6 Overview of IFRS 4

Section	Details
IFRS 4	IFRS 4 addresses insurance contracts. As the IFRS Board (2012) stated, The objective of this IFRS is to specify the financial reporting for *insurance contracts* by any entity that issues such contracts (described in this IFRS as an *insurer*) until the Board completes the second phase of its project on insurance contracts. In particular, this IFRS requires: (a) limited improvements to accounting by insurers for insurance contracts. (b) the disclosure that identifies and explains the amounts in an insurer's financial statements arising from insurance contracts and helps users of those financial statements understand the amount, timing and uncertainty of future cash flows from insurance contracts. An insurance contract is a contract under which one party (the insurer) accepts significant insurance risk from another party (the policyholder) by agreeing to compensate the policyholder if a specified uncertain future event (the insured event) adversely affects the policyholder (p. 1).

Table 3.7 Overview of IFRS 5

Section	Details
IFRS 5	IFRS 5 pertains to non-current assets held for sale and discontinued operations. According to the IFRS Board (2012), The objective of this IFRS is to specify the accounting for assets held for sale, and the presentation and disclosure of discontinued operations. In particular, the IFRS requires: (a) assets that meet the criteria to be classified as held for sale to be measured at the lower of carrying amount and fair value less costs to sell, and depreciation on such assets to cease; (b) an asset classified as held for sale and the assets and liabilities included within a disposal group classified as held for sale to be presented separately in the statement of financial position; and (c) the results of discontinued operations to be presented separately in the statement of comprehensive income (p. 1).

Table 3.8 Overview of IFRS 6

Section	Details
IFRS 6	IFRS 6 pertains to the exploration for, and valuation of, mineral resources. According to the IFRS Board (2012), IFRS 6 Requires entities recognizing exploration and valuation assets to perform an impairment test on those assets when facts and circumstances suggest that the carrying amount of the assets may exceed their recoverable amount (p. 1). IFRS 6 is more technical and focused than the other IFRSs and applies solely to a small subset of companies (such as mining and energy companies) that have an interest in mineral resources.

- Criterion 2: Use of reliable and relevant values: IFRS 13 provides guidance, both quantitative and qualitative, about how to plug reliable and relevant values into fair value calculations.
- Criterion 3: Recognition of the allocation and magnitude of risks: IFRS 13 does not address risk.

Table 3.9 Overview of IFRS 7

Section	Details
IFRS 7	IFRS 7 pertains to disclosures of financial instruments. According to the IFRS Board (2012), The objective of this IFRS is to require entities to provide disclosures in their financial statements that enable users to evaluate: (a) the significance of financial instruments for the entity's financial position and performance; and (b) the nature and extent of risks arising from financial instruments to which the entity is exposed during the period and at the end of the reporting period, and how the entity manages those risks. The qualitative disclosures describe management's objectives, policies and processes for managing those risks. The quantitative disclosures provide information about the extent to which the entity is exposed to risk, based on information provided internally to the entity's key management personnel. Together, these disclosures provide an overview of the entity's use of financial instruments and the exposures to risks they create (p. 1).

Table 3.10 Overview of IFRS 8

Section	Details
IFRS 8	IFRS 8 pertains to operating segments. According to the IFRS Board (2012), The IFRS specifies how an entity should report information about its operating segments in annual financial statements and, as a consequential amendment to IAS 34 *Interim Financial Reporting*, requires an entity to report selected information about its operating segments in interim financial reports. It also sets out requirements for related disclosures about products and services, geographical areas and major customers (p. 1). IFRS 8 is highly important, as it prevents companies from resorting to segmenting their operations in a manner that disguises any aspect of financial performance.

Table 3.11 Overview of IFRS 9

Section	Details
IFRS 9	IFRS 9, like IFRS 7, pertains to financial instruments. The difference between the two IFRSs is that IFRS 7 is about the disclosure of financial instruments whereas IFRS 9 consists of more detailed guidance about how to "classify and measure financial assets and financial liabilities" (IFRS Board 2012, p. 1). IFRS 7 and 9 are similar enough in conception and detail that the earlier analysis of IFRS 7 also applies to IFRS 9. For this reason, IFRS 9 will not be analyzed, as doing so would be redundant.

- Criterion 4: Provision of comparable financial statements: IFRS 13 directly addresses comparable financial statements by ensuring that fair values are provided.
- Criterion 5: Provision of clear and understandable financial statements: The requirements for IFRS 13 ensure that actual values appear in financial statements, thus making those statements more clear and understandable.
- Criterion 6: Portrayal of the financial situation: IFRS 8 specifies that any disclosure of the financial situation of companies includes the performance of operating segments.

Table 3.12 Overview of IFRS 10

Section	Details
IFRS 10	IFRS 10 pertains to consolidated financial statements. This IFRS is of special importance, as it addresses the core topic of how companies that control one or more entities should prepare financial statements. According to the IFRS Board (2012), the goals of IFRS 10 are as follows: The objective of this IFRS is to establish principles for the presentation and preparation of consolidated financial statements when an entity controls one or more other entities. To meet the objective, this IFRS: (a) requires an entity (the parent) that controls one or more other entities (subsidiaries) to present consolidated financial statements; (b) defines the principle of control, and establishes control as the basis for consolidation; (c) sets out how to apply the principle of control to identify whether an investor controls an investee and, therefore, must consolidate the investee; and (d) sets out the accounting requirements for the preparation of consolidated financial statements (p. 1).

Table 3.13 Overview of IFRS 11

Section	Details
IFRS 11	IFRS 11 pertains to what are known as joint arrangements. According to the IFRS Board (2012), the purpose of this IFRS is to establish principles for financial reporting by entities that have an interest in arrangements that are controlled jointly (i.e. joint arrangements). The IFRS requires a party to a joint arrangement to determine the type of joint arrangement in which it is involved by assessing its rights and obligations arising from the arrangement (p. 1). Because IFRS 11 is close in principle and substance to IFRS 8 and IFRS 10, it will not be discussed further. Suffice it to note that IFRS 11, like IFRS 8 and 10, is designed to ensure that a company's reporting responsibilities extend to every entity that it controls or, in the case of IFRS 11, partly controls.

Table 3.14 Overview of IFRS 12

Section	Details
IFRS 12	IFRS 12 pertains to the disclosure of interests in other entities. According to the IFRS Board (2012), The objective of the IFRS is to require an entity to disclose information that enables users of its financial statements to evaluate: (a) the nature of, and risks associated with, its interests in other entities; and (b) the effects of those interests on its financial position, financial performance and cash flows (p. 1). IFRS 12 is close enough to IFRS 11, IFRS 8, and IFRS 10 in spirit and substance to preclude further discussion since what was noted in these earlier IFRS sections also applies to IFRS 12.

- Criterion 7: Alignment of accounting rules and sound risk management practices: IFRS 13 does not address risk management.
- Criterion 13: Promotion of a forward-looking recognition of risks: IFRS 13 does not directly address a forward-looking recognition of risks.

Table 3.15 Overview of IFRS 13

Section	Details
IFRS 13	IFRS 13 pertains to fair value management, which is defined as follows: Fair value is a market-based measurement, not an entity-specific measurement. For some assets and liabilities, observable market transactions or market information might be available. For other assets and liabilities, observable market transactions and market information might not be available. However, the objective of a fair value measurement in both cases is the same—to estimate the price at which an *orderly transaction* to sell the asset or to transfer the liability would take place between *market participants* at the measurement date under current market conditions (i.e. an *exit price* at the measurement date from the perspective of a market participant that holds the asset or owes the liability). When a price for an identical asset or liability is not observable, an entity measures fair value using another valuation technique that maximizes the use of relevant *observable inputs* and minimizes the use of *unobservable inputs*. Because fair value is a market-based measurement, it is measured using the assumptions that market participants would use when pricing the asset or liability, including assumptions about risk. As a result, an entity's intention to hold an asset or to settle or otherwise fulfill a liability is not relevant when measuring fair value (IFRS Board 2012, pp. 3–4).

- Criterion 9: Avoidance of negative externalities and promotion of positive externalities. IFRS 13 might generate positive externalities through boosting market confidence in financial statements.
- Criterion 10: Enhancement of market confidence and corporate governance: IFRS 13 promotes market confidence and corporate governance by pushing for a fair and transparent use of the value concept.

3.3 Further Discussion of Valuation in IFRS 13

IFRS 13 pertains to fair value measurement. Because fair value measurement is at once, a complex and highly important concept, without which no accounting system can be properly evaluated, the IFRS Board's definition of fair value has been quoted at length. This measurement will be employed in the fourth chapter of the study, where there is an assessment of the Turkish and Romanian accounting systems' adherence to fair value.

IFRS defines fair value as *"the amount for which an asset could be exchanged, a liability settled, or an equity instrument granted could be exchanged between knowledgeable, willing parties in an arm's length transaction (IFRS 2, Appendix A)."* As a nominal adherent of IFRS, Turkey employs this definition. The filings of Turkish companies tend to make extensive use of the fair value concept. For example, the Turkish Agricultural Bank (Ziraat Bankasi 2007) has an accounting policy in which fair value is used for all derivative transactions.

FASB defines Fair Value through ASC 820–10-05-1B that *"Fair value is a market-based measurement, not an entity-specific measurement. For some assets and liabilities, observable market transactions or market information might be available. For other assets and liabilities, observable market transactions and market information might not be available. However, the objective of a fair value measurement in both cases is the same—to estimate the price at which an orderly transaction to sell the asset or to transfer the liability would take place between market participants at the measurement date under current market conditions."* (i.e. *an exit price at the measurement date from the perspective of a market participant that holds the asset or owes the liability (IFRS 13 paragraph 2; FASB ASC 820–10-05-1B)).*

FASB defines the steps of the fair value perspective that *"When a price for an identical asset or liability is not observable, an entity measures fair value using another valuation technique that maximizes the use of relevant observable inputs and minimizes the use of unobservable inputs. Because fair value is a market-based measurement, it is measured using the assumptions that market participants would use when pricing the asset or liability, including assumptions about risk. As a result, an entity's intention to hold an asset or to settle or otherwise fulfill a liability is not relevant when measuring fair value. (FASB ASC 820)."*

There are a number of concepts in IFRS 13 that will be applied to the analysis and evaluation of the Turkish and Romanian accounting systems to follow in Chap. 4. To begin with, the criterion of transactional and market information represents a basic test focused on a single question: Is there already information about how to measure an asset or a liability based on existing data? This question is more complex than it appears at first because the reporting company has to be making some kind of judgment based on whether the data is applicable to its case. In other words, some subjectivity can enter the analysis on the basis of determining whether an IFRS reporter's asset or liability is strictly comparable to an asset or liability in the marketplace. Answering this question is, in a way, more dependent on a country's accounting case law than on the letter of IFRS. For example, in the U.S., there is a rich body of civil and criminal law that has served as a de facto means of determining the limits of fair value. Similar laws have to be examined in the context of Turkey and Romania to determine where the bounds of fair value in those countries lie.

Next, IFRS 13 touches on the question of how to estimate fair value in the absence of actual transactions or other relevant data. Here, IFRS offers a formula in which the use of observable inputs is maximized while the use of unobservable inputs is minimized. This formula, too, is open to a wide range of interpretations, and only decisions in key accounting cases can lay bare how Turkish and Romanian authorities have allowed companies to calculate fair value.

The section of IFRS that is most relevant to valuation in IFRS 13, which provides a detailed definition of fair market valuation. However, other sections in IFRS also address the topic of how to evaluate or value a company's assets. IFRS 1 touches on how to evaluate all assets and liabilities, IFRS 2 focuses on share-based payments, IFRS 3 addresses how a company's valuation can change based on its associated businesses, IFRS 5 mentions the role of non-current assets and IFRS mentions the role of mineral rights. All of these emphases touch on valuation in some way. Cumulatively, the goal of IFRS is to create a single standard whereby a reporting entity can recognize, account for, and disclose its value, with a focus on insuring that

(a) every important component of value appears in the reporting and (b) every important component of value is evaluated in a uniform way by all IFRS adopters, enabling relatively easy investor comparison of IFRS-compliant companies.

European Accounting Standards (EAS) on Valuation in Accounting
European Accounting Standards are now obsolete. As Walton and Aerts (2005) noted, "The IAS Regulation (2002) requires the use of IFRS for consolidated financial statements of European quoted companies by 1 January 2005" (p. 24). For this reason, a separate discussion of European Accounting Standards and accounting valuation principles is unnecessary.

3.4 Settling of Financial Valuation in Accounting

For intangible assets, specifically for goodwill, IAS 36 has needed to execute yearly impairment tests. The application of IAS 36 conducts the systems of the impairment test and disclosures of the issue. That means IAS 36 brings the firms a very vital and strategic concept. By the application of IAS 36, the interest groups are assured that *the value of the goodwill is at least equal to the value of that in the balance sheet.* That means the book value of the goodwill counts on the financial valuation and methodical amortization is no more in use.

The target of the impairment test is to test that the book value of an intangible asset is less than its retrievable value. IAS 36 specifies the retrievable value as bigger in between value in use, and fair value less cost to sell. The loss of the value is registered when the retrievable value is less than the book value.

The barometer studies the effectiveness and trust of financial disclosure of the firms of the SBF 120 Index (The index is prepared on the base of the 120 most actively traded stocks registered in Paris, French Stock Market). These analyzes are built on the yearly reports of 2006 to 2009 of the SBF 120 (i.e. 360 reports). The analysis was run by analyzing 51 paired questions that reflect the quantity and the quality of the information disclosed according with IAS 36. The results of the questions are presented briefly as a conclusion of scoring out of 10 per firm per year.

3.4.1 *Evaluation of the IAS 36 Disclosures*

2009 Barometer's specifications.

Most of the companies prepare the necessary conditions of IAS 36. Very few of the companies present even the suggestions of IAS 36. In analyzing we can see that:

- Most of the average values: 42% of values between 4/40 and 6/10
- Some unusual values: 9 values above 8/10 and below 2/10

The changes from 2007 to 2009:

- A barometer on the rise: average value rose from 4.6/10 in 2007 to 4.9/10 in 2008 and 5.4/10 in 2009.
- Developing of combined values: difference from the lowest value to the highest value has increased.

3.4.2 The Determinative Factors for the Highest and Lowest Scores

The quantitative studies identify that some factors became the reasons for better financial disclosures:

- **High-level impairment of the goodwill:** the value of the disclosures is growth on IAS 36 because the test direct to impairment of the asset.
- **Decreased floating capital:** If the companies have the little-floating capital they disclose in annual reports. The other companies improve other points of disclosure such as having meetings together with analysts, sending letters to the shareholders, and so on.
- **The existence of a powerful institutional of shareholders:** Associated shareholders demand systematized disclosures for comparison of their different investments.
- **Earlier studies with American standards:** Some US listed companies before using of IFRS collects higher scores comparing other, listed in the United States before the entry of IFRS gets higher scores than others, corresponding of the US GAAP and IFRS.
- **An independent auditor from the main audit companies.**
- **An auditor from the leading auditing firms.**

3.4.3 Settlement Between Accounting and Valuation

Studies identify that accounting and valuation are not concluded for reconciliation. Two main difficulties can be noted:

- Some points left to be clarified regarding the concept that were introduced by the standard (i.g. fair value and the value in usage)
- The obvious exciting choice for WACC, as observed in the disclosure of companies, usually hides unclear discount rates, the principal criterion, and the companies hesitate to expose this vital information.

3.4.4 *The Meaning of High Score According with the Accuracy: Paris Dauphine Barometer?*

IAS 36 is very important for auditors and financial managers because its main target is to provide the stability of an item (goodwill) increases weighing in the balance sheet of the company. The target of this disclosure according with the IAS 36 is to show the strength of the valuation application has been performed. It is not necessary for disclosing valuation items aimed for financial analysts, shareholders or investors.

Therefore, if a company gets a higher score according with the Accuracy—Paris-Dauphine Barometer that can be considered as a good result as far as significant accuracy and transparency are concerned in the eyes of the external inspector.

3.4.5 *Financial Disclosures to Be Chosen According with IAS 36*

According with IAS 36 for investors, inspectors, and analysts the disclosure of some items is a forecast of future cash flows, discount rates, the forecast of growth rate, etc.

We should accept that in daily usage, the disclosed information is mostly very restricted and useless for the external evaluator. The reason is, because of hesitating of exposing the company's information to outside of the company, accountants and auditors decrease the level of information because of sensitivity. For this reason, companies just disclose the requested disclosures of IAS 36, and they do not want to disclose the principal parameters of valuation.

As it can be accepted that according with the companies, all level of information is considered delicate and confidential, and they shouldn't be exposed voluntarily. For this reason, accounting departments and financial auditors try to escape of preparing the level of detail disclosed on these issues.

3.5 Observing of Romania and Turkey for Valuation Perspective and IFRS Adaption

Both Turkey and Romanian are adopters of IFRS. Although IFRS evolved later than U.S. GAAP, it is now the default accounting system in much of the world outside the United States. The purpose of this section of the literature review is to offer a discussion of the 13 sections of IFRS. This discussion is important because the sections of IFRS are both the theoretical and, at least in some cases, the practical basis on which accounting evaluation is carried out in Turkey and Romania. The empirical portion of the study to follow in chapter four will examine (a) how well the provisions of IFRS satisfy the European Central Bank's (2006) criteria of accounting standards and (b) how well Turkey and Romania, in particular, have succeeded in enacting both the letter and the spirit of the IFRS in a manner that satisfies the European Central Bank's criteria. This empirical analysis requires a fairly thorough documentation and discussion of the IFRS provisions, especially IFRS 10 (Consolidated Financial Statements) and IFRS 13 (Fair Value Measurement).

Interestingly, the histories of Turkey and Romania are partially intertwined, as Romania was under Ottoman Turkish role for over three centuries; it was only in 1877 that Romania declared independence from the Ottomans. In modern times, the history of Romania has been characterized by a clash between the interests of more powerful surrounding peoples (such as the Ottomans and Habsburgs, and later the Russians) who have imposed their will on Romania, and the character and aspirations of the Romanian people themselves (Hentea 2007).

According to the United Nations (2008), Turkey has done well with the concept of fair value, but Romania has not done as well—due largely to internal disputes about the concept of fair value. In this sense, Turkey has benefited from an accounting system that has been closer to the concept of fair value than Romania.

Accounting principles are rooted in accounting standards (Cline 2010), and the two most widespread standards are the U.S. generally-accepted accounting standards (GAAP) and international financial reporting standards (IFRS). Thus, it is appropriate to begin any discussion of the literature on accounting assessment with an overview of both U.S. GAAP and IFRS.

After this overview is complete, the literature review will examine IFRS in greater detail (since IFRS is now the core of Romanian and Turkish accounting standards) and touch on each of the areas in which, according to the European Central Bank (2006), accounting standards should be evaluated: (1) Reliance on principles-based standards, (2) use of reliable and relevant values, (3) recognition of the allocation and magnitude of risks, (4) provision of comparable financial statements, (5) provision of clear and understandable financial statements, (6) portrayal of the financial situation, (7) alignment of accounting rules and sound risk management practices, (8) promotion of a forward-looking recognition of risks, (9) avoidance of negative externalities and promotion of positive externalities, and (10) enhancement of market confidence and corporate governance. Points (3), (7), and (8) will collapse into a single discussion of risk; every other point in the European Central Bank's list will be considered in its own section.

As the focus of this study is in Turkey and Romania, special attention will be paid to the accounting systems in these two countries after the overview of GAAP and IFRS. The conclusion of the literature review will summarize the points of consensus and controversy in the literature and prepare the way for the third chapter, the discussion of methodology. Before proceeding to the accounting-specific portions of the literature review, a brief economic overview of both Turkey and Romania will be offered, adding important background context to the study (and providing data that will be relied on in the fourth chapter of the study, the assessment of the Turkish and Romanian accounting systems).

3.5.1 Accounting Policies and Choices for Valuation in Romania

According to Kumar (2010), the distinction between reliability and relevance is as follows: "*While relevance signals the potential of fair value to impact the decisions of the financial statement users, reliability ensures that the reported fair value represents what it is purported to represent" (p. 70).* It is possible for accounting systems to leave the door open for both reliability and relevance to be used in potentially misleading ways. For example, as Kumar argued, fair market value of assets can be hidden by using reliable numbers (for example, numbers that reliably represent the nominal value of an asset) rather than relevant numbers (for example, numbers that represent what an asset would be likely to sell for under current market conditions).

Despite the fact that Romania is now a member of the European Union and a functional, vibrant democracy, the accounting system remains weak in many respects. There persists a system of dual accounting in Romania; just as the country has hesitated to accept the Euro, it has also hesitated to make a strong commitment to IFRS. In addition to the complexity created by the system of dual accounting, Romania is also troubled by the relative lack of accounting experts in IFRS who are also familiar with Romanian accounting. Certain concepts introduced by IFRS are still somewhat alien to the vocabulary of Romania accounting as it evolved, in a fairly haphazard way, after 1989. In Turkey, the activities of the KGK have served as a means of translating (both figuratively and literally) the requirements of the IFRS for the specific Turkish legislative, bureaucratic, and business environment. Romania's rough equivalent of this body is CECCAR, or the Body of Expert and Licensed Accountants of Romania. As its name implies, CECCAR is limited to accounting (unlike KGK, which is also a standards enforcement and general market oversight body) and is also a bottom-up organization in the sense that its activities are driven by accountants themselves, without the same degree of government, legal, and business input that KGK receives.

According to the European Commission (2012, p. 5, 6), the general accounting principles followed in Romania are as follows:

- ***Going concern;*** *It is presumed that the entity is a going concern and will continue in operation without liquidating or curtailing materially the scale of its operations.*
- ***Consistency;*** *Measurement methods and accounting principles should be applied consistently from one accounting period to the next.*
- ***Prudence;*** *Assets and revenues should not be overstated, and liabilities and expenses should not be understated. However, the exercise of prudence does not allow, for example, the creation of excessive provisions, the deliberate understatement of assets or revenues, or the deliberate overstatement of liabilities or expenses.*

- ***Independence;*** *All revenues and expenses relating to the financial year should be taken into account, irrespective of the date of receipt or payment of such revenues or expenses.*
- ***Separation;*** *The components of asset and liability items should be measured separately.*
- ***Intangibility;*** *The opening balance sheet for each financial year should correspond to the closing balance sheet of the previous financial year.*
- ***Non-compensation of asset and liability items;*** *Asset and liability items or revenue and expense items should not be offset.*
- ***Substance over form;*** *Balance sheet and profit or loss items are presented taking into account the economic substance of the underlying transactions and not merely their legal form.*
- ***Materiality threshold;*** *Certain balance sheet and profit or loss items may be combined if: they are immaterial in amount; or such combination makes for greater clarity, provided that the items combined are presented separately in the notes to the financial statements.*

Manea (2011) argued that, in contrast to Turkey, Romanian accounting has only recently become acquainted with the concept of fair value, largely after the country's accession to the EU. One of the problems faced by Romania in this regard is that the IFRS's lack of extensive guidance has made it difficult for Romanian accountants, who come from an accounting tradition in which the concept of fair value is absent, to quantify fair value (Manea). Irina and Sabina's (2010) meta-analysis of the Romanian accounting literature discovered that Romanian accounting scholars had not even reached a consensus on the definition of fair value. "*The term, known in Romanian as "valoare justa", is the translation of the phrase "fair value" which, literally speaking corresponds to "genuine value" rather than "fair value." When speaking of the contents of the concept, there are some opinions that attributes its quality of assessment base, others who claim that represents a particular application of market value, others it considers some convention or accounting principle, finally it is also shown that fair value is an estimate and not a finding, as in the case of the market value. Another variant of the previous definition is the sum for which an asset could be exchanged in a balanced transaction, between parties informed and determined, different than in a forced liquidation sale (*Irina and Sabina 2010, *p. 465)."*

In Romania, then, the problem is that scholars are still trying to conceptualize and quantify fair value, which indicates that there is not yet a national consensus on where to set the balance between reliability and relevance. In Turkey, on the other hand, there is a firmer tradition of using relevant as well as reliable numbers in the national accounting system, which in turn has facilitated the adoption of IFRS principles of relevance.

According to Vinals (2010), the Romanian accounting systems remains "heavily rules-based" (p. 21) despite the institutionalization of IFRS in the European Union, of which Romania is a member. Vinals pointed out that Romania has a dual accounting system, employing the principle-based IFRS in order to meet EU requirements (as in the case of public companies doing business in the EU) and retaining the rules-based Romanian system for domestic use. This dual system means that the Romanian accounting system should not be assessed as performing well on the European Central Bank (2006) criterion of reliance on performance-based standards.

3.5.2 Features of Valuation in the Accounting System of Turkey

For Turkey, the adoption of IFRS has been driven by a number of interests. Initially, IFRS adoption was seen as a means of signaling that Turkey was ready to the join the European Union (EU), of which it has been a candidate member for several years. Lately, after many Turks began to despair of being admitted into the EU, IFRS adoption began to be seen as a boon to Turkish business interests in an era of globalization and liberalization. In recent years, Turkish economic growth has been extremely rapid, often second only to China (Pope and Pope 2011). In this environment, Turkish businesses have proven to be increasingly important investment opportunities for individuals and organizations from all over the world. Thus, the adoption of IFRS is a means of ensuring Turkish competitiveness in a global investment landscape, given that so many investors are already familiar with IFRS.

In Turkey and Romania, the national accounting standards in place before IFRS did not address the allocation and magnitude of risks. In Turkey, matters of risk disclosure will, after January 1, 2013, be governed by a combination of the Turkish Commercial Code and IFRS 7 (Pricewaterhouse Coopers 2012). In Romania, risk disclosure is governed by IFRS 7, at least for those companies that have adopted the IFRS standard. The Romanian national accounting system before IFRS did not focus attention on risk disclosures (Manea 2011). As a country that languished under Communism for nearly half a century (Deletant 1999), the Romanian accounting system was never as well-developed as that of the essentially capitalist Turkey, which is probably a factor in the lack of attention to risk principles in the Romanian national accounting system before the influence of IFRS.

One of the problems with the Turkish accounting system in this regard is that it only recently began to abandon a rules-based accounting approach for the principle-based IFRS approach, and this transition has imposed a heavy burden on auditors, students, and businesses (OECD 2006). According to the OECD, Turkey's accounting system was adopted from older European models and was reliant on rules; however, during the process of Turkish candidacy to the European Union, the country adopted IFRS. Turkey's recent adoption of IFRS has resulted in a number of problems, including the failure of universities to graduate sufficient numbers of accounting trained in the new system and an over-reliance on foreign auditors (OECD). At the same time, Turkey's reliance on IFRS has been undermined by the somewhat capricious exercise of power by the government, which has imposed both fines and audits on political enemies. Thus, the best way to assess the Turkish accounting system vis-à-vis reliance on principles is as follows: The letter of the IFRS standard, as adopted in Turkey, is robust, but the environment in which auditing and enforcement take place is poor.

3.5.3 IFRS Adoption in Romania and Turkey

The evaluation of accounting systems is a difficult endeavor, partly because of the subjectivity of interpretation. This subjectivity exists on multiple levels of analysis. For example, there is widespread agreement (European Central Bank 2006) that transparency ought to be a central feature of financial statements, and there is also agreement that IFRS has made transparency a core principle in the reporting of financial statements (see for example IFRS 10, which applies to Consolidated Financial Statements). The difficulty in analysis arises when attempting to quantify or otherwise objectively determine how well IFRS 10 and other applicable parts of IFRS satisfy the criterion for transparency. In a way, this question is a variation of the chicken-and-egg riddle. What accountants mean by transparency is, in a sense, derived from the letter of accounting standards, which put add a layer of concrete operational definition to the otherwise vague concept of transparency. On the other hand, the concept of transparency also exists separately from standards, as a general principle to which a standard gives voice. Determining how well a particular accounting standard satisfies a general accounting principle is, therefore, imprecise, subjective, and philosophically difficult, as a clear distinction has to be made between a principle and its application in the standard. In this study, the source of principles according to which standards can be evaluated is the European Central Bank's (2006) criteria, and the standard is the IFRS. Keeping the principles and the standards distinct is one way in which to confer methodological validity on an evaluation of accounting systems.

Another challenge in determining how to evaluate an accounting system arises from the multiplicity and complexity of inputs into the analysis. The comparison of accounting standards and principles (for example, the use of the European Central Bank's 2006 criteria against which to evaluate IFRS) is, after all, just the first level of analysis. When considering two specific countries, attention has to be paid not only to how these countries formally interpret and implement IFRS, but also to how legislative, legal, bureaucratic, economic, political, social, and even historical forces impact these acts of interpretation and implementation. Fortunately, this project can be eased by following existing models in the literature. For example, there is a rich body of literature on the evolution of accounting standards in the U.S. that takes stock of many factors in the development and evaluation of these standards. Such literature hardly exists for either Turkey or Romania; however, one of the purposes of surveying the literature on American accounting so thoroughly in the second chapter was to create a methodological model that could be used in the study of Turkey and Romania.

Ultimately, the methodology employed in this study is qualitative rather than quantitative in nature. One way of distinguishing between these two orientations is through Windelband's (1913) terminology. Windelband argued that all scholarly work could ultimately be divided into two categories: Nomothesis, which was the search for, and application of, laws and generalities; and idiography, which was the study of isolated phenomena based on both subjective and local facts. The country-specific assessment and evaluation of accounting is, in Windelband's terminology, an act of idiography similar to a historical narrative. The purpose of such a methodology should be the generation of a narrative allowing the evaluation of a country's accounting system, as will be presented in the chapter four.

What can be done to improve the Turkish and Romanian accounting systems in light of the knowledge generated by answering a research question? There are two main themes that emerged from the research. The first theme was that Turkey, although possessing a fairly sophisticated accounting system, also possesses a business structure that has availed itself of complex and sometimes illegal or unethical relationships between entities in order to hide risk, distort financial statements, and perpetrate fraud (Harrison and Wessels 2009).

According to Vinals (2010), the Romanian accounting systems remains "heavily rules-based" (p. 21) despite the institutionalization of IFRS in the European Union, of which Romania is a member. Vinals pointed out that Romania has a dual accounting system, employing the principle-based IFRS in order to meet EU requirements (as in the case of public companies doing business in the EU) and retaining the rules-based Romanian system for domestic use. This dual system means that the Romanian accounting system should not be assessed as performing well on the European Central Bank (2006) criterion of reliance on performance-based standards.

IFRS adoption in Turkey has, in the technical sense, been relatively easy, since IFRS adoption coincides with the interests of large segments of the Turkish population and the stated policies of the Turkish government (Pope and Pope 2011). The main problems associated with IFRS adoption in Turkey have been related to corruption (Gregoriou 2009). Turkey has its own accounting standards board, which is actually part of a larger organization: The Market Oversight, Accounting, and Standards Compliance Division (Kamu Gozetimi, Muhasebe ve Denetim Standartlari Kurumu, or KGK for short). Today, the KGK supports IFRS adoption in Turkey and publishes various documentation to assist Turkish companies to make the transition. However, KGK is a new organization, and it is not year clear whether it can perpetuate a culture respect of IFRSs 8, 10, 11, and 12 in Turkey. KGK ought to be strengthened so that it can help to bring about the necessary changes in Turkish culture to generate organic support for these four IFRSs in particular.

The Romanian economy has undergone inflation and other economic problems in the years since 1989 (Hentea 2007). In Turkey, there arose a positive feedback loop in which the country's liberalization efforts (including the adoption of IFRS) helped lead to economic growth, which in turn solidified the country's commitment to liberalization. In Romania, no such virtuous circle has yet been established. The Romanian economy has improved in fits and starts, the project of full integration with Europe has been put off (as exemplified by the country's reluctance to adopt the Euro in 2007, and postponement of that decision until 2015 at the earliest), and Romania has also suffered because of the slow emergence of business interests and a civil society capable of counteracting the influence of decades of Communist role. All of these factors play a role in the evaluation of Romania's accounting system and the slow adoption of IFRS, which is handicapped not so much by an absence of will as by an absence of practical knowledge and experience. What Romanian accounting needs, therefore, is better education, training, and time.

References

Andrews DM (2008) Orderly change: international monetary relations since Bretton Woods. Cornell University Press, Ithaca, NY

Bird G, Rajan RS (2002) Does FDI guarantee the stability of international capital flows? Evidence from Malaysia. Dev Policy Rev 20(2):1–12

Bogui FB (2009) Handbook of governmental accounting. CRC Press, New York, NY

Bragg SM (2005) The ultimate accountants' reference. Wiley, New York, NY

Braiotta LB Jr, Gazzaway T (2010) The audit committee handbook. Wiley, New York, NY

Brice S (2008) Are there lessons to be learned from Europe? Retrieved from http://www.cpa2biz.com/Content/media/PRODUCER_CONTENT/Newsletters/Articles_2008/CPA/Oct/Conversion.jsp

Camfferman K, Zeff SA (2007) Financial reporting and global capital markets. Oxford University Press, Oxford

Clark GL, Hebb T, Wojcik D (2007) Institutional investors and the language of finance: the global metrics of market performance. In: Godfrey JM, Chalmers K (eds) Globalization of accounting standards. Edward Elgar, London, pp 15–33

Clarke T (2009) European corporate governance: readings and perspectives. Taylor & Francis, London

Cline WR (2010) Financial globalization, economic growth, and the crisis of 2007–09. Peterson Institute, Washington, DC

Collins PS (2011) Regulation of securities, markets, and transactions. Wiley, New York, NY

Deletant D (1999) Romania under Communist rule. Center for Romanian Studies, Bucharest

Epstein BJ, Jermakowicz EK (2008) Integration and application of international accounting and financial reporting standards. Wiley, New York, NY

European Central Bank (2006) Assessment of accounting standards from a financial stability perspective. Retrieved from http://www.ecb.int/pub/pdf/other/assessmentaccountingstandards2006en.pdf

European Commission Retrieved from Romania (2012). http://ec.europa.eu/enterprise/policies/sme/business-environment/files/annexes_accounting_report_2011/romania_en.pdf

Gibson CH (2010) Financial reporting, and analysis. Cengage, New York, NY

Godfrey JM, Chalmers K (2007) Globalization of accounting standards. Edward Elgar, London

Gomez P-Y, Moore R (2009) Board members and management consultants: redefining the boundaries. IAP, New York, NY

Gregoriou GN (2009) Emerging markets: performance, analysis, and innovation. CRC Press, Toronto

Guzman AT, Sykes AO (2007) Research handbook in international economic law. Edward Elgar Publishing, New York, NY

Harrison J, Wessels B (2009) Mediating Europe. Bergahn Books, New York, NY

Hentea C (2007) Brief Romanian history. Scarecrow Press, New York, NY
Hughes SB, Sander JF (2007) A U.S. manager's guide to differences between IFRS and U.S. GAAP. Manage Account Q 8(4):4–17
IFRS Board (2012) Standards and technical summaries. Retrieved from http://www.ifrs.org/IFRSs/IFRS.htm
Irina AI, Sabina JA (2010) Does fair value represent a concern for Romanian researchers? Retrieved from http://anale.steconomiceuoradea.ro/volume/2010/n1/072.pdf
Kaufman C (2003) Ideas for action: relevant theory for radical change. South End Press, London
Kimmel PD, Kieso DE, Weygandt J (2010) Financial accounting: tools for business decision making. Cengage, New York, NY
Kose MA, Prasad E, Rogoff K, Wei S-J (2007) Financial globalization beyond the blame game. Finance Dev 9–13
Krugman P, Wells R (2009) Economics. Worth Publishers, New York, NY
Kumar BA (2010) Studies in accounting and finance. Pearson Education India, New Delhi
Lamoureux C (2010) Transparency and corporate integrity. Retrieved from docsotppcom/CICA_ClaudeLamoureux_Sept07pdf
Manea M (2011) The fair value representation of the market value in accounting. CES Working Pap 3(2):277–292
Mankiw NG (2011) Principles of economics. Cengage, New York, NY
Needles BE, Powers M (2010) International financial reporting standards: an introduction. Cengage, New York, NY
Nikolai LA, Bazley JD, Jones JP (2009) Intermediate accounting. Cengage Learning, New York, NY
Niskanen WA (2007) Bureaucracy and representative government. Atherton Press, Aldine
Norton CL, Diamond MA, Pagach DP (2006) Intermediate accounting: financial reporting and analysis. Cengage, New York, NY
Organization of Economic Cooperation Development (2006) Corporate governance in Turkey: a pilot study. OECD, London
Palepu KG, Healy PM, Peek E, Bernard VL (2007) Business analysis and valuation. Cengage, New York, NY
Pope N, Pope H (2011) Turkey unveiled: a history of modern Turkey. Overlook Press, London
Porter GA, Norton CL (2012) Using financial accounting information. Cengage, New York, NY
Pounder B (2009) Convergence guidebook for corporate financial reporting. Wiley, New York, NY
Prasad ES, Rajan RG, Subramanian A (2007) Foreign capital and economic growth. NBER National Bureau of Economic Research, Working Paper 13619. https://doi.org/10.3386/w13619. https://www.nber.org/papers/w13619
Previts GJ, Walton P, Wolnizer P (2011) A global history of accounting, financial reporting, and republic policy. Emerald Group Publishing, New York, NY
Pricewaterhouse Coopers (2012) New Turkish commercial code. Retrieved from http://www.pwc.com/tr/tr/publications/assets/TTK-A_blueprint_for_the_future.pdf
Reda JF, Reifler S, Thatcher LG (2007) Compensation committee handbook. Wiley, New York, NY
Roehl-Anderson JM (2010) IR best practices for financial managers. Wiley, New York, NY
Saudagaran SM (2009) International accounting: a user perspective. CCH, New Delhi
Schroeder RG, Clark MW, Cathey JM (2010) Financial accounting theory and analysis. Wiley, New York, NY
Securities and Exchange Commission (2008) Roadmap for the potential use of financial statements prepared in accordance with international financial reporting standards by U.S. issuers. Retrieved from http://www.sec.gov/rules/proposed/2008/33-8982.pdf
Spero JE, Hart JA (2009) The politics of international economic relations. Cengage, New York, NY
Thomas R, Gup BE (2010) The valuation handbook. Wiley, New York, NY

Tracy JA (2004) How to read a financial report: wringing vital signs out of the numbers. Wiley, New York, NY

Vinals J (2010) Romania: financial sector stability assessment. International Monetary Fund, Washington, DC

Walton P (2011) An executive guide to IFRS. Wiley, New York, NY

Warren CS, Reeve JM, Duchac J (2011) Accounting. Cengage, New York, NY

West BP (2003) Professionalism and accounting rules. Psychology Press, New York, NY

Windelband W (1913) Encyclopedia of the philosophical sciences. Macmillan, New York, NY

Wolf RC (2004) Trade, aid, and arbitrate: the globalization of western law. Ashgate Publishing, Aldershot

Zack GM (2009) Fair value accounting fraud: new global risks and detection techniques. Wiley, New York, NY

Ziraat Bankasi (2007) Unconsolidated financial statements together with review report. Retrieved from www.ziraat.com.tr/en/s/d/financials.doc

Chapter 4
Accounting Evaluation between Certainty of Past Costs and Uncertainty of Future Values and Measurement in Accounting

The purpose of this chapter is to discuss accounting evaluation in light of financial and management accounting principles and theories and discussions regarding fair value and historical cost. The main hypothesis defended in the chapter is that the decision between fair value and the historical cost is a decision between IFRS and other kinds of GAAP.

In order to relate some of these general neoclassical ideas about value to specific practices in accounting, and to move the discussion away from the innate value of accounting and towards how accounting assigns value to goods and services, take the concept of fair value. In accounting theory, fair value is the price of an asset, good, or service that most accurately reflects current and realistic conditions (Previts et al. 2011). Fair value can be distinct from other kinds of value, such as market value and historical value. The market value of a manufacturing plant might be $1 billion, but fair value might be considerably lower—perhaps because of the small number of potential number of buyers of such a plant, combined with the fact that potential buyers might already have plants of their own. Thus, the fair value of the manufacturing plant would be lower than its market price. The same kind of reasoning applies to the historic price. For example, the historic price of a parcel of land might be $ten million, but appreciation in real estate might mean that the land can easily be sold at $50 million. The fair value principle would, in such a scenario, require the value of the land to be recorded at $50 million rather than at $ten million.

These examples demonstrate that value is a floating concept rather than a fixed one. Accounting is the framework through which value is expressed and assigned (Saudagaran 2009). Thus, having understood the roots of value in economic theory and having introduced the role of accounting as an arbiter of value, it remains to offer a more precise examination of how measurement and evaluation function within the discipline of accounting.

I. Mert, *Assessment of Accounting Evaluation Practices*, Contributions to Finance and Accounting, https://doi.org/10.1007/978-3-030-98486-1_4

4.1 Theoretical Discussions

Yuji Ijiri's Theory of Accounting Measurement is important for a number of reasons. First, Ijiri argued forcefully in favor of accountability as the main goal of all accounting functions, the theoretical orientation that helps to simplify some of the functions of measurement within accounting. Second, Ijiri defended the historic cost approach; since the historic cost is not currently a popular means of measurement, it is all the more important to be able to survey strong defenses of this approach. Third, Ijiri had a number of worthwhile points to make about both the theoretical and empirical attributes of different kinds of measurement.

4.1.1 The Function of Evaluation

In Ijiri's view, management is the steward of resources and is, therefore, responsible for making an account of how these resources are used, both to internal and external stakeholders.

Ijiri thus claimed that settling on the function of accounting as stewardship, with management as the so-called accountor, was a way of clarifying the way in which accounting should be carried out. However, this view is subject to numerous possible critiques. For example, the notion of stewardship is not necessarily helpful when comparing and contrasting (a) managers who are shareholders in a corporation and (b) managers who are true managers, that is, who are managing resources on behalf of others without having as much of a vested stake in the company.

An example can clarify this problem further. A manager who possesses millions of shares in a company has a perverse incentive to raise share prices in the short term, for example through the use of questionable or aggressive accounting methods, because such action can be personally enriching. Since the manager has advance notice, and an insider's knowledge, of what is happening, he or she can take actions that injurious to a company in the long term in order to gain personal enrichment in the short term. On the other hand, a manager who draws a salary from a company but who owns no stock has a more rational incentive to keep the company solvent over a longer period of time, thus enriching himself or herself at the same as presiding over the longer-term interests of stockholders.

In this scenario, the manager without shares and the manager with shares are both stewards of the company's resources and functioning in the role of what Ijiri called the accountor. However, merely placing someone in the role of stewardship does not guarantee that he or she will choose a specific approach to accounting. Stewards can have many different kinds of incentives to apply accounting in particular ways. As such, *pace* Ijiri, it might not necessarily serve the purpose of clarity to claim that accounting begins with stewardship. Unless or until it can be demonstrated that stewardship locks the steward into a specific approach to accounting (which is certainly not the case), the idea of accounting for resource management is not specific enough to serve as a theoretical orientation.

In particular, establishing the function of accounting as stewardship does not result in the kind of support for historic cost accounting that Ijiri assumed. A steward could decide to use or dispense with historic cost accounting for reasons that have to do with personal enrichment and not conscientious reporting to stakeholders. Since Ijiri never answered this potential objection, an objection that looms large in the contemporary era of golden parachutes and stockholding CEOs, there is no compelling reason to assign a much theoretical value to the idea of stewardship. Certainly, in theory, it can be acknowledged that accounting is meant to function as a form of stewardship, but it is not stewardship itself that decides how and why certain forms of measurement might be used as part of an accounting system.

A more practical and realistic appraisal of this topic was presented in Contemporary Issues in Accounting, in which the choice of measurement is described as being informed by a combination of (a) accounting standards, (b) framework and qualitative characteristics, (c) management motivations and objections, and (d) current economic conditions or other circumstances. Stewardship as Ijiri described it falls into category (c) and, for the above-mentioned reasons, is not a sufficient explanation for how measurement approaches are chosen and implemented within companies.

4.1.2 The Case for Historic Cost

Ijiri was aware of the classic critiques of the historic cost method; however, Ijiri recommended the use of historic cost as long as it was accompanied by an adjustment in purchasing power.

In order to understand why Ijiri recommended a price-level-adjusted version of historic cost, it is also necessary to understand Ijiri's theoretical orientation. Ijiri wished to see accounting reorganized along more scientific lines, an orientation that placed an emphasis on objectivity (a quality that is invariably associated with historic cost) over subjectivity (a quality associated with the other popular measurement alternatives). The choice of historic cost as a measurement approach thus met Ijiri's criterion of objectivity; however, being aware of the problems of accuracy and relevance raised by the use of historic cost, Ijiri recommended a purchasing power adjustment.

The choice of adjustment criterion is important for two reasons. First, the use of an adjustment helps to recuperate historic cost from the charge of being irrelevant or inaccurate since a price adjustment could, in theory, make the historic cost much more accurate. Second, the specific choice of purchasing power adjustment fits closely with Ijiri's theoretical orientation since the purchasing power is also an objective variable that is precisely measured in every country. Thus, the combination of purchasing power adjustment and historic cost results in a cost estimate that is both objective and accurate, and that therefore supports Ijiri's general program of bringing more scientific rigor to the use of measurement in accounting.

Since the core of Ijiri's work is a defense of the historic cost method, and since Ijiri's main proposed alteration to historic cost is purchasing power adjustment, particular attention should be devoted to a description and critique of this component of Ijiri's work.

Ijiri suggested that purchasing power adjustments can be made to the value of assets purchased at historic costs. However, there are several problems with this suggestion. First, purchasing power is generally measured in terms of asset classes; for example, in the United States, purchasing power is measured as the ability for (a) a dollar to purchase a bucket of goods (such as selected consumer goods) and (b) a dollar to purchase a limited set of goods or even a single good (such as oil). Technically, inflation is measured through an analysis of the change in purchasing power relative to a bucket of goods.

Even though the measurement of purchasing power through inflation is based on objective criteria, it is still necessary to note that these criteria are based on changes in the price of consumer assets rather than business assets. For the purchasing power adjustment recommended by Ijiri to be valid, it would have to be based on a measured appreciation or decline in either (a) the price of the actual asset in question or (b) the price of a larger basket of business assets that were, however tangentially, related to the asset in question. In the absence of the kind of analysis required in option (b), it is not necessarily appropriate to depreciate or appreciate the value of a business asset based on the general inflation rate. Meanwhile, option (a) is already fairly close to the current cost method of measurement, which undercuts Ijiri's recommendation for the historic cost. If option (a) were chosen, there would be no need for Ijiri's two-step method of adjusting the historic cost for inflation since the actual change in market price could be consulted instead.

Even if data existed in order to allow option (b) to be exercised, there are still numerous possible objections to the use of Ijiri's price adjustment. For example, it could be the case that the value of an asset is no longer in line with historic cost * purchasing power changes. Some assets can be rare, valuable, impaired, or otherwise in a state that makes their genuine value significantly different from historic cost multiplied by purchasing power adjustment. The larger point behind this critique is that the market is likely to be a far better arbiter of the cost of an asset than the historic cost multiplied by a purchasing power adjustment. In the time elapsed since the purchase of an asset, there could be special factors that have increased or decreased the value of an asset far beyond what would be predicted by general changes in purchasing power. When current cost or fair value approaches are used, these factors are already accounted for by appealing to the intelligence of the market, which appears to be a far better indicator of value than historic cost, whether or not it is adjusted by purchasing power or any other criterion.

These kinds of vulnerabilities in Ijiri's argument have resulted in the diminished popularity of the historic cost approach. The purchasing power adjustment suggestion has not been acted upon in any widespread accounting standard, and Ijiri's work remains of interest more for its theoretical defense of historic cost than as a living document for the practice of accounting. Nonetheless, analyzing and critiquing Ijiri's approach to historic cost accounting in particular is a way to build a more robust understanding of how and why the market has come to be the preferred source for valuation in accounting theory and practice.

Ijiri's larger project was to align accounting with science. This project has not necessarily met with wide approval among accountants. For example, Contemporary Issues in Accounting suggested that scientific rigor is one of the several desiderata in accounting, but that science cannot be the only input into accounting in general or the selection of measurement methods in particular.

Along these lines, one critique of Ijiri's project of reorganizing accounting scientific lines is that, even if purely objective measures of value could be found and implemented (a scenario that, for reasons described in the critique of Ijiri's approach to historical cost, is highly unlikely in the first place), accounting exists as part of a necessarily unscientific system. Physics and other sciences discuss deterministic physical systems that, at least, in theory, can be understood and modeled at great length. Accounting exists as part of a market system that can never be deterministic. For example, it will likely never be the case that perfect information symmetry will exist in markets; there will always be some investors who know more than others, or who know before others, or who have more relevant information than others. Indeed, it is the very existence of such differences that allows money to be made in financial markets. If all investors were in a state of perfect information symmetry with each other, then it is hardly likely that there would be a market for stocks, bonds, and other financial instruments.

Thus, even if financial statements could somehow be rendered objective through the kind of scientific means proposed by Ijiri, financial statements would continue to exist in a world in which they would be interpreted differently by different investors. Of course, the benefit of such a scientific revolution in accounting would, at least, in theory, be a much greater level of comparability between companies, but, for reasons discussed in the critique of Ijiri's approach to historic cost, would not in fact be as comparable in practice.

It should also be noted that the market already provided a scientific approach to valuation in particular. While no individual market actor is likely to be right, the judgment of a large and free market is nearly always accurate. Modern markets are quick to reward companies that deserve reward and punish companies that deserve punishment because the sum of insights that are possessed by millions of individual market participants carry a great deal of force. It is not clear that this special quality of markets needs to be replaced by the kinds of objective principles or programs discussed in Ijiri's work; indeed, since Ijiri assumes the input of historic cost (which is itself determined by potentially subjective market forces), his model simply cannot stand at a distance from the workings of the market, whether objective or subjective.

In conclusion, while Ijiri's work is valuable for its strong defense of historic cost, Ijiri did not necessarily present a compelling reason to accept the historic cost approach.

4.2 Measurement in Accounting

The discipline of accounting has a history that extends into the early Middle Ages. However, the most appropriate starting point for a discussion of contemporary accounting practices is the late nineteenth century. It was at this time that accounting scholars began to be aware of the fundamental conflict between various stakeholders in the accounting process, and to begin the process of defining accounting in a way that smoothed over some of these conflicts (Stickney et al. 2009). It was also at this time that the aim of accounting was first defined as a means of holding managers accountable for the performance of capital under their control. From the nineteenth century onwards, there has been a conflict—sometimes intense, sometimes muted—over the use of accounting as a means of hiding information versus the use of accounting as a means of disclosing information (Walton 2011).

The reason that such a conflict is possible in the first place is that any accounting system of sufficient complexity contains ambiguities and interpretative space within which some form of adversarial relationship between the managers and providers of capital can unfold (Spero and Hart 2009). Such relationships are not necessarily adversarial by nature; however, the fact that managers and providers of capital can have different kinds of vested interest can result in tension. Indeed, such tensions exist not only between managers of capital and holders of capital, but amongst holders of capital themselves (Thomas and Gup 2010). For example, in modern stock markets, there are stark differences between capital holders whose goal is to keep stocks for long periods of time and derive dividends, and those whose goal is to sell stock for quick profit in a limited timeframe. Capital holders with a long-horizon ownership strategy have a greater vested interest in accounting regimes of full disclosure, since there is empirical proof that companies that embrace maximum transparency in accounting are rewarded by the stock market over the long run. On the other hand, capital owners seeking to make money quickly have an innate interest in suppressing corporate information that could depress the value of a stock in the short term (Thomas and Gup 2010).

Because of these incompatible strategies of capital ownership, even stockholders of the same company will tend to have divergent interests. Accounting regimes are one venue in which capital owner's fight to ensure that their interests are represented (Warren et al. 2011). Over time, some interests become more powerful than others and are enshrined as part of accounting practice. In the U.S., for example, the accounting reforms of the 1930s closed the door to certain practices that had allowed managers to hide more readily or misrepresent financial underperformance (Warren et al. 2011). The change in U.S. accounting practice reflected an emerging political, social, and economic consensus that the combination of transparency and long-term corporate value building was more important than secrecy and short-term profit-taking. On the other hand, for much of the nineteenth century, the U.S. attitude to accounting—like the country's attitude to banking and corporate organization in general—was highly *laissez faire,* a legacy of the significant sovereignty enjoyed in individual American states and a national distrust of federal regulation (Mankiw 2011; Warren et al. 2011).

It is important to begin with a historical and structural overview because the application of specific measurement and evaluation frameworks only makes sense in light of these considerations. For example, the idea of fair value reflects a specific historical concept of fairness, one in which the interest of the stockholder or other capital owner trumps the interest of the insider or capital manager in determining the nature of a balance sheet (Mirza et al. 2011). Today the major principles in accounting tend to reflect the higher priority to the interests of non-insiders (Mirza et al. 2011).

There are numerous answers to the question of what the goals of accounting ought to be. One set of answers was provided by the European Central Bank (2006), according to which the overall goal of accounting standards and practices is to provide financial stability, and the ten constituent goals in support of this major goal are as follows: (1) reliance on principles-based standards, (2) use of reliable and relevant values, (3) recognition of the allocation and magnitude of risks, (4) provision of comparable financial statements, (5) provision of clear and understandable financial statements, (6) portrayal of the financial situation, (7) alignment of accounting rules and sound risk management practices, (8) promotion of a forward-looking recognition of risks, (9) avoidance of negative externalities and promotion of positive externalities, and (10) enhancement of market confidence and corporate governance. Starting from the major and constituent goals, the European Central Bank (2006) then examined how IFRS allows these goals to be achieved, and where IFRS falls short.

It can legitimately be asked why there is a need to determine why the perspective of an outside party such as the European Central Bank (2006) is necessary to determine the standards of accounting evaluation. In fact, the approach taken by the European Central Bank (2006) is just one possible approach to the evaluation and measurement in accounting system. What different approaches to measurement and evaluation have in common is the enumeration of goals and the adoption of gap analysis. All mainstream approaches to measurement and accounting posit some particular set of goals as the foundation for accounting and then examine how particular standards live up to or fail to live up to, such goals (Kimmel et al. 2010). In performing these kinds of analysis, there is certainly potential for disagreement. For example, historically, there has been considerable disagreement over what the goals of accounting ought to be. Even in the twentieth century, during which the profession of accounting came to be standardized in many ways, has seen a great deal of flux, starting from the pre-1929 prioritization of capital managers' ability to use accounting for purposes of distortion to the post-Great Depression recognition of the information rights of stockholders (Kimmel et al. 2010; Mirza et al. 2011). Thus, there is by no means a consensus on what the goals of accounting are or should be. Even after the goals of accounting are defined by a particular group, such as the European Central Bank (2006), the question of how these goals are accommodated by a particular standard is fraught with difficulties. For example, both IFRS and U.S. GAAP recognize the principle of fair value and have adopted a common definition and disclosure standard for fair value, but there is still disagreement over whether the disclosure standard is appropriate (Gibson 2010).

The use of measurement and evaluation in accounting is a contentious endeavor. It is unlikely that consensus will form around any one approach. However, regardless of differences in goals and evaluation structures, measurement and evaluation approaches can all be described as a combination of goal articulation and gap analysis guided by the following questions: (1) What should be the goals of accounting? (2) To what extent do existing accounting practices and standards address the goals of accounting? (3) What can be done to improve the ways in which accounting practices and standards address the goals of accounting?

4.2.1 Importance of Information in Measurement

Theodore J. Mock's Measurement and Accounting Information Criteria describes measurement as an attempt to bring about the correspondence between certain empirical objects and certain numbers. The purpose of the numbers is to quantify the empirical objects. This position initially appears to be a bold one, perhaps close to the spirit of Ijiri's Theory of Accounting Measurement in terms of its scientism, but on further consideration also has much in common with the systems-oriented, descriptive approach of Raymond Chambers in Accounting, Evaluation, and Economic Behavior. Mock's position is also worth examining at length because of its central importance to any theoretical formulation of accounting.

First, what does it mean to suggest that accounting measurement is the measurement of empirical objects? The claim can be illustrated through the use of examples. If Asset A is a computer that was bought for $1000, the empirical object is the computer. However, Asset B might be intangible, for example in the form of intellectual property or a brand. Asset B can be accommodated in Mock's scenario by tying it to another empirical object. For example, a brand could be reduced to a series of empirical objects (such as trademarks, copyrights, &c.) that have some kind of tangibility. Even though the concept of the empirical object can be somewhat stretched when understood in terms of intangible assets, Mock's point stands. Value (and other numbers within accounting) attaches to objects, or to ideas that are directly associated with objects, in a manner that can be quantified.

According to Mock, the purpose of measurement is to communicate something fundamental about empirical objects to an audience, which could consist of stockholders, managers, policy-makers, or others. This aspect of Mock's argument is similar to Chamber's' position in Accounting, Evaluation, and Economic Behavior. Like Chambers, Mock suggests that measurement cannot be understood out of the context of a system of communication between the entities that Ijiri called the accountor (that is, the company) and the audience.

One difference between Chambers and Mock is that Mock paid more attention to the characteristics of decision-making and how the use of certain kinds of measurement informs such decision-making. Since decision-making is the ultimate form of economic behavior associated with accounting, it is worthwhile to recapitulate Mock's discussion of this phenomenon.

Mock approaches decision-making from the perspective of systems design, which overlaps closely with the kinds of communication theory discussed by Chambers. As described by Mock, a good information system is one that sends the right signal at the right time to the right audience. This simple but powerful formulation suggests that measurement is not an objective mathematical exercise in the manner favored by Ijiri, but rather a form of complex information communication between the accountor and the audience. Hence, the same theories and empirical techniques that can be applied to information systems design and communication can also be applied to the measurement.

It seems that one position shared by Mock, Chambers, and Ijiri—despite the other major differences between their works—is that the accountor is a conscientious information steward. To be sure, the history of accounting can be understood from the viewpoint of conscientious; companies have disclosed more and more in response to both pressure and expectations from audiences as varied as stockholders and regulators. There are many objective and reliable measures of how companies have provided more and higher-quality financial information. However, the assumption of conscientious need not be universal. For example, Mock's Measurement and Accounting Information Criteria suggests that companies are engaged in a process of improving their information systems, such as by choosing more accurate measurement systems such as fair value. However, it is by no means clear that this assumption is warranted. Companies can certainly choose approaches to accounting that are designed to conceal rather than reveal information; in fact, even a strategy based on revealing a great deal of information can be designed to defy interpretation, since some investors will doubtlessly struggle with being able to cut through the mass of information to find what is important to them.

It is for this reason that Mock's emphasis on decision-making is warranted. For example, if it is possible for scholars to understand how and why people make investment decisions are made, then it is possible for companies to choose approaches to accounting and measurement that are in alignment with these methods of decision-making. Indeed, in recent years, there has been a great deal of research on the connection between investor decision-making strategies and the provision of accounting information. It is likely that much of this work has been inspired, whether directly or directly, by Mock's emphasis on decision-making in Measurement and Accounting Information Criteria. However, when Measurement and Accounting Information Criteria was published nearly 40 years ago, decision-making was a little-studied emphasis in accounting theory.

While decision-making might seem somewhat remote from core issues of measurement approaches, there is, in fact, a link between these phenomena. In particular, Mock argued that one of the shared characteristics of decision-making among those who act on accounting information is more of a focus on current and future events, and less of a focus on past events. By this criterion of decision-making, the use of historic cost measurement would appear to be less relevant than fair value, current cost, or other current- and forward-looking approaches to measurement.

Mock made a strong argument that information usefulness in accounting is connected to what such information conveys about the present and future of the company. Of course, this observation does not in itself solve the various problems of measurement raised in Contemporary Issues in Accounting. For example, perhaps the most forward-looking approach to measurement discussed in Contemporary Issues in Accounting was the present value method, in which the value of an asset is calculated as the sum of forecast cash flows associated with the asset. In terms of Mock's theory, the present value approach to measurement would have a great deal of relevance to decision-makers because of its future focus. However, as pointed out in Contemporary Issues in Accounting, the present value measurement system is rife with the potential for bias and inaccuracy, given not only the innate interest of companies in inflating the future productivity capacity of an asset but also the natural likelihood of unanticipated developments over the course of enough time.

One of the weaknesses in Mock's Measurement and Accounting Information Criteria was the absence of a framework for balancing decision-makers' need for measurement systems that offered future-relevant data versus the innate biases and inaccuracies that come with longer time spans.

In fact, the same critique can be applied to so-called current-relevant decision criteria. Current cost and fair value are both systems of measurement that provide decision-makers with information about the current value of an asset. However, there are very significant differences between these methodologies. In this sense, suggesting that decision-makers need current- and future-relevant data is not necessarily a point that has major implications for measurement theory. To be sure, Mock further undermines the case for the use of historic cost as a system of measurement, but his discussion of decision-making criteria does not offer a practical way to understand, much less choose between, the remaining alternative approaches to decision-making.

Leaving aside the weaknesses in the decision-oriented approach to understanding measurement systems, the idea of information usefulness, an idea that plays a central role in both Chambers' Accounting, Evaluation, and Economic Behavior and Mock's Measurement and Accounting Information Criteria, is itself vulnerable to critique on a number of fronts. One of the weaknesses of this idea is that it does not specify the exact role of the decision-maker. For example, it can be assumed that a company issues a series of financial statements that are highly accurate but extremely complex in their application of the fair value system, so much so that most investors are not able to act upon the information conveyed therein in order to amend their portfolios. In such a scenario, both Chambers and Mock would be committed to critiquing the appropriateness of fair value as a system of measurement, because their systemic approach means that the response of the audience has a key effect in the overall effectiveness of a measurement system.

This kind of systems approach is open to critique because the market very rapidly corrects bad decisions and punishes good ones. Thus, there is no real need to take a systems view of measurement that includes the decisions of stockholders. If a company offers accurate information that is initially misunderstood or glossed over by a majority of stockholders, then the few stockholders who actually understand and act upon this information will make money and tilt the market in their favor. At that point, other investors will also come to understand what the initial investors understood. This dynamic can perhaps be seen every day in every market of note, as there are always investors who are ahead of the pack, just as there are always lagging investors who learn certain information too late. If this central function of marketplaces is respected, then it appears that Mock's focus on decision-making might be less relevant than Measurement and Accounting Information Criteria suggests.

Another critique is that innate differences between investors might make the choice of specific measurement approaches irrelevant. One of the implicit assumptions in Measurement and Accounting Information Criteria is that there are aspects of measurement that can be readily understood by the majority of an audience. However, financial statements are complex enough regardless of what kinds of measurement systems they employ, and single financial statements do not necessarily convey actionable information about a company. True experts might pore through hundreds of financial statements, and other sources of financial information, as fodder for their market decisions (such as buying, selling, or holding stock). There is likely to be a disparity between expert investors and inexpert investors regardless of what kind of measurement system is chosen, how simple the information design is, or how useful a communication framework between managers and audiences happens to be. This disparity exists not because of the information itself, but because of basic cognitive differences and other kinds of differences (such as information asymmetries) between individuals. These differences exist because biology itself dictates wide variation in characteristics such as information processing speed, working memory, and synthetic intelligence. Other differences (such as the difference between wealthy investors who have the time and resources to access the best stock information and poor investors who lack time and resources) appear to be just as intractable. If this point is granted, then it can be argued that (a) the quest for an ideal best method of measurement is misguided and (b) the systems-inspired approach to accounting championed by Chambers as well as by Mock is unnecessary. No matter what system of measurement is used, it is likely that the same subgroup of expert investors who beat the market will keep beating the market. Moreover, there appears to be little point in aligning the choice of a measurement method with the decision-making preferences of a specific audience, given that markets would function just as efficiently in any case (because they would continue to disproportionately reward people who tend to be right and punish people who tend to be wrong).

In a way, despite their implicit as well as explicit support for free markets and other artifacts of capitalism, Chambers and Mock appear to be making an argument for the anti-capitalist approach of equalism, that is, the use of accounting to try to flatten differences between investors. In communication, it is both practical and laudable to engineer a message so that it can be understood by a majority of people upon initial exposure to the message. It is simply not clear, as Chambers and Mock assume that financial information is like this, or ought to be like this. Mock's commitment to equalism appears to be irreconcilable with the belief in a free and efficient market subjects to the decisions of investors with widely varying skill sets.

4.2.2 Modern-era Subjects in Measurement

Contemporary Issues in Accounting contains a thorough overview of theories of measurement, including a detailed analysis of (a) historical cost, (b) current cost, (c) fair value, (d) present value, and (e) deprival value. The purpose of this discussion is to offer an overview of each of these measurement approaches, along with an analysis of its strengths and weaknesses. First, however, it would be helpful to provide a more general overview of theories of measurement.

Overview of Accounting Measurement

According to Contemporary Issues in Accounting, measurement can be described as follows:

> Measurement in an accounting context, therefore, refers to the way the figures on the financial statements are determined. It is interesting to note that the definitions refer to measurement as an act or process. This act or process may involve calculations to determine the quantity of a particular asset held by the entity—for example, inventory. The act or process of accounting measurement can also involve making estimates and comparisons—for example, determination of fair value of an item by reference to market prices or by calculating the net current value of the future cash inflows expected to be derived from an item.

With this definition in mind, Contemporary Issues in Accounting situated the choice of measurement protocol (including historical cost, current cost/replacement cost, fair value, present value, and deprival value) as informing both the quality of accounting information and the usefulness for decision making. The inputs into the choice of measurement are (a) accounting standards, (b) framework and qualitative characteristics, (c) management motivations and objections, and (d) current economic conditions or other circumstances. Finally, the problems associated with measurement are the additivity problem, flexibility, comparability, choice, and subjectivity.

Problems with Accounting Measurement

The problems with measurement, in general, notwithstanding the specific kind of measurement chosen, are additivity, flexibility, comparability, choice, and subjectivity. Each of these problems was discussed in turn in Contemporary Issues in Accounting, creating a framework from which to critique each of the specific kinds of measurement approaches.

The problem of choice is, simply put, that there are many kinds of measurement approaches (with five major alternatives recognized in Contemporary Issues in Accounting), and no global consensus on which approach is the best, even though of late there has been a shift towards IFRS. The problem of choice has two dimensions. The first dimension pertains to standards. There might not be objective reasons for choosing between, say, U.S. Generally Accepted Accounting Principles (GAAP) and IFRS, both of which have quite different approaches to measurement. The second dimension pertains to inter-standard choice issues. When a single standard offers accountants the opportunity to choose from multiple measurement approaches, then there might once more fail to be an objective standard for choosing, and it might also be the case that assets evaluated with different measurement systems might not be easily comparable.

The second problem, which is somewhat connected to the problem of measurement, is the problem of comparability. In order to function properly, markets require investors and other key decision-makers to be able to compare companies as fairly and transparently as possible. In the absence of such fair, transparent comparisons, the efficiency of markets is impaired, and various distortions can enter into transactions. At heart, the comparison is the comparison of measurements, and it is simply not clear whether two companies that employ different measurement systems (for example, historical cost versus fair value) can truly be compared. Thus, the existence and usage of multiple approaches to measurement renders decision-making more difficult.

The third problem is subjectivity. Subjectivity is more of a problem when it comes to fair value and other kinds of measurement that can require accountants to make untested assumptions about market demand, costs of sale, future productivity, and other unknowns. However, the opposite of subjectivity, namely objectivity, is just as much of a problem; for example, while the use of the historical cost method can be objective, it might prove to be inaccurate. Thus, both subjectivity and objectivity both present unique kinds of problems in terms of measurement.

The fourth problem is flexibility. When companies can choose which kinds of measurement to apply in which cases, they might do so in an opportunistic manner that conveys misleading information to markets. Even when a company has chosen a single measurement approach couched in a single standard, flexibility within standards allows companies to choose the method of measurement that might not necessarily be the most accurate, but that is likely to portray the company in the most favorable light.

The additivity problem has two premises. The first premise is that, if total assets are measured by adding together individual assets whose values might have been calculated through the use of different kinds of measurement, then the total figure is essentially useless, since it is invalid to mix historical costs and fair values to yield a single figure. The second premise is that, even if the same measurement standard is applied to every single asset, then the fact that asset values might have been measured at different times still creates a validity problem with the final sum.

In sum, it appears that the problems with measurement noted by Contemporary Issues in Accounting are cumulatively insoluble; there does not appear to be any ironclad solution to all of these problems. For example, the subjectivity problem might be solved through the application of the historical cost measurement approach, but then there is an accuracy issue associated with objectivity. The additivity problem is also insoluble; even if a company could be completely strict in the application of the same measurement standard to each and every asset (a very unlikely scenario in itself), it is still the case that asset values cannot all be measured at exactly the same time.

With this point of insolubility in mind, it should be concluded that the function of specific measurement techniques (choosing from among the alternatives of historical cost, current cost, fair value, present value, and deprival value) is to manage, not solve, the problems of measurement. Since no system of measurement is perfect, management must make its decision based on a mix of factors, including not only an evaluation of how well a chosen measurement method will allow a company to manage the five problems of measurement but also the existing regulatory and legal climate).

Types of Accounting Measurement

Contemporary Issues in Accounting listed five kinds of measurement, including historical cost, current cost, fair value, present value, and deprival value.

In historical cost, the value is determined on the basis of an actual transaction. For example, if $100 were paid for Asset A, then the value of Asset A is recorded as $100.

In current cost, the value of Asset A would be recorded as either the amount that needs to be paid to purchase Asset A currently, or else the lowest amount that needs to be paid to acquire an asset identical or similar to Asset A in its capability to deliver the same expected future benefits as Asset A. Thus, if the current market price of Asset A were $125, then the value of Asset A under current cost would be recognized as $125 rather than $100. If Asset A were no longer obtainable on the market, but Asset B provided extremely similar benefits at a cost of $110, then the value of Asset A would be recorded as $110.

In fair value, what matters is market price for Asset A. A company using fair value has to find some means of obtaining a market price for Asset A, for example by checking existing commodity prices, bid amounts, or similar transactions, or even by extending a request for bids from potential buyers. For example, assume that an item extremely similar to Asset A now sells in the secondary market for $87. The value of Asset A would have to be recognized as $87 under fair value. Of course, it could also be the case that the value of Asset A has appreciated over time to $113, in which case a value of $113 would be recognized. In whatever case, the will of the market would be respected.

It can be seen that there are some similarities between current cost and fair value. In particular, both of these approaches focus on market transactions and allow the market to assign value. However, there are also key differences worth remarking. First, current cost has more alternatives; under fair value, only the market value of Asset A is of import, whereas, under current value, the value of Asset B can be used as a substitute for the value of Asset A as long as a case can be made that Asset A and Asset B provide similar or identical benefits. In this sense, the current cost can be said to have more flexibility than fair value.

Under the present value approach, the value of Asset A would be recognized as the present value of the discounted value of all future net cash flows associated with Asset A.

Finally, under the deprival value, the value of Asset A would be the loss that the company would have suffer if the asset is deprived.

Discussion of the Types of Accounting Measurement

Contemporary Issues in Accounting provided critiques of each of the types of measurement.

The main critique of historic cost was that it lacked both accuracy and relevance to decision-making, as the historic cost for a given asset might well have been established years or even decades ago. These disadvantages most likely outweigh the benefit of objectivity that comes with a historic cost.

The main critique of current cost was that it does not necessarily indicate the value of the asset over time. However, Contemporary Issues in Accounting praised the market-based objectivity of this approach to measurement. The market-based objectivity of fair value was also praised, but only in those circumstances in which it is readily possible to obtain a market price for an asset. Fair value can remain somewhat subjective if there is not an active market for an asset. Additionally, Contemporary Issues in Accounting noted that markets can be volatile and that fluctuations in value might not represent the genuine value of an asset.

Finally, Contemporary Issues in Accounting critiqued both the present value and deprival value approaches fairly extensively. Present value was said to lack subjectivity because of the innate difficulties in estimating future cash flows (including lack of subjectivity in choosing discount rates), and also because the cash flows said to be generated be a specific asset might in fact also require the use of other assets to be realized. Ultimately, though, the present value method is most flawed because it presents an opportunity for management bias to present itself in the estimation of how long, and with what productivity, an asset can continue to function. Deprival value also suffers from similar kinds of subjectivity.

Based on the analysis presented in Contemporary Issues in Accounting, it appears that fair value has perhaps the most strengths, and the fewest weaknesses, of any of the five presented approaches to measurement. One of the main weaknesses of fair value, as presented in Contemporary Issues in Accounting, is that markets are not fallible. There can be information asymmetries and other distortions in markets that prevent the fair value from functioning as an appropriate form of measurement. However, this critique should not be thought to apply to fair value alone; although Contemporary Issues in Accounting did not make this point, it should be noted that market anomalies can also be responsible for distortions in historic cost and current cost. Nonetheless, Contemporary Issues in Accounting did go on to present a number of arguments on behalf of fair value, arguments that cumulatively suggested that fair value does better in resolving the sum of the five measurement problems (additivity, flexibility, comparability, choice, and subjectivity) than historic cost, current cost, present value, and deprival value.

4.2.3 Evaluation for Measurement of Accounting

Raymond J. Chambers' Theory of Accounting Measurement takes what might be described as an ethnographic and historical approach to accounting. Instead of setting out to identify the best or most appropriate method of measurement or evaluation, in the manner of Ijiri, Chambers' purpose differed in the following manner:

Our purpose is not to seek principles of universal validity in all institutional settings. It is to examine the features of the institutional setting of the present insofar as they provide the conditions for accounting that is appropriate to that setting. There may emerge some principles that we deem to be valid in a much wider setting and over a range of different historical contexts. But this is incidental. (p. 18).

As is clear from this passage in the introduction to Theory of Accounting Measurement, Chambers approaches accounting from an almost Darwinian perspective, that is, with a view to examining how accounting has evolved to meet the needs of its specific circumstances. The Darwinian metaphor is apt because, just as evolution has resulted in the generation of certain systems and organs that play a less important role in the lines of contemporary organisms than they played in the lives of these organisms' ancestors, some accounting principles also exist merely because they are relics of the past. Chambers thus cautions scholars of accounting against the assumption that whatever exists today in accounting theory and practice plays a specific and useful function. On the other hand, Chambers does emphasize that the contemporary role of accounting theory and practice is in large measure the outcome of a sort of evolutionary adaptation. Understood from this point of view, accounting in general (and measurement and valuation in particular) can be thought of as answers to certain problems that have arisen in different environments and different ways.

For example, in England, modern accounting probably arose in response to satisfy the needs of owners of joint-stock companies, such as the British East India Company, that could not raise capital until they assured the marketplace of potential investors that they were making good use of their existing resources. On the other hand, in the Ottoman Empire, the theoretical ownership of all state assets by the Emperor retarded the development of complex accounting, since there was no significant body of stakeholders to appeal to for funds or to satisfy. These examples illustrate what Chambers had in mind by claiming that accounting, despite sharing core characteristics across countries, is not a monolithic entity but a series of local practices.

Implicit in Chambers' argument is the role of global capitalism and free trade, as a result of which the market needs of stakeholders in different countries are becoming increasingly similar to each other. As capital spreads globally, accounting in general, and measurement and valuation, in particular, are converging towards the same set of needs that were discussed in Contemporary Issues in Accounting. These needs are, once again, transparency, comparability, accuracy, and relevance. While acknowledging the distinct influences that have resulted in shaping accounting in different ways in different national contexts, Chambers' theory also relies on an implicit assumption of global convergence to accounting approaches, a convergence that is based on the seemingly irresistible momentum of capitalism itself.

Another emphasis of Chambers' book, one that is recognized in the title, is the relationship between accounting and economic behavior. This relationship makes more sense if understood from the perspective of Chambers' discussion of information and information processing and can be illustrated by means of a generic example of how corporations tend to work; especially in free market settings (such corporations are also called open organizations in business theory).

The open organization is one that acts on inputs, via a transformative process, to create outputs. For example, a tire company might take the input of rubber and place it into the transformative process of a factory to produce the output of a tire. This process is a loop. The tire company might discover that it costs $1 to produce a tire that sells for $1.25 and decide to lower the costs of production so as to gain more profit. In the open systems theory of organization, obtaining data about the costs of production and deciding to lower them counts as an example of feedback. The organization constantly monitors its production loop in order to identify and eliminate waste and add other efficiencies. In order to do, the company must be able to understand its processes, wring data out of them, and be disciplined enough to alter its productive cycle (in this hypothetical case, with the purpose of lowering the cost of per-tire production).

Chambers' Accounting, Evaluation, and Economic Behavior suggests that accounting is perhaps the key component of the open systems cycle, as accounting is the function that determines budgetary commitment, monitors processes for costs and margins, and otherwise determines if any particular strategic move of the company is profitable or not.

Money is the lifeblood an organization—the one key factor that determines whether an organization can act or not, depending on strategic circumstances. Thus, accounting (and, in particular, management accounting) is tremendously strategic and sits right on the foundation of the organizational theory of open systems and is an important determinant of nearly every kind of economic behaviour within an organization.

In other words, without accounting, there is no empirical standard for feedback on the model of open organizations; the corporation that functions without this sort of accounting foundation will, according to the theory defended by Chambers in Accounting, Evaluation, and Economic Behavior, not be able to continually refine its productive cycle in order to add efficiency, eliminate waste, and lower costs. Indeed, given that these three functions are very important for the functioning of a company, it is likely that a company of sufficient size without adequate accounting at its foundation would probably collapse. Thus, there is strong support for Chambers' argument that accounting is the foundation of economic behaviour, not only within a firm but also with respect to the firm and its investors.

Chambers' Accounting, Evaluation, and Economic Behavior was also important for its application of the theoretical frames of information and communication to accounting in general and measurement in particular. If Chambers is correct, then the right approach to measurement is not so much to ask which kind of measurement is correct in itself (a project that was undertaken by Ijiri in Contemporary Issues in Accounting); rather, the usefulness of specific kinds of measurement ought to be considered in light of the information that this kind of measurement is communicating to stakeholders.

As Chambers argued, both information and communication theory take a systems view; the quality of communication, for example, can be judged not only by the qualities of the message itself (for example, the syntax and semantics of the message) but also by how well the message achieves its function of communicating information to the audience. Thus, the ultimate test of communicating information is whether such communication is understandable and useful within the framework of the relationship between the communicator (in this case, the company) and the audience (in this case, the stockholder examining financial statements in order to make investment decisions, or perhaps the CEO examining assets in order to determine a strategic direction for the company).

If the kind of systems view recommended by Chambers is taken, then there is a need to judge measurement systems not only on the basis of their own innate characteristics (such as subjectivity, accuracy, etc.) but also on the basis of how well such measurement systems convey information to stakeholders. The logical conclusion of Chambers' theory is that best way of determining how well measurement conveys information to stakeholders is to examine the quantity and quality of information exchange, and then to relate these data to the actual economic behavior of stakeholders. Economic behavior is one of the most important themes in Chambers' book and can be used as a proxy indicator of how well a measurement system is working, but only if there is some consistency in place.

For example, assume that the same company uses the same measurement system (which, for the sake of argument, can be fair value) to value its assets for 5 years in a row. If there is a marked decline in assets in year 5, and the position of the company is otherwise unchanged, then it is expected that the stock value of the company would decline, as the result of a successful signaling mechanism to the market. However, for accounting to have this kind of measurable and immediate impact on economic behavior, there needs to be consistency in the kind of measurement system that is used. As was pointed out in Contemporary Issues in Accounting, accounting comparisons of this sort can only be meaningful if they are based on the same methodology of measurement. If five different kinds of measurement are used in 5 years, then, in practice, it is difficult to evaluate the link between the accounting system and economic behavior.

This point raises vulnerability in Chambers' theory. If accounting is both a form of, and a precursor to, different kinds of economic behavior, then we cannot know what effect accounting has had until or unless we can observe economic behavior. Even if we can observe economic behavior, one of the unintended consequences of Chambers' theory about the roles of information and communication in accounting is that observed economic behavior does not necessarily allow onlookers to make judgments about the usefulness of measurement systems in and of themselves. For example, if a company's stockholders take a justified action (such as dumping the company's stock) even in the absence of a transparent measurement system, then there is not necessarily a strong motivation for changing the measurement system.

On the other hand, stockholders could also make the wrong economic decision in the wake of an accurate use of measurement. If one measures the quality of accounting as part of a larger system of information communication, then, in cases such as these, it is possible that not enough weight is placed on the innate robustness of the measurement system. In this sense, approaching accounting from the theoretical orientations of information and communication might create complications for regulators, scholars, and others who need to determine how exactly to calibrate measurement systems.

Ultimately, Chambers suggests that controversies over measurement and valuation are likely to be settled based on the needs, capabilities, and constraints of the larger system, a system that consists of stockholders, managers, regulators, and many other market participants. Chambers also suggests that accounting practices reflect, however imperfectly or inefficiently, what local circumstances dictate. As such, it is possible to think of Chambers' work as providing a descriptive rather than a prescriptive account of the formation of measurement philosophies. Instead of trying to prescribe specific kinds of measurement, Chambers describes the circumstances in which different kinds of measurement have arisen. Moreover, if the Darwinian metaphor of evolution implicit in Accounting, Evaluation, and Economic Behavior is taken to its logical conclusion, then whatever system of measurement is most widely adopted deserves to be widely adopted. Measurement appears to subject to some kind of Darwinian force that is winnowing out less useful techniques (such as historical cost) in favor of more useful techniques (such as fair value). If so, then Accounting, Evaluation, and Economic Behavior can be taken to support the position that whatever kind of measurement approach is currently most prominent in the accounting landscape deserves its prominence, and little effort should be made to defend less popular positions (such as the defense of historic cost mounted in Ijiri's work.

4.2.4 The Conditions in Measurement

One of the accounting studies points out that there is a common thought in the accounting literature (see, Ijiri 1975; Willett 1987; Chambers 1997; Musvoto 2008) accounting studies could not prepare the theories regarding accounting measurement from the daily usages of accounting. On the other hand, in accounting, measurements should mention the theory of measurement (see, Luce et al. 1971).

The measurement theory was first improved by Scott and Suppes (1958). The theory's essential side says that measurements should have a calibration regulated by the points of a scale that is composed with quality and empirically existed in abstract. Besides that, Steven says (1951) that measurement can't be saved if the strict rules conditions of an assignment are not existing. According with the conclusion from above, a measurement scale is necessary. Another conclusion is that well-regulated fundamentals are appreciated and that are focused on statements for an empirical paradox for the purpose of empirical clarity. This aspect of measurement is steady along with the modernized descriptions of homomorphism of measurement that needs to have common acceptance in the social science environment. The actuality and distinctiveness theorems should be confirmed possibly with the defined values. IASB declared (2009) that measurement in accounting is characterized as of stage of authorizing monetary values to the items of financial tables amounts where they are reviewed.

There are two critique warnings for accounting measurement as far as homomorphism explication is concerned. The warnings claim that supporting points for the explication of measurement is not wide enough for accounting defined numerical issues except other assigned numerical values of financial statements. Another claim is that accounting measurement is too wide, and it is not able to prevent monetary charges to the items of the financial statements. If the situation is analyzed by comparing past and present practices, we can say that defining accounting measurement by writing numbers to the items of the financial statements, the supporters of the accounting measurement theory have connected to clear vital points in accounting measurement. In spite of this, characterization of accounting measurement is anyhow a vital side of the measurement. Narens (2002) claims that the alteration of an empirical connection form into a numerical connection form by a homomorphism. IASB has a point also (2009) that the recognized accounting measurement needs to be limited to writing values to the items of the financial statements. The significant point of accounting measurement is the facts of the financial statements give a smooth and acceptable ideal foundation for defining the financial movements of an entity. For summarizing, it is not correct to claim that the other perspectives of accounting measurements are not measuring anything in accounting with the reason that these perspectives are not converted to the monetary values to the items of the financial statements. Another point, it is different comparing monetary values in the other disciplines for defining an empirical connection form is not very different from assigning monetary values as a hypothetical form that confirms the value of an item in the financial statements.

Continuously, the assigning of a specific hypothetical form of monetary values for confirming a specific empirical connectional form cannot be employed as a description of measurement. One of the claimers is Musvoto (2008), and he also says the accounting description of measurement is extremely wide.

Errors

There are, certainly, some criticisms regarding accounting measurement. The criticisms argue with the method of treating measurement models. Probabilities refer the identification of the items in the financial statements. In this perspective, the idea of probabilities is utilized in the identification parameter for implying the level of ambiguity that further interests regarded with the element will draw to or from the entity. The explanation of the perspective of the probability's outcomes three issues regarding the applications of error that are closely combined with the perspective of accounting measurement.

Orbach (1978) was claiming that expected things have valid assets for the current time that can be measured. That implies that probabilities point out the studies that are concluded. The first problem argues that a method does not exist in the accounting field to examine the measurement principles that point out the probabilities. The fact made this worse that the illustrative measurement theory couldn't succeed enough improvements to form a method that can test the measurement principles pointing out the probabilities (Falmagne 1980; Michell 1986).

The criticisms focused on some problems, and the first of the problems argues that no a testing method for measurement principles that points out the probabilities.

The mostly known concept considered is to presume that possibilities are samples of a matching alive mentioning random variable where the biggest value defines the choice. As an instance, in the accounting world, an average thorough is presumed where both definitions of order are produced and companies are linked to a format new ones understood to be demonstrating showing the same abilities in value. As an example, the current assets of financial statements, the assumed values of exclusive current elements are considered to design a new company, total current assets that demonstrate the same value by also considering snow.

In the accounting world, it is widely accepted (see, Tinker 1985), Ryan et al., Musvoto 2008; Stamp 1981) that value is basically a tool for change. On the other hand, Luce and Narens (1994) think that figures are stable random variables. According to this, the principle discussion is focusing on defining if the variable of the recognized figures of the asset (value) is a basic for that or built on the observed data that the definition of accounting literature for that is unfinished.

The definition of meaningfulness in accounting measurement couldn't get enough concentration for the necessity of charging monetary numbers to the value of the items to get enough attention, but the conclusion that it couldn't get progress. The establishment of meaningfulness couldn't be verified or analyzed completely. As an instance, the IASB (2009) identifies that accounting information system should be arranged with a method that provides it easy to be used for its users. For the representational measurement (Luce 1990), accounting measurement results are beneficial if they are provided meaningful. By continuing, if accounting is a measurement fact as indicated in the literature, that refers that accounting information should assist the representational measurement idea of meaningfulness. The ability could not get enough support in the accounting as the need to turn the monetary numbers to the value of the items to succeed recognition. The representational concept of measurement balances the meaningfulness by empirical importance. That shows that qualitative relation instructing the connection of the empirical form of value should be explainable empirically with the condition of early usages of the empirical form of value if accounting information needs to be recognized meaningful. Another indication is that relations of non-meaningful qualitative connections of the empirical connection form of value are non-empirical as far as early usages are concerned. On the other hand, Ryan et al. (2002), Stamp (1981) and Musvoto (2008) indicate that the qualitative form of value is not definite and doubtful, that means, defining the connection between value and monetary units is not possible. That refers that the measure of value is not empirically important, meaning, value measures are not balanced. That refers that the determination of meaningfulness of accounting information by balancing with empirical importance is not possible. On the other if it is considered that accounting information needs to be applicable to the applicants that mean that accounting information should have a realistic or utilitarian value in the frame of the applicants. As a conclusion, accounting should be light, not dark for the applicants as far as accounting information flow is concerned if it is a measurement discipline.

Psychological and Physical Theory

The mission of monetary elements to the value of an item of the financial statements demands that the figure corresponds the character of the value in the empirical connection form of value with the character of money in the empirical connection form of money. Orderly, we need to have two physical forms with disciplines V and M; provided that monetary elements as the symbolizing are a wide and each of the physical needs a rate series sample. According to this, the psychological instruction can be explained like this: for every sign v in discipline V, some m exists in discipline M by connection with the figure m corresponds v. Ryan et al. (2002) and Musvoto (2008) claims that implied connection does not exist and it correlates value to monetary elements that refers that two probable physical connection that are combined with only psychological connection. This means, in case, value and monetary are moved to be that are established on the rating series as mentioned in the accounting literature, an evaluation of the corresponding in between the two may be defined as authority connection. On the other hand, Musvoto (2008) argues that the concept of value is somehow theoretical and the all-measurement studies of the concept of value couldn't be concluded yet. That means that we have a physical connection combined with a hypothetical idea by a psychological connection. For this reason, that demands someone to search the contributor of the authority connection. Luce and Narens point out a base of agreement in between the two physical wide forms like this:

> For any translation t of X, a corresponding translation exists as rt of S, such that for all x which is inside of X and for all s which is S: xMs if and only if t(x) M rt(s).

The result suggests that the two physical wide forms have agreement disciplines if moving a character in one discipline corresponds moving a character in another discipline. That translates that the connection M combining the two physical wide forms is only psychological. Luce and Narens (1994) say that the corresponding connection may be introduced empirically as an authority connection (for the first evaluation) between the two physical rate-series measures. That implies that aspect of the multipliable stable of the connection needed the exponent applied. Additionally, the performing of the base of agreement between the two disciplines is clearly unique for a distinguished case. It is needed in the accounting domain to describe the concept of value and the concept of money and right after the describing, corresponding may appear between elements of these two concepts. In case the value is a hypothetical idea as indicated, that explains that the agreement between the concept of value and monetary elements cannot be explained as value is not a physical form. Furthermore, even though agreement of the concept of value with the concept of monetary elements is special for a particular case, the phenomenon of searching which psychological rules are agreement with the explanation of the elements of the concept of value and elements of the concept of monetary elements is accustomed base in the science of accounting.

References

Chambers RJ (1997) Whose reality really counts? Putting the first last, Intermediate Technology Development Group. London. ISBN 1-85339-386-X

European Central Bank (2006) Assessment of accounting standards from a financial stability perspective. Retrieved from http://www.ecb.int/pub/pdf/other/assessmentaccountingstandards2006en.pdf

Falmagne JC (1980) A probabilistic theory of extensive measurement. Philos Sci 47:277–296

Gibson CH (2010) Financial reporting, and analysis. Cengage, New York, NY

Ijiri Y (1975) Theory of accounting measurement. Studies in Accounting Research #10, ASIN: B002FOFO2M. Sarasota, FL: American Accounting Association Publishing

International Accounting Standards Board (IASB) (2009) International Financial Reporting Standards (IFRS) (2009): Including International Accounting Standards (IAS) and interpretations as at 1 July 2009

Kimmel PD, Kieso DE, Weygandt J (2010) Financial accounting: tools for business decision making. Cengage, New York, NY

Luce RD (1990) Rational versus plausible accounting equivalences in preference judgments. Psychol Sci 1(4):225–234

Luce RD, Narens L (1994) Fifteen problems concerning the representational theory of measurement. http://www.Imbs.uci.edu/personnel/Luce/1994/Luce&Narens_Book%20Chapter_1994.pdf. Accessed June 2013

Luce RD, Krantz DH, Suppes P, Tversk A (1971) Foundations of measurement, (Vol 1) additive and polynomial representations. Academic Press, New York

Mankiw NG (2011) Principles of economics. Cengage, New York, NY

Michell J (1986) Measurement scale and statistics: a clash of paradigms. Psychol Bull 100:398–407

Mirza AA, Holt G, Knorr L (2011) Wiley IFRS. Wiley, New York, NY

Musvoto SW (2008) Applying the representational theory of measurement to accounting, PhD thesis, University of Pretoria, Pretoria

Narens L (2002) A meaningful justification for the representational theory of measurement. J Math Psychol 46:746–768

Orbach KN (1978) Accounting as a mathematical measurement theoretic discipline. Texas A&M University. https://hdl.handle.net/1969.1/DISSERTATIONS-637414

Previts GJ, Walton P, Wolnizer P (2011) A global history of accounting, financial reporting, and republic policy. Emerald Group Publishing, New York, NY

Ryan B, Scapens RW, Theobald M (2002) Research method and methodology in finance and accounting, 2nd edn. International, Padstow, Cornwall, Mitcham, Surrey

Saudagaran SM (2009) International accounting: a user perspective. CCH, New Delhi

Scott D, Suppes P (1958) Foundational aspects of theories of measurement. J Symb Log 23:113–128

Spero JE, Hart JA (2009) The politics of international economic relations. Cengage, New York, NY

Stamp E (1981) Why can accounting not become a science like physics? Abacus, June 13–27

Stickney CP, Weil RL, Schipper K, Francis J (2009) Financial accounting: an introduction to concepts, methods, and uses. Cengage Learning, New York, NY

Thomas R, Gup BE (2010) The valuation handbook. Wiley, New York, NY

Tinker T (1985) Paper prophets, a social critique of accounting. Praeger, New York
Walton P (2011) An executive guide to IFRS. Wiley, New York, NY
Warren CS, Reeve JM, Duchac J (2011) Accounting. Cengage, New York, NY
Willett R (1987) An axiomatic theory of accounting measurement. Account Bus Res Spring:155–171

Chapter 5
Event Study on the Impact of Fair Value Evaluation

An empirical analysis was conducted on 56 companies. The purpose of this chapter is to present and report on the results of this analysis; to form conclusions about accounting evaluation on the basis of the results; and to fill gaps in the current empirical literature.

5.1 Methodology

The study was conducted on 56 publicly-listed companies in Turkey and Romania. The following data were gathered (Table 5.1):

Data on the country, fair value use, revenue, profit margin, share growth, and industry were drawn from publicly-available databases of listed companies in Turkey and Romania. Data on optimism, likeliness to buy, and company transparency were gathered from a survey of 56 investors, 28 from Turkish markets and 28 from Romanian markets. Each investor held stock in exactly one of the companies evaluated in the study.

The population of the study consisted of investors in Turkish and Romanian companies. It is unknown how many people (or institutions) are investors in such companies, so a power analysis could not be conducted to calculate the generalizability of the sample to the population. The sample was obtained by the following means. First, the social media sites Facebook and LinkedIn were used to identify both individuals and organizations who were involved in investing in both Turkish and Romanian companies. Next, messages were sent to the identified organizations and individuals to solicit participation in the research study; these messages were sent in the Turkish and Romanian languages in order to increase the response rate. A total of 79 messages were sent, yielding the final sample of 56 individuals (response rate = 70.88%).

In order to be recruited into the study, respondents had to electronically complete and return an informed consent form disclosing the nature of the research, the

I. Mert, *Assessment of Accounting Evaluation Practices*, Contributions to Finance and Accounting, https://doi.org/10.1007/978-3-030-98486-1_5

Table 5.1 Variables in empirical study

Variable name	Description and coding
Company	There were 56 companies in the study; each was assigned a number from 1 to 56
Country	1 = Turkey; 2 = Romania
Fair value	0 = does not use fair value; 1 = uses fair value
Revenue	Annual revenue in millions of USD
Profit margin	Profit margin over most recent fiscal year
MOM share growth	Month-over-month increase in stock price
YOY share growth	Year-over-year increase in stock price
Industry	1 = manufacturing, 2 = holding company, 3 = telecommunications, 4 = agriculture, 5 = technology, 6 = financial services, 7 = logistics, 8 = construction
Optimism	A measure of investors' optimism about the company, with 1 = not at all, 2 = no, 3 = not really, 4 = neutral, 5 = a little bit, 6 = yes, 7 = absolutely
Likely to buy	A measure of investors' likelihood of buying further stock in the company, with 1 = not at all, 2 = no, 3 = not really, 4 = neutral, 5 = a little bit, 6 = yes, 7 = absolutely
Company transparent	A measure of how transparent investors find the company to be, with 1 = not at all, 2 = no, 3 = not really, 4 = neutral, 5 = a little bit, 6 = yes, 7 = absolutely

conditions of participation, and their rights to refuse or withdraw participation at any time and without penalty. In accord with the principles of ethical data collection (Creswell 2009), no data collection or analysis took place until each member of the sample returned the informed consent form. These forms did not subjects' names or other identifying information and were stored on an encrypted laptop.

After obtaining consent from subjects, the next step in the empirical study was to direct participants to an electronic survey. This survey was structured as follows. First, the subjects were directed to frame their responses based on their on investment in only one company of their choice; this company had to be publicly listed in either Turkey or Romania. Since many subjects doubtlessly had investment holdings in several companies, they were asked to choose the one public Turkish or Romanian company in which they had the largest degree of investment.

Next, the subjects were asked three questions about the company they had chosen, as follows:

1. Are you generally optimistic about the company's stock price increasing?
2. Are you likely to buy more stock in the company?
3. Do you find the company to be transparent concerning the information it discloses to you via prospectus?

No effort was made to define the variables of optimism or transparency. Since optimism and belief in a company's transparency are both subjective, the decision was made to allow subjects to define these concepts in whichever ways made sense to them.

After subjects nominated their 1 allotted company and disclosed their degrees of optimism, likelihood of buying, and evaluation of transparency, additional research took place in order to identify the following variables as they pertained to each company: (1) Did the company use fair value accounting? (2) What was the annual revenue of the company for the most recently-concluded fiscal year? (3) What was the month-over-month increase in stock price for the company, with the starting point being July 1, 2012, and the ending point being July 31, 2012? (4) What was the year-over-year share growth for the company, with the starting point being January 1, 2011 and the ending point being December 31, 2011? (5) What industry is the business in? These questions were answered through a combination of public company database analysis and follow-up emails to each of the companies in the survey.

Once these data were collected, it was possible to answer the research questions posed by the study in the appropriate manner.

5.2 Descriptive Statistics of the Study

This section of the study consists of an overview of the descriptive, non-inferential statistics associated with the study. The purpose of the section is to offer further insight into the data gathered for the study prior to presenting and discussing the inferential statistics (Table 5.2).

The sample consisted of 56 companies, 28 of which were Romanian and 28 of which were Turkish. Choosing an equal number of companies from each country facilitated the statistical analysis (Fig. 5.1).

Of the companies in the sample, 28 used fair value and 28 did not use fair value. Choosing an equal number of companies from each value facilitated the statistical analysis. Moreover, each country had an equal number of fair value-using and non-fair value-using companies (Tables 5.3, 5.4, 5.5, Figs. 5.2 and 5.3).

Revenue data were collected for all the countries in the sample:

Table 5.2 Country statistics

Statistics		
N	Valid	56
	Missing	0

Country					
		Frequency	Percent	Valid percent	Cumulative percent
Valid	Turkey	28	50.0	50.0	50.0
	Romania	28	50.0	50.0	100.0
	Total	56	100.0	100.0	

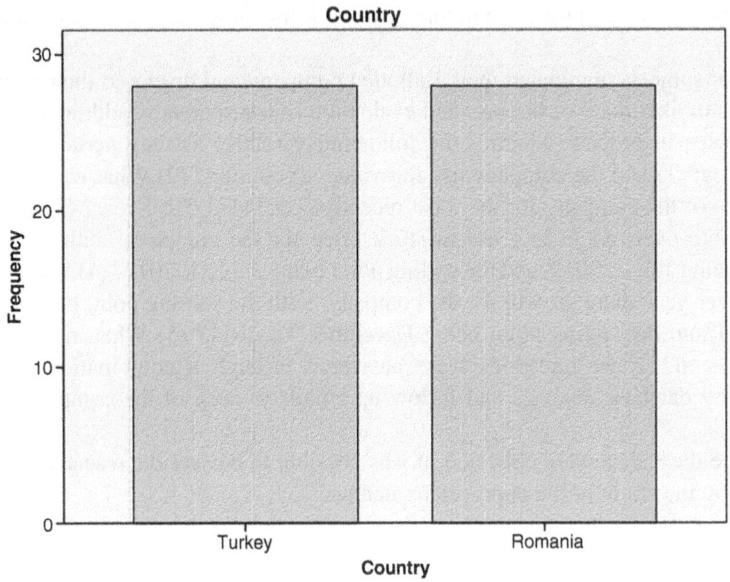

Fig. 5.1 Bar chart of country representation

Table 5.3 Fair value statistics

Statistics		
Fair value		
N	Valid	56
	Missing	0

Fair value					
		Frequency	Percent	Valid percent	Cumulative percent
Valid	Does not use fair value	28	50.0	50.0	50.0
	Uses fair value	28	50.0	50.0	100.0
	Total	56	100.0	100.0	

Table 5.4 Cross-tabulations, fair value used by country

Case processing summary						
	Cases					
	Valid		Missing		Total	
	N	Percent	N	Percent	N	Percent
Country * fair value	56	100.0%	0	0.0%	56	100.0%

Country * fair value cross-tabulation				
Count				
		Fair value		
		Does not use fair value	Uses fair value	Total
Country	Turkey	14	14	28
	Romania	14	14	28
Total		28	28	56

Table 5.5 Descriptive statistics, revenue

Revenue		
N	Valid	56
	Missing	0
Mean		464.64
Std. deviation		753.485
Skewness		3.988
Std. error of skewness		0.319
Kurtosis		16.072
Std. error of kurtosis		0.628
Range		3941
Percentiles	25	177.75
	50	308.00
	75	387.25

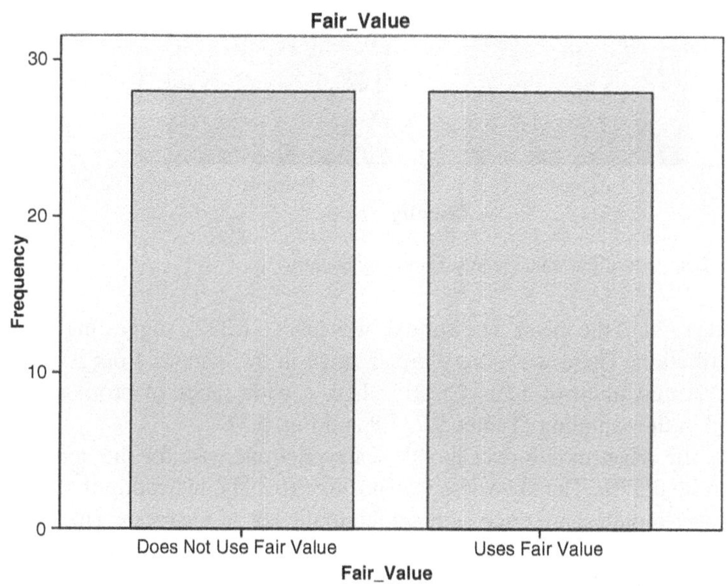

Fig. 5.2 Bar chart of fair value representation

The mean revenue for companies in the sample was $464.64 million per year. The skewness was positive (3.988), indicating that most of the revenue values fell to the left of the mean. The kurtosis was high (16.072), suggesting a sharp peak in the distribution. There was a very broad range in the sample, from a minimum of $59 million to a maximum of $4 billion (see Table 5.21). Clearly, then, a wide range of revenues was captured in the sampling (Table 5.6 and Fig. 5.4).

Next, the mean profit margin for companies in the sample was 4.93%. The skewness was negative (−0.048), indicating that most of the profit margin values

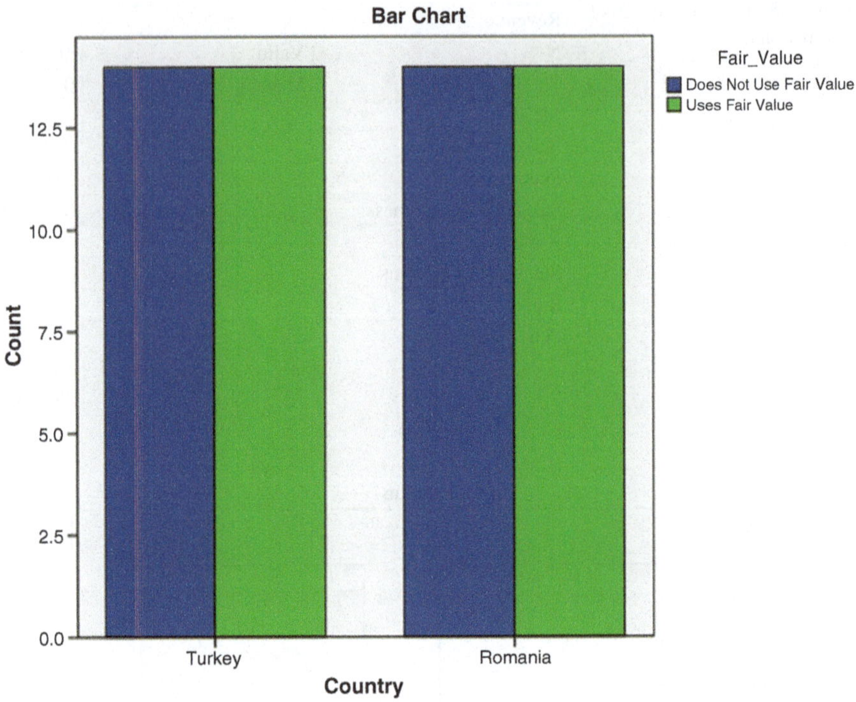

Fig. 5.3 Bar chart of fair value representation by country

fell to the right of the mean. The kurtosis was low (−1.272), suggesting a flat top for the distribution. There was a very broad range in the sample, from a minimum of −2% to a maximum of 12%. Clearly, then, a wide range of profit margins was captured in the sampling (Tables 5.7, 5.8 and Fig. 5.5).

Next, the mean month-over-month share price increase for the companies was found to be 0.57%. The skewness was positive (0.191), indicating that most of the month-over-month share price increase fell to the left of the mean. The kurtosis was low (−1.420), suggesting a flat top for the distribution. The range was from −2% to 4% (Tables 5.9, 5.10 and Fig. 5.6).

Next, the mean year-over-year share price increase for the companies was found to be 5.61%. The skewness was positive (0.009), indicating that most of the month-over-month share price increase fell to the left of the mean. The kurtosis was low (−1.522), suggesting a flat top for the distribution. The range was from −3% to 14% (Tables 5.11, 5.12 and Fig. 5.7).

Next, data were collected to tabulate the industries of the companies in the sample. There were eight industries represented in the sample, distributed as follows (Table 5.13 and Fig. 5.8):

Next, data were gathered on investor optimism. A plurality (13) of the respondents were not really optimistic about the company in which they had invested (Table 5.14 and Fig. 5.9).

Table 5.6 Frequencies, revenue

		Frequency	Percent	Valid percent	Cumulative percent
Valid	59	1	1.8	1.8	1.8
	60	1	1.8	1.8	3.6
	64	1	1.8	1.8	5.4
	71	1	1.8	1.8	7.1
	77	1	1.8	1.8	8.9
	93	1	1.8	1.8	10.7
	98	1	1.8	1.8	12.5
	101	1	1.8	1.8	14.3
	133	1	1.8	1.8	16.1
	158	1	1.8	1.8	17.9
	167	1	1.8	1.8	19.6
	172	1	1.8	1.8	21.4
	176	1	1.8	1.8	23.2
	177	1	1.8	1.8	25.0
	180	1	1.8	1.8	26.8
	195	1	1.8	1.8	28.6
	227	1	1.8	1.8	30.4
	232	3	5.4	5.4	35.7
	250	1	1.8	1.8	37.5
	255	1	1.8	1.8	39.3
	260	1	1.8	1.8	41.1
	288	1	1.8	1.8	42.9
	299	1	1.8	1.8	44.6
	302	1	1.8	1.8	46.4
	304	1	1.8	1.8	48.2
	306	1	1.8	1.8	50.0
	310	1	1.8	1.8	51.8
	311	1	1.8	1.8	53.6
	323	1	1.8	1.8	55.4
	326	1	1.8	1.8	57.1
	334	1	1.8	1.8	58.9
	337	1	1.8	1.8	60.7
	357	1	1.8	1.8	62.5
	359	1	1.8	1.8	64.3
	364	2	3.6	3.6	67.9
	370	1	1.8	1.8	69.6
	375	1	1.8	1.8	71.4
	381	1	1.8	1.8	73.2
	385	1	1.8	1.8	75.0
	388	1	1.8	1.8	76.8
	411	1	1.8	1.8	78.6
	413	1	1.8	1.8	80.4

(continued)

Table 5.6 (continued)

		Frequency	Percent	Valid percent	Cumulative percent
	415	1	1.8	1.8	82.1
	419	1	1.8	1.8	83.9
	420	1	1.8	1.8	85.7
	429	1	1.8	1.8	87.5
	431	1	1.8	1.8	89.3
	437	1	1.8	1.8	91.1
	452	1	1.8	1.8	92.9
	1711	1	1.8	1.8	94.6
	2130	1	1.8	1.8	96.4
	3900	1	1.8	1.8	98.2
	4000	1	1.8	1.8	100.0
	Total	56	100.0	100.0	

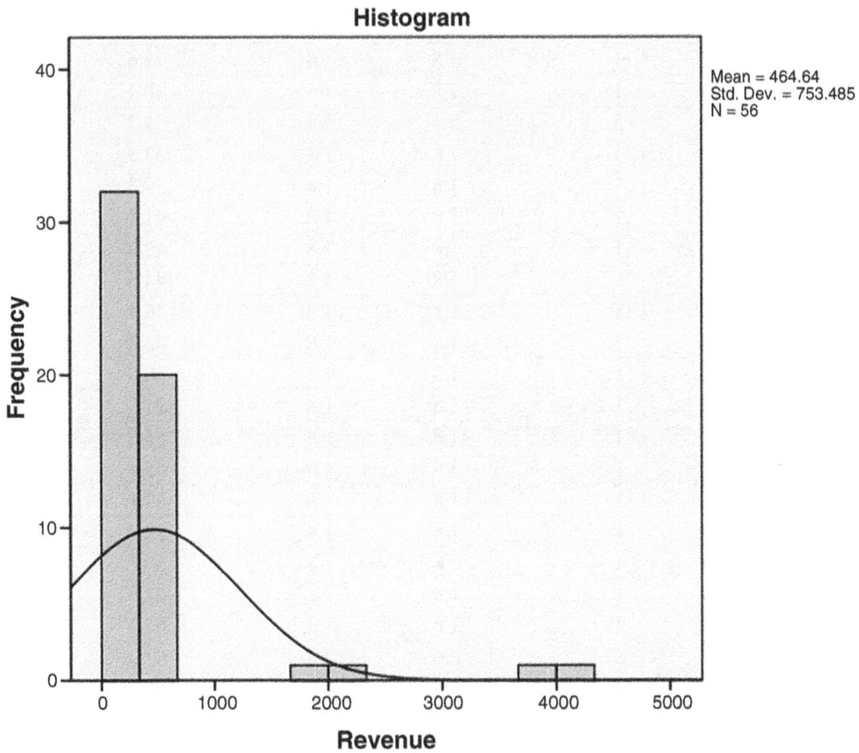

Fig. 5.4 Histogram of revenue distribution (normal curve superimposed)

Table 5.7 Descriptive statistics, profit margin

Profit Margin		
N	Valid	56
	Missing	0
Mean		4.93
Std. deviation		4.212
Skewness		−0.048
Std. error of skewness		0.319
Kurtosis		−1.272
Std. error of kurtosis		0.628
Range		14
Percentiles	25	1.00
	50	5.00
	75	8.75

Table 5.8 Frequencies, profit margin

Profit margin					
		Frequency	Percent	Valid percent	Cumulative percent
Valid	−2	3	5.4	5.4	5.4
	−1	4	7.1	7.1	12.5
	0	4	7.1	7.1	19.6
	1	4	7.1	7.1	26.8
	2	4	7.1	7.1	33.9
	3	5	8.9	8.9	42.9
	4	1	1.8	1.8	44.6
	5	5	8.9	8.9	53.6
	6	3	5.4	5.4	58.9
	7	3	5.4	5.4	64.3
	8	6	10.7	10.7	75.0
	9	5	8.9	8.9	83.9
	10	2	3.6	3.6	87.5
	11	6	10.7	10.7	98.2
	12	1	1.8	1.8	100.0
	Total	56	100.0	100.0	

Next, data were gathered on investor likelihood of buying further stock in the company. A plurality (15) of the respondents were not really likely to buy more stock in the company in which they had invested (Table 5.15 and Fig. 5.10).

Next, data were gathered on investor evaluation of the company as transparent. A plurality (13) of the respondents did not really believe that the companies in which they had invested were transparent (Table 5.16 and Fig. 5.11).

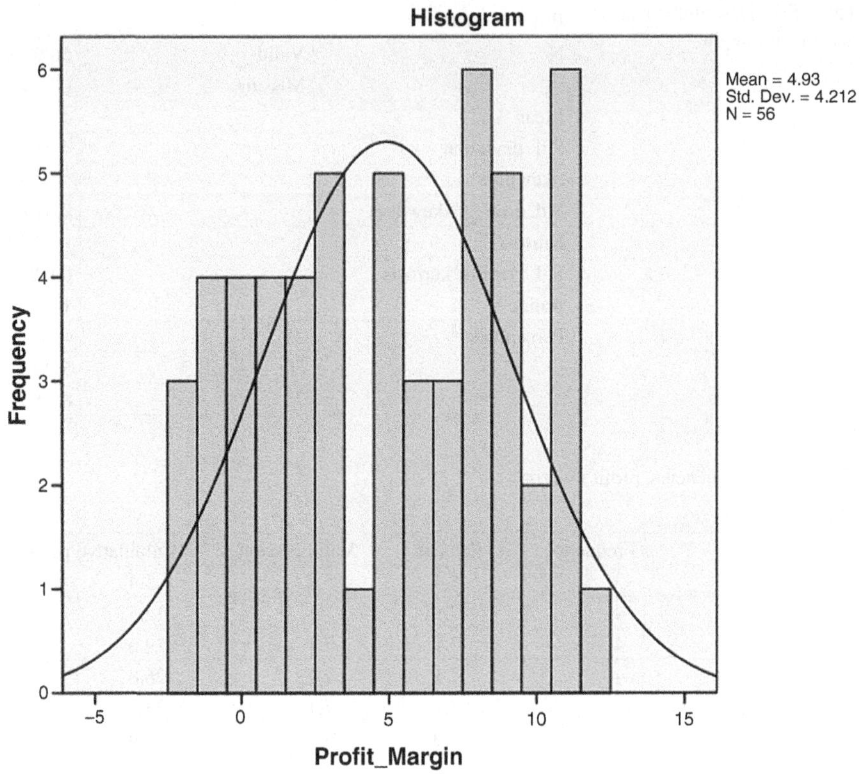

Fig. 5.5 Histogram of profit margin distribution (normal curve superimposed)

Table 5.9 Descriptive statistics, month-over-month share price increase

Month-over-month stock price growth		
N	Valid	56
	Missing	0
Mean		0.57
Std. deviation		2.096
Skewness		0.191
Std. error of skewness		0.319
Kurtosis		−1.420
Std. error of kurtosis		0.628
Range		6
Percentiles	25	−1.00
	50	0.00
	75	2.75

Table 5.10 Frequencies, month-over-month share price increase

		Frequency	Percent	Valid percent	Cumulative percent
Valid	−2	13	23.2	23.2	23.2
	−1	10	17.9	17.9	41.1
	0	6	10.7	10.7	51.8
	1	5	8.9	8.9	60.7
	2	8	14.3	14.3	75.0
	3	9	16.1	16.1	91.1
	4	5	8.9	8.9	100.0
	Total	56	100.0	100.0	

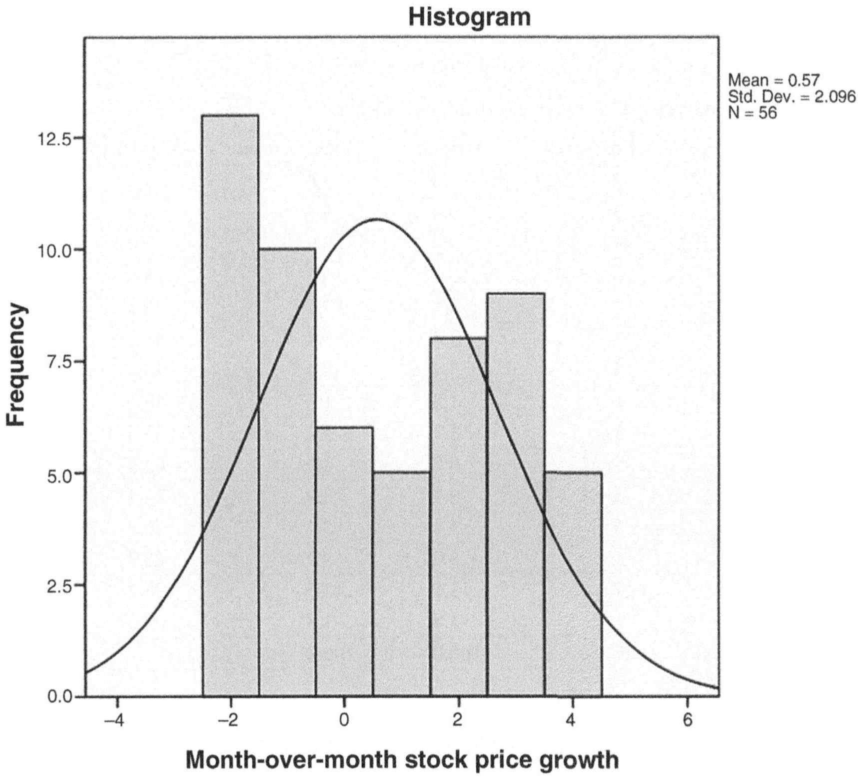

Fig. 5.6 Histogram of month-over-month share price increase distribution (normal curve superimposed)

Table 5.11 Descriptive statistics, year-over-year share price increase

Year-over-year stock price growth		
N	Valid	56
	Missing	0
Mean		5.61
Std. deviation		5.549
Skewness		0.009
Std. error of skewness		0.319
Kurtosis		−1.522
Std. error of kurtosis		0.628
Range		17
Percentiles	25	0.00
	50	6.00
	75	11.00

Table 5.12 Frequencies, year-over-year share price increase

		Frequency	Percent	Valid percent	Cumulative percent
Valid	−3	2	3.6	3.6	3.6
	−2	3	5.4	5.4	8.9
	−1	5	8.9	8.9	17.9
	0	6	10.7	10.7	28.6
	1	4	7.1	7.1	35.7
	3	3	5.4	5.4	41.1
	4	3	5.4	5.4	46.4
	5	1	1.8	1.8	48.2
	6	3	5.4	5.4	53.6
	7	5	8.9	8.9	62.5
	10	5	8.9	8.9	71.4
	11	3	5.4	5.4	76.8
	12	5	8.9	8.9	85.7
	13	7	12.5	12.5	98.2
	14	1	1.8	1.8	100.0
	Total	56	100.0	100.0	

5.3 Inferential Statistics of the Study: Fair Value

The first set of inferential tests conducted in the study involved determining whether the use of fair value accounting was associated with more or less (1) revenue, (2) profit margin, (3) month-over-month stock price growth, (4) year-over-year stock price growth, (5) investor optimism, (6) investor likelihood to buy more stock, and (7) investor evaluation of a company's transparency. These tests were conducted using the independent samples t-test methodology, in which there were two data points of note: The difference in means between fair value and non-fair

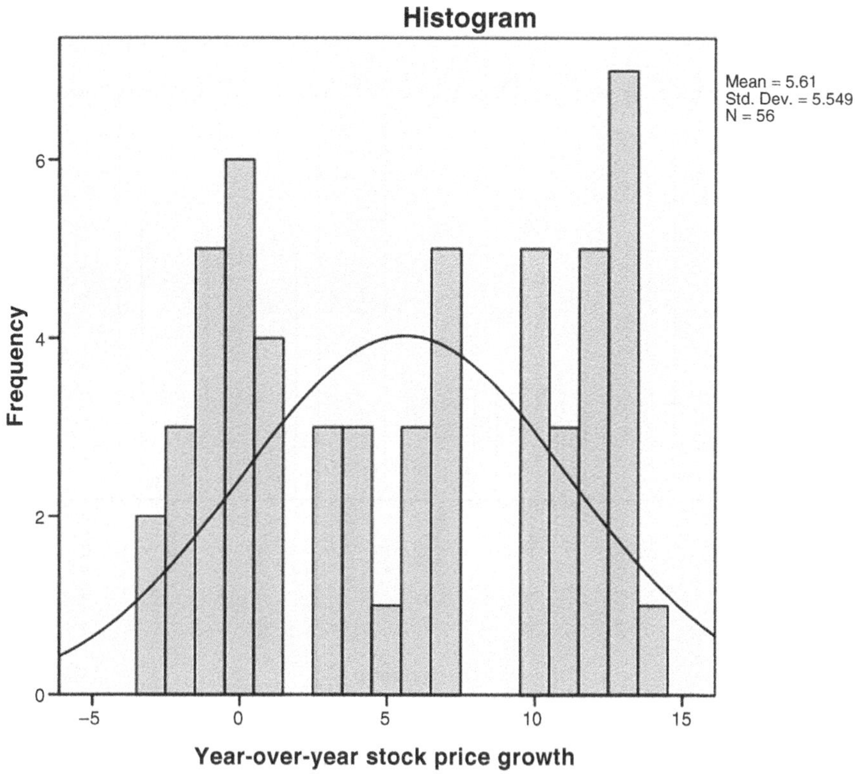

Fig. 5.7 Histogram of year-over-year share price increase distribution (normal curve superimposed)

Table 5.13 Industry representation in the sample: Frequencies

		Frequency	Percent	Valid percent	Cumulative percent
Valid	Manufacturing	10	17.9	17.9	17.9
	Holding company	4	7.1	7.1	25.0
	Telecommunications	3	5.4	5.4	30.4
	Agriculture	3	5.4	5.4	35.7
	Technology	10	17.9	17.9	53.6
	Financial services	7	12.5	12.5	66.1
	Logistics	8	14.3	14.3	80.4
	Construction	11	19.6	19.6	100.0
	Total	56	100.0	100.0	

value companies in each of the seven points of comparison listed above; and the *p* value, or significance, of this difference (which the SPSS software used to conduct this analysis reports as Sig.). If the *p* value for any of these comparisons was above

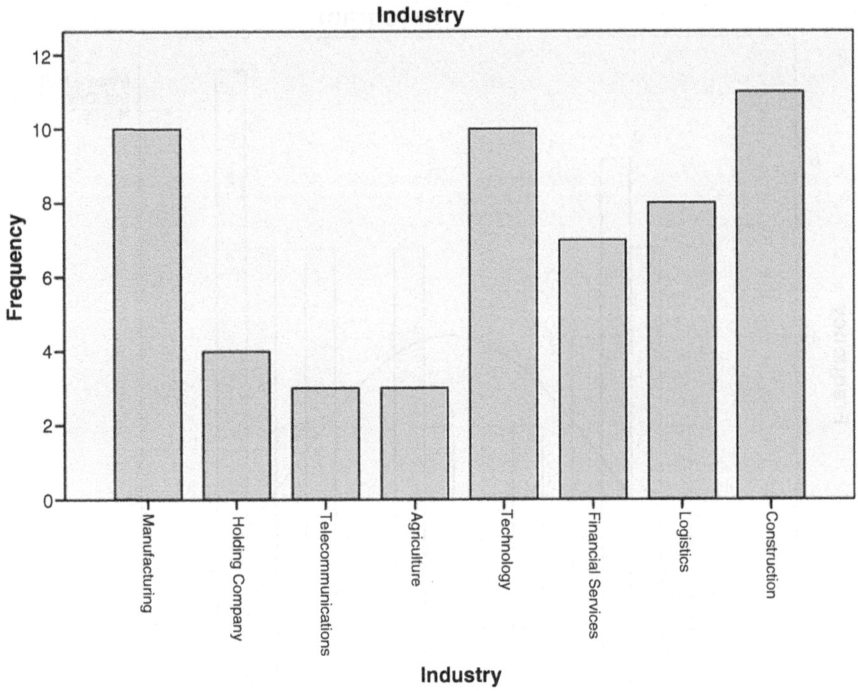

Fig. 5.8 Industry representation in the sample: Bar chart

Table 5.14 Investor optimism: Frequencies

		Frequency	Percent	Valid percent	Cumulative percent
Valid	No	8	14.3	14.3	14.3
	Not really	13	23.2	23.2	37.5
	Neutral	10	17.9	17.9	55.4
	A little bit	9	16.1	16.1	71.4
	Yes	9	16.1	16.1	87.5
	Absolutely	7	12.5	12.5	100.0
	Total	56	100.0	100.0	

.05, then it meant that fair use was not associated with any significant differences in the variables being measured. If the p value was below .05, then there was a significant difference, one that was isolated further through the use of cross-tabulations and Chi-square analysis. The assumption carried into the inferential statistics was that using fair value was associated with higher revenue, profit, month-over-month stock price changes, year-over-year stock price changes, investor optimism, investor likelihood of buying, and investor evaluation of company transparency (Table 5.17).

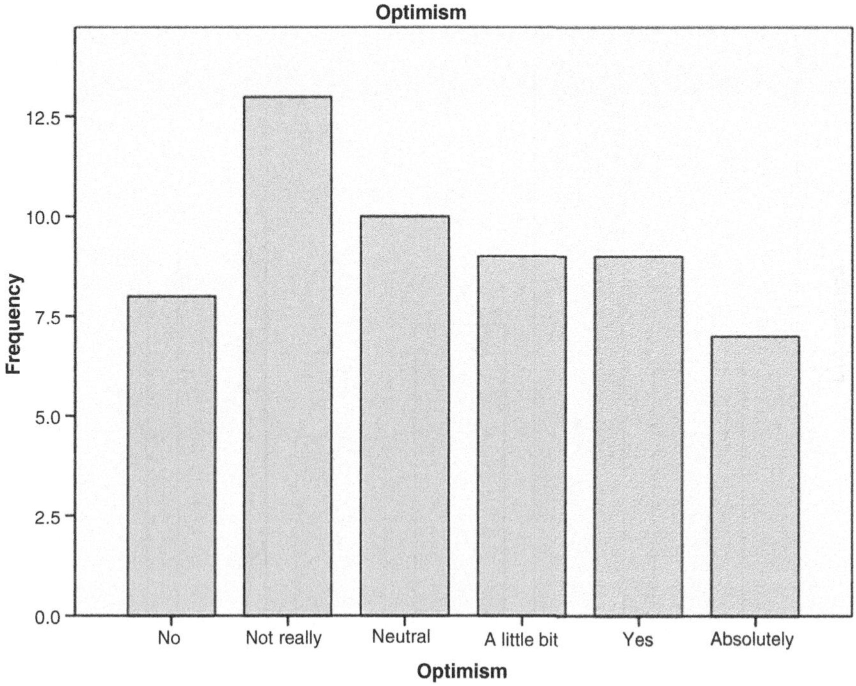

Fig. 5.9 Optimism representation in the sample: Bar chart

Table 5.15 Investor likelihood to buy: Frequencies

		Frequency	Percent	Valid percent	Cumulative percent
Valid	No	7	12.5	12.5	12.5
	Not really	15	26.8	26.8	39.3
	Neutral	8	14.3	14.3	53.6
	A little bit	5	8.9	8.9	62.5
	Yes	11	19.6	19.6	82.1
	Absolutely	10	17.9	17.9	100.0
	Total	56	100.0	100.0	

The difference in revenue mean of fair-value-using and non-fair-value-using companies was not significant ($p = 0.743$). Fair value use was therefore not associated with having higher or lower revenues (Table 5.18).

The difference in profit margin mean of fair-value-using and non-fair-value-using companies was not significant ($p = 0.346$). Fair value use was therefore not associated with having higher or lower profit margins (Table 5.19).

The difference in a month-over-month stock price increase for fair-value-using and non-fair-value-using companies was not significant ($p = 0.801$). Fair value use

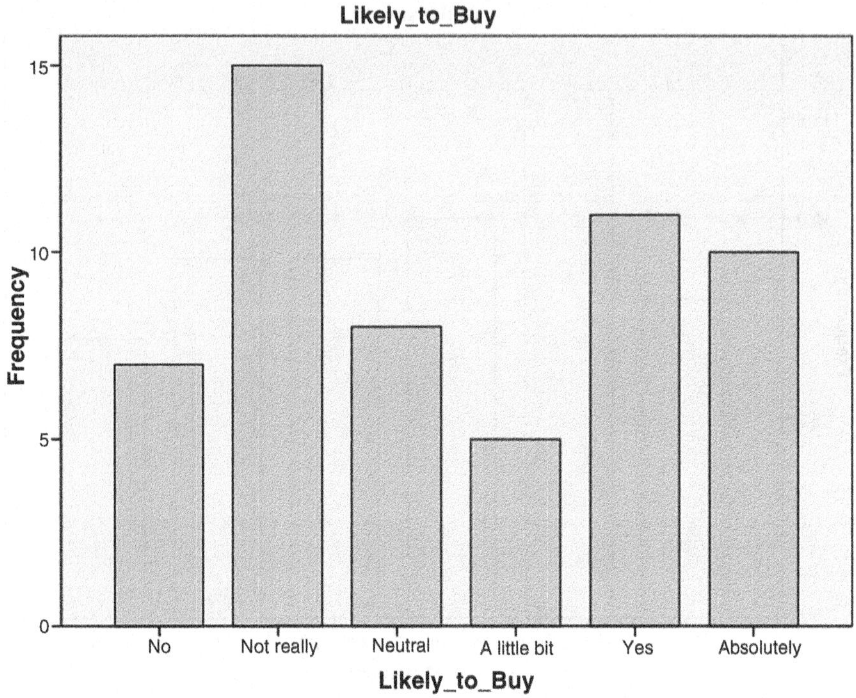

Fig. 5.10 Likelihood to buy representation in the sample: Bar chart

Table 5.16 Investor evaluation of company transparency: Frequencies

Company transparent					
		Frequency	Percent	Valid percent	Cumulative percent
Valid	No	7	12.5	12.5	12.5
	Not really	13	23.2	23.2	35.7
	Neutral	9	16.1	16.1	51.8
	A little bit	12	21.4	21.4	73.2
	Yes	11	19.6	19.6	92.9
	Absolutely	4	7.1	7.1	100.0
	Total	56	100.0	100.0	

was therefore not associated with having higher or lower month-over-month stock price increases (Table 5.20).

The difference in a year-over-year stock price increase for fair-value-using and non-fair-value-using companies was not significant ($p = 0.505$). Fair value use was therefore not associated with having higher or lower year-over-year stock price increases.

Next, Chi-square analysis was used to determine whether the fair value use was equally distributed among industries (Table 5.21 and Fig. 5.12).

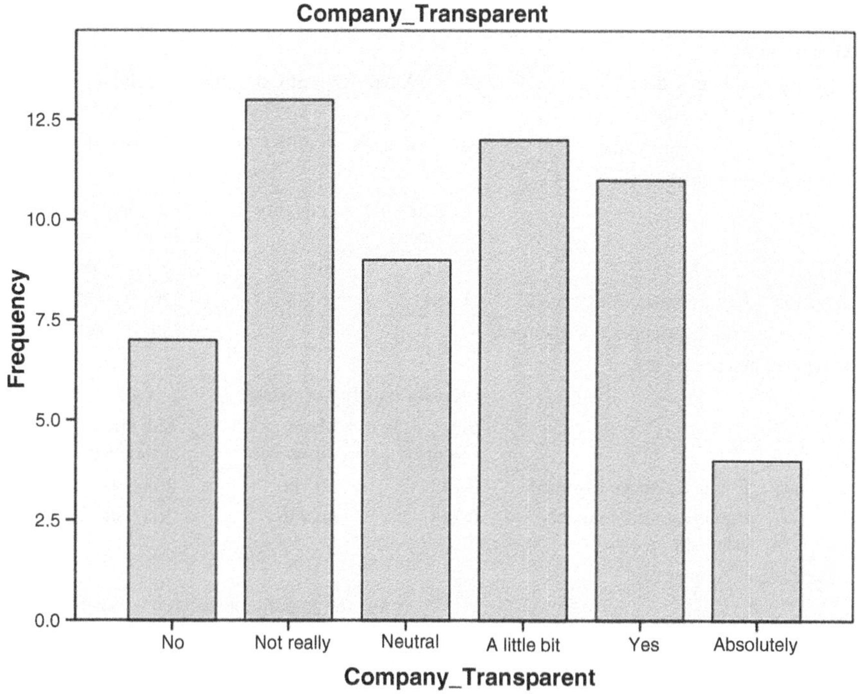

Fig. 5.11 Investor evaluation of transparency: Bar chart

Fair value use was approximately evenly distributed across industries because the p value of the Pearson Chi-square figure was 0.312. Had this figure been less than 0.05, it could have been concluded that fair value users were concentrated in one or more industries in a manner that could have lowered the validity of the study. As it was, the even distribution of fair value use means that the empirical study's conclusions apply generally, not to any one industry (Table 5.22).

Mean investor optimism was much higher for companies that used fair value ($M = 5.04$, $s = 1.503$) than for companies that did not use fair value ($M = 3.64$, $s = 1.471$). This difference was statistically significant ($p = 0.001$). Chi-square analysis was used to analyze further the difference between investor optimism levels in companies that used fair value versus companies that did not use fair value (Table 5.23).

Chi-square analysis confirmed that investor optimism was unevenly distributed across companies that used fair value versus companies that did not use fair value ($p = 0.006$) (Fig. 5.13).

The bar chart above clearly depicts the trend observed in the t-test, which is that there are higher levels of investor optimism for companies that use fair value versus companies that do not use fair value. Next, t-tests were used to determine whether the use of fair value was also associated with higher investor likelihood of buying more stock and better investor evaluations of company transparency (Table 5.24).

Table 5.17 Independent samples T-Test, revenue and fair value use

Group statistics					
	Fair value	N	Mean	Std. deviation	Std. error mean
Revenue	Does not use fair value	28	498.04	809.895	153.056
	Uses fair value	28	431.25	705.879	133.399

Independent samples test					
		Levene's test of equality for variances		t-test of equality for means	
		F	Sig.	t	df
Revenue	Equal variances assumed	1.164	0.285	0.329	54
	Equal variances not assumed			0.329	53.011

Independent samples test				
		t-test for equality of means		
		Sig. (2-tailed)	Mean difference	Std. error difference
Revenue	Equal variances assumed	0.743	66.786	203.030
	Equal variances not assumed	0.743	66.786	203.030

Independent samples test			
		t-test for equality of means	
		95% confidence interval of the difference	
		Lower	Upper
Revenue	Equal variances assumed	−340.265	473.836
	Equal variances not assumed	−340.439	474.011

Mean investor likelihood to buy more stock was higher for companies that used fair value (M = 5.25, s = 1.624) than for companies that did not use fair value (M = 3.75, s = 1.555). This difference was statistically significant (p = 0.001). Chi-square analysis was used to analyze further the difference between investor likelihood to buy more stock in companies that used fair value versus companies that did not use fair value (Table 5.25).

Chi-square analysis confirmed that investor likelihood to buy more stock was unevenly distributed across companies that used fair value versus companies that did not use fair value (p = 0.002) (Fig. 5.14).

The bar chart above clearly depicts the trend observed in the t-test, which is that there are higher levels of investor likelihood to buy from companies that use fair value versus companies that do not use fair value. Next, a t-test was used to determine whether the use of fair value was also associated with better investor evaluations of company transparency (Table 5.26).

The difference in investor evaluations of company transparency for fair-value-using and non-fair-value-using companies was not significant (p = 0.189). However, Chi-square analysis revealed that there were still meaningful differences between the distribution of company transparency evaluations based on fair value usage (Table 5.27).

Table 5.18 Independent samples T-Test, profit margin and fair value use

Group statistics

	Fair value	N	Mean	Std. deviation	Std. error mean
Profit margin	Does not use fair value	28	5.46	4.078	0.771
	Uses fair value	28	4.39	4.349	0.822

Independent samples test

		Levene's test of equality for variances		t-test of equality for means	
		F	Sig.	t	df
Profit margin	Equal variances assumed	0.226	0.636	0.951	54
	Equal variances not assumed			0.951	53.778

Independent samples test

		t-test for equality of means		
		Sig. (2-tailed)	Mean difference	Std. error difference
Profit margin	Equal variances assumed	0.346	1.071	1.127
	Equal variances not assumed	0.346	1.071	1.127

Independent samples test

		t-test for equality of means	
		95% confidence interval of the difference	
		Lower	Upper
Profit margin	Equal variances assumed	−1.187	3.330
	Equal variances not assumed	−1.188	3.330

It is true that there not a statistically significant difference between investor evaluations of company transparency for fair-value-using and non-fair-value-using companies. However, the significance of the Chi-square analysis ($p = 0.005$) revealed that the distribution of investor evaluations was still not random. A bar chart revealed the patterns in the survey response data (Fig. 5.15):

It was interesting to note that the only companies to receive 'absolutely' responses to the question of whether they were transparent were also companies that had fair value accounting; similarly, only companies that did not use fair value received the 'no' rating. These differences were too small to register significance in the t-test, but should still be noted.

5.4 Inferential Statistics of the Study: Country Effects

The second set of inferential tests conducted in the study involved determining whether a company's being in Turkey or Romania was associated with more or less (1) revenue, (2) profit margin, (3) month-over-month stock price growth,

Table 5.19 Independent samples T-Test, month-over-month stock price growth, and fair value use

Group statistics

	Fair value	N	Mean
Month-over-month stock price growth	Does not use fair value	28	0.50
	Uses fair value	28	0.64

Group statistics

	Fair value	Std. deviation	Std. error mean
Month-over-month stock price growth	Does not use fair value	1.953	0.369
	Uses fair value	2.264	0.428

Independent samples test

		Levene's test of equality for variances	
		F	Sig.
Month-over-month stock price growth	Equal variances assumed	2.752	0.103
	Equal variances not assumed		

Independent samples test

		t-test of equality for means		
		t	df	Sig. (2-tailed)
Month-over-month stock price growth	Equal variances assumed	−0.253	54	0.801
	Equal variances not assumed	−0.253	52.862	0.801

Independent samples test

		t-test of equality for means	
		Mean difference	Std. error difference
Month-over-month stock price growth	Equal variances assumed	−0.143	0.565
	Equal variances not assumed	−0.143	0.565

Independent samples test

		t-test of equality for means	
		95% confidence interval of the difference	
		Lower	Upper
Month-over-month stock price growth	Equal variances assumed	−1.276	0.990
	Equal variances not assumed	−1.276	0.991

(4) year-over-year stock price growth, (5) investor optimism, (6) investor likelihood to buy more stock, and (7) investor evaluation of a company's transparency.

One purpose of this set of inferential tests, vis-à-vis the study of fair value use that was presented earlier in the analysis, was to exclude company location as a more important predictor of investor sentiment than the use of fair value. Treating the

Table 5.20 Independent samples T-Test, year-over-year stock price growth, and fair value use

Group statistics

	Fair value	N	Mean
Year-over-year stock price growth	Does not use fair value	28	5.11
	Uses fair value	28	6.11

Group statistics

	Fair value	Std. deviation	Std. error mean
Year-over-year stock price growth	Does not use fair value	5.315	1.004
	Uses fair value	5.827	1.101

Independent samples test

		Levene's test of equality for variances	
		F	Sig.
Year-over-year stock price growth	Equal variances assumed	0.699	0.407
	Equal variances not assumed		

Independent samples test

		t-test of equality for means		
		t	df	Sig. (2-tailed)
Year-over-year stock price growth	Equal variances assumed	−0.671	54	0.505
	Equal variances not assumed	−0.671	53.550	0.505

Independent samples test

		t-test of equality for means	
		Mean difference	Std. error difference
Year-over-year stock price growth	Equal variances assumed	−1.000	1.490
	Equal variances not assumed	−1.000	1.490

Independent samples test

		t-test of equality for means 95% confidence interval of the difference	
		Lower	Upper
Year-over-year stock price growth	Equal variances assumed	−3.988	1.988
	Equal variances not assumed	−3.989	1.989

country variable as a sorting variable was thus a way to determine whether location was more important than fair value use, especially in terms of measuring investor optimism, likelihood to buy more stock and evaluations of company transparency. A second purpose of the country-based statistical tests was to gather more data on the differences between Turkish and Romanian companies, a topic on which there is very little if any, empirical literature.

First, it was discovered that mean revenue was higher for Turkish companies (M = \$666.75 million, s = 1028.153) than for Romanian companies (M = \$262.54

Table 5.21 Chi-Square analysis, fair value use * industry * fair value cross-tabulation

Count				
		Fair value		
		Does not use fair value	Uses fair value	Total
Industry	Manufacturing	6	4	10
	Holding company	2	2	4
	Telecommunications	3	0	3
	Agriculture	2	1	3
	Technology	4	6	10
	Financial services	5	2	7
	Logistics	2	6	8
	Construction	4	7	11
Total		28	28	56

Chi-square tests

	Value	df	Asymp. Sig. (2-sided)
Pearson Chi-Square	8.237[a]	7	.312
Likelihood ratio	9.554	7	.215
Linear-by-linear association	2.370	1	0.124
N of valid cases	56		

[a] Ten cells (62.5%) have expected count less than 5. The minimum expected count is 1.50

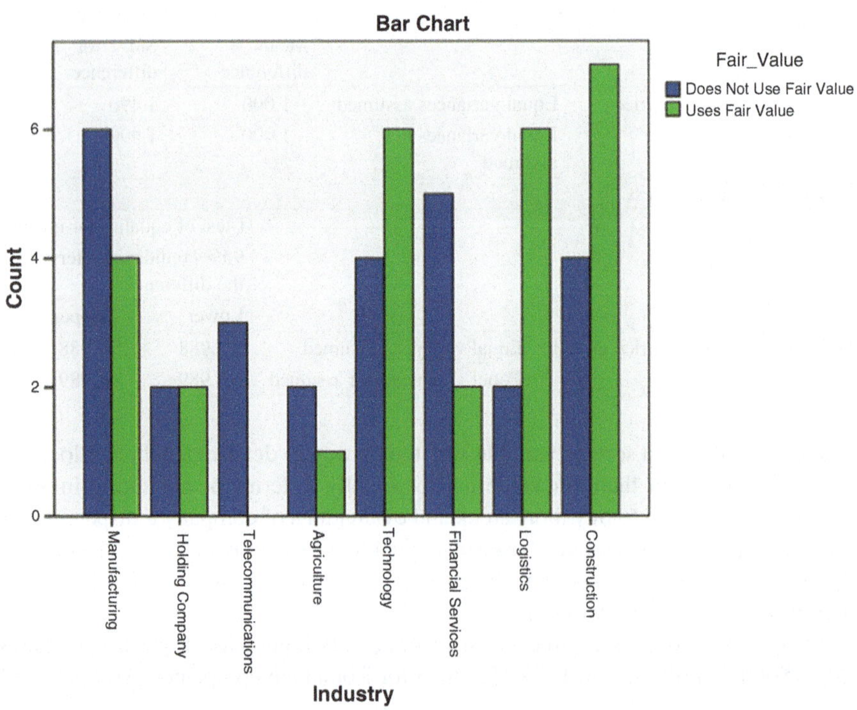

Fig. 5.12 Fair value use by industry: bar chart

Table 5.22 Independent samples T-Test, investor optimism, and fair value use

Group statistics

	Fair value	N	Mean	Std. deviation	Std. error mean
Optimism	Does not use fair value	28	3.64	1.471	0.278
	Uses fair value	28	5.04	1.503	0.284

Independent samples test

		Levene's test of equality for variances		t-test of equality for means	
		F	Sig.	t	df
Optimism	Equal variances assumed	0.000	0.990	−3.505	54
	Equal variances not assumed			−3.505	53.976

Independent samples test

		t-test of equality for means		
		Sig. (2-tailed)	Mean difference	Std. error difference
Optimism	Equal variances assumed	0.001	−1.393	0.397
	Equal variances not assumed	0.001	−1.393	0.397

Independent samples test

		t-test of equality for means 95% confidence interval of the difference	
		Lower	Upper
Optimism	Equal variances assumed	−2.190	−0.596
	Equal variances not assumed	−2.190	−0.596

Table 5.23 Chi-Square analysis, fair value use * optimism

Count

		Fair value		
		Does not use fair value	Uses fair value	Total
Optimism	No	8	0	8
	Not really	7	6	13
	Neutral	5	5	10
	A little bit	3	6	9
	Yes	5	4	9
	Absolutely	0	7	7
Total		28	28	56

Chi-square tests

	Value	df	Asymp. Sig. (2-sided)
Pearson Chi-Square	16.188[a]	5	0.006
Likelihood ratio	22.002	5	0.001
Linear-by-linear association	10.193	1	0.001
N of valid cases	56		

[a] Eight cells (66.7%) have expected count less than 5. The minimum expected count is 3.50

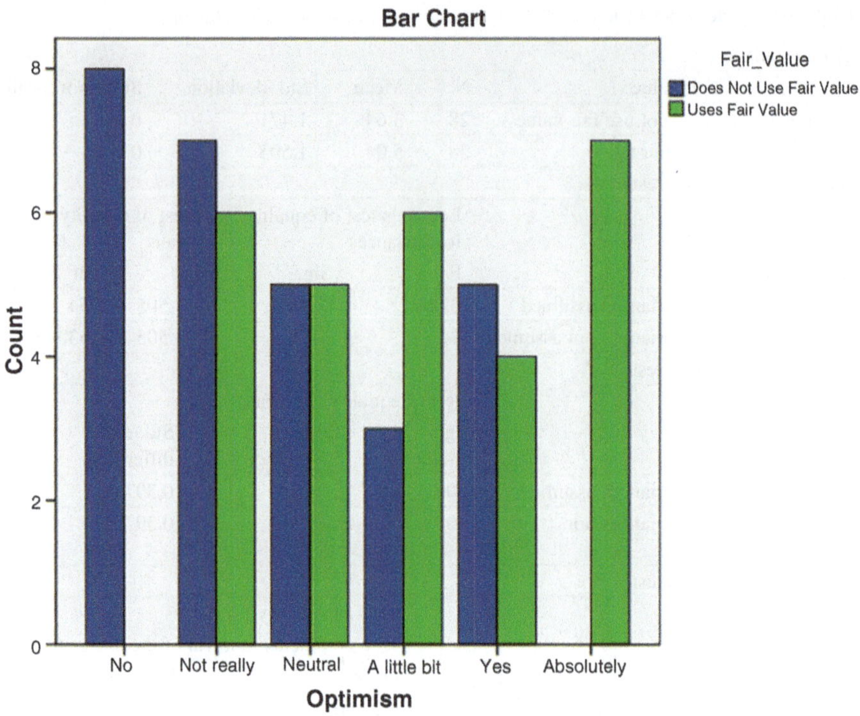

Fig. 5.13 Optimism by fair value: Bar chart

million, $s = 121.191$). This difference was statistically significant ($p = 0.048$). Turkish companies thus appear to generate more revenue than Romanian companies. These results are formally presented in Table 5.28:

Mean profit margin was higher for Turkish companies (M = 6.25, $s = 3.758$) than for Romanian companies (M = 3.61, $s = 4.289$). This difference was statistically significant ($p = 0.017$). Turkish companies thus appear to generate more profit margin than Romanian companies. These results are formally presented in Table 5.29:

Month-over-month stock price growth was higher for Turkish companies (M = 1.29, $s = 2.070$) than for Romanian companies (M = −0.14, $s = 1.900$). This difference was statistically significant ($p = 0.009$). Turkish companies had thus been enjoying better stock market improvements over the past month than Romanian companies at the time the data were gathered. These results are formally presented in Table 5.30:

Next, Chi-square analysis was conducted in order to gather more data about the distribution of month-to-month stock price growth by country (Table 5.31).

The significance of the Chi-square analysis ($p = 0.046$) revealed that the distribution of month-to-month stock price growth was not random. A bar chart revealed the patterns in the survey response data (Fig. 5.16):

Table 5.24 Independent samples T-Test, investor likelihood to buy more stock and fair value use

Group statistics

	Fair value	N	Mean	Std. deviation	Std. error mean
Likely to Buy	Does not use fair value	28	3.75	1.555	0.294
	Uses fair value	28	5.25	1.624	0.307

Independent samples test

		Levene's test of equality for variances		t-test of equality for means	
		F	Sig.	t	df
Likely to Buy	Equal variances assumed	0.349	0.557	−3.530	54
	Equal variances not assumed			−3.530	53.896

Independent samples test

		t-test of equality for means		
		Sig. (2-tailed)	Mean difference	Std. error difference
Likely to Buy	Equal variances assumed	0.001	−1.500	0.425
	Equal variances not assumed	0.001	−1.500	0.425

Independent samples test

		t-test of equality for means	
		95% confidence interval of the difference	
		Lower	Upper
Likely to Buy	Equal variances assumed	−2.352	−0.648
	Equal variances not assumed	−2.352	−0.648

Table 5.25 Chi-Square analysis, fair value use * Investor likelihood to buy more stock

Count

		Fair value		
		Does not use fair value	Uses fair value	Total
Likely to buy	No	7	0	7
	Not really	9	6	15
	Neutral	3	5	8
	A little bit	2	3	5
	Yes	7	4	11
	Absolutely	0	10	10
Total		28	28	56

Chi-Square tests

	Value	df	Asymp. Sig. (2-sided)
Pearson Chi-Square	19.118[a]	5	0.002
Likelihood ratio	25.706	5	0.000
Linear-by-linear association	10.312	1	0.001
N of valid cases	56		

[a] Six cells (50.0%) have expected count less than 5. The minimum expected count is 2.50

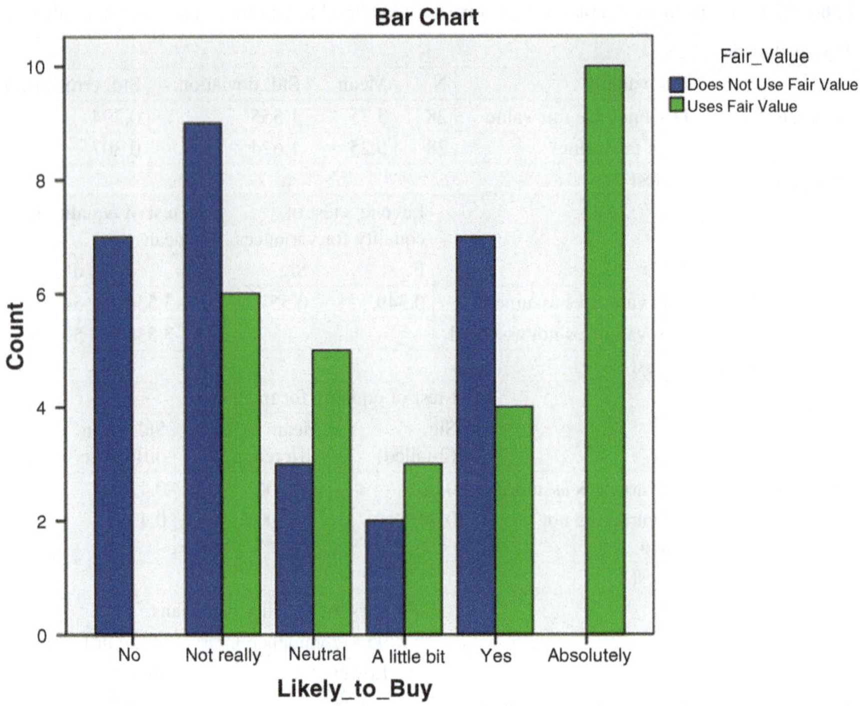

Fig. 5.14 Likelihood to buy at fair value: Bar chart

The final three t-tests at the country level focused on investor optimism, investor likelihood to buy more stock, and investor evaluations of company transparency (Table 5.32).

The difference in the means of year-over-year stock growth for companies in Turkey versus companies in Romania was not significant ($p = 0.601$) (Table 5.33).

The difference in the means of investor optimism in Turkey versus investor optimism in Romania was not significant ($p = 0.373$) (Table 5.34).

The difference in the means of investor likelihood to buy more stock in a Turkish company versus investor likelihood to buy more stock in a Romanian company was not significant ($p = 0.171$) (Table 5.35).

The difference in the means of investor evaluation of company transparency for Turkish companies versus investor evaluation of company transparency for Romanian companies was not significant ($p = 0.794$).

Table 5.26 Independent samples T-Test, investor evaluation of company transparency and fair value use

Group statistics

	Fair value	N	Mean
Company transparent	Does not use fair value	28	4.07
	Uses fair value	28	4.61

Group statistics

	Fair value	Std. deviation	Std. error mean
Company_Transparent	Does not use fair value	1.538	0.291
	Uses fair value	1.474	0.279

Independent samples test

		Levene's test of equality for variances	
		F	Sig.
Company_Transparent	Equal variances assumed	0.008	0.929
	Equal variances not assumed		

Independent samples test

		t-test of equality for means		
		t	df	Sig. (2-tailed)
Company_Transparent	Equal variances assumed	−1.331	54	0.189
	Equal variances not assumed	−1.331	53.904	0.189

Independent samples test

		t-test of equality for means	
		Mean difference	Std. error difference
Company_Transparent	Equal variances assumed	−0.536	0.403
	Equal variances not assumed	−0.536	0.403

Independent samples test

		t-test of equality for means	
		95% confidence interval of the difference	
		Lower	Upper
Company_Transparent	Equal variances assumed	−1.343	0.271
	Equal variances not assumed	−1.343	0.271

Table 5.27 Chi-Square analysis, fair value use * Investor evaluation of company transparency

Count

		Fair value		
		Does not use fair value	Uses fair value	Total
Company transparent	No	7	0	7
	Not really	3	10	13
	Neutral	6	3	9
	A little bit	5	7	12
	Yes	7	4	11
	Absolutely	0	4	4
Total		28	28	56

Chi-square tests

	Value	df	Asymp. Sig. (2-sided)
Pearson Chi-Square	16.921[a]	5	0.005
Likelihood ratio	21.409	5	0.001
Linear-by-linear association	1.746	1	0.186
N of valid cases	56		

[a] Six cells (50.0%) have expected count less than 5. The minimum expected count is 2.00

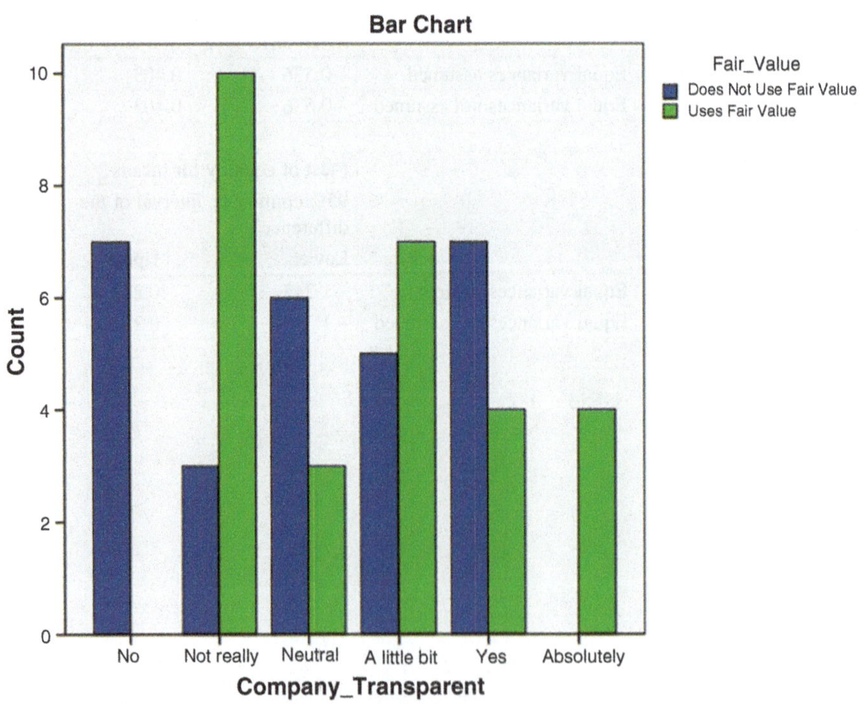

Fig. 5.15 Company transparency evaluation by fair value: Bar chart

Table 5.28 Independent samples T-Test, revenue and country

Group statistics

	Country	N	Mean	Std. deviation	Std. error mean
Revenue	Turkey	28	666.75	1028.153	194.303
	Romania	28	262.54	121.191	22.903

Independent samples test

		Levene's test of equality for variances		t-test of equality for means	
		F	Sig.	t	df
Revenue	Equal variances assumed	13.415	0.001	2.066	54
	Equal variances not assumed			2.066	27.750

Independent samples test

		t-test of equality for means		
		Sig. (2-tailed)	Mean difference	Std. error difference
Revenue	Equal variances assumed	0.044	404.214	195.648
	Equal variances not assumed	0.048	404.214	195.648

Independent samples test

		t-test of equality for means	
		95% confidence interval of the difference	
		Lower	Upper
Revenue	Equal variances assumed	11.964	796.465
	Equal variances not assumed	3.285	805.143

Table 5.29 Independent samples T-Test, profit margin, and country

Group statistics

	Country	N	Mean	Std. deviation	Std. error mean
Profit_Margin	Turkey	28	6.25	3.758	0.710
	Romania	28	3.61	4.289	0.811

Independent samples test

		Levene's test of equality for variances		t-test of equality for means	
		F	Sig.	t	df
Profit_Margin	Equal variances assumed	0.775	0.383	2.452	54
	Equal variances not assumed			2.452	53.082

Independent samples test

		t-test of equality for means		
		Sig. (2-tailed)	Mean difference	Std. error difference
Profit_Margin	Equal variances assumed	0.017	2.643	1.078
	Equal variances not assumed	0.018	2.643	1.078

Independent samples test

		t-test of equality for means	
		95% confidence interval of the difference	
		Lower	Upper
Profit_Margin	Equal variances assumed	0.482	4.803
	Equal variances not assumed	0.481	4.804

Table 5.30 Independent samples T-Test, month-over-month stock price growth, and country

Group statistics

	Country	N	Mean	Std. deviation	Std. error mean
Month-over-month stock price growth	Turkey	28	1.29	2.070	0.391
	Romania	28	−0.14	1.900	0.359

Independent samples test

		Levene's test of equality for variances	
		F	Sig.
Month-over-month stock price growth	Equal variances assumed	0.937	0.337
	Equal variances not assumed		

Independent samples test

		t-test of equality for means		
		t	df	Sig. (2-tailed)
Month-over-month stock price growth	Equal variances assumed	2.690	54	0.009
	Equal variances not assumed	2.690	53.605	0.009

Independent samples test

		t-test of equality for means	
		Mean difference	Std. error difference
Month-over-month stock price growth	Equal variances assumed	1.429	0.531
	Equal variances not assumed	1.429	0.531

Independent samples test

		t-test of equality for means	
		95% confidence interval of the difference	
		Lower	Upper
Month-over-month stock price growth	Equal variances assumed	0.364	2.493
	Equal variances not assumed	0.364	2.493

Table 5.31 Chi-Square analysis, country * month-to-month stock price growth

Count

		Country		
		Turkey	Romania	Total
Month-over-month stock price growth	−2	4	9	13
	−1	4	6	10
	0	2	4	6
	1	2	3	5
	2	5	3	8
	3	8	1	9
	4	3	2	5
Total		28	28	56

Chi-square tests

	Value	df	Asymp. Sig. (2-sided)
Pearson Chi-Square	9.334[a]	6	0.046
Likelihood ratio	10.162	6	0.118
Linear-by-linear association	6.501	1	0.011
N of valid cases	56		

[a] Ten cells (71.4%) have expected count less than 5. The minimum expected count is 2.50

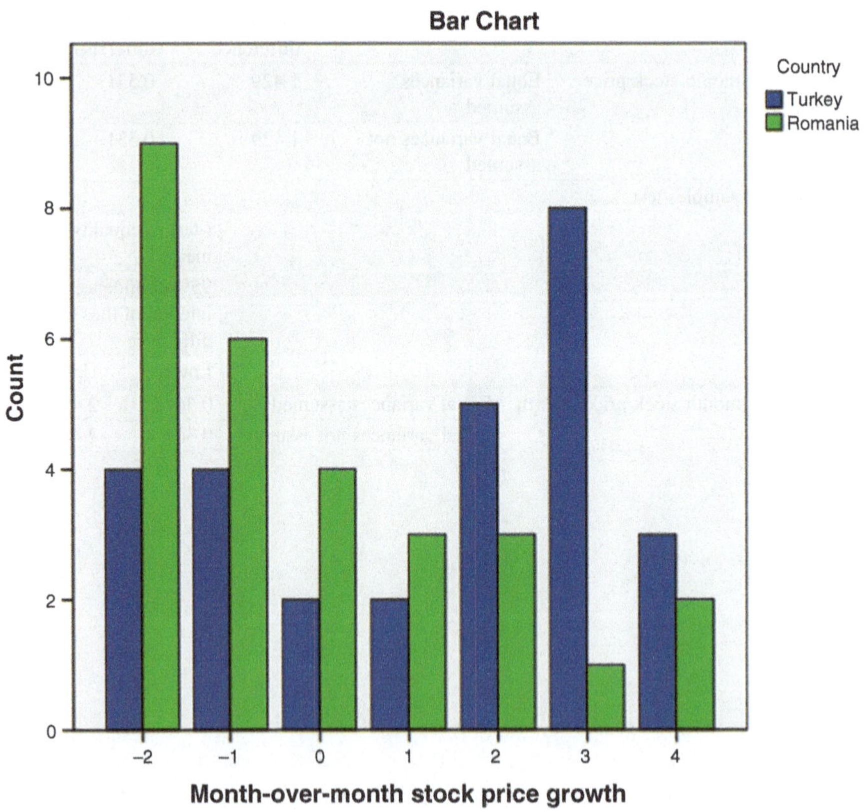

Fig. 5.16 Month-to-month stock price growth by country: Bar chart

Table 5.32 Independent samples T-Test, year-over-year stock price growth, and country

Group statistics

	Country	N	Mean	Std. deviation	Std. error mean
Year-over-year stock price growth	Turkey	28	5.21	6.045	1.142
	Romania	28	6.00	5.084	0.961

Independent samples test

		Levene's test of equality for variances	
		F	Sig.
Year-over-year stock price growth	Equal variances assumed	2.435	.124
	Equal variances not assumed		

Independent samples test

		t-test of equality for means		
		t	df	Sig. (2-tailed)
Year-over-year stock price growth	Equal variances assumed	−0.526	54	0.601
	Equal variances not assumed	−0.526	52.459	0.601

Independent samples test

		t-test of equality for means	
		Mean difference	Std. error difference
Year-over-year stock price growth	Equal variances assumed	−0.786	1.493
	Equal variances not assumed	−0.786	1.493

Independent samples test

		t-test of equality for means	
		95% confidence interval of the difference	
		Lower	Upper
Year-over-year stock price growth	Equal variances assumed	−3.779	2.207
	Equal variances not assumed	−3.781	2.209

Table 5.33 Independent samples T-Test, investor optimism, and country

Group statistics

	Country	N	Mean	Std. deviation	Std. error mean
Optimism	Turkey	28	4.54	1.710	0.323
	Romania	28	4.14	1.557	0.294

Independent samples test

		Levene's test of equality for variances		t-test of equality for means	
		F	Sig.	t	df
Optimism	Equal variances assumed	0.196	0.660	0.899	54
	Equal variances not assumed			0.899	53.530

Independent samples test

		t-test of equality for means		
		Sig. (2-tailed)	Mean difference	Std. error difference
Optimism	Equal variances assumed	0.373	0.393	0.437
	Equal variances not assumed	0.373	0.393	0.437

Independent samples test

		t-test of equality for means	
		95% confidence interval of the difference	
		Lower	Upper
Optimism	Equal variances assumed	−0.483	1.269
	Equal variances not assumed	−0.484	1.269

Table 5.34 Independent samples T-Test, investor likelihood to buy more stock and country

Group statistics

	Country	N	Mean	Std. deviation	Std. error mean
Likely to Buy	Turkey	28	4.18	1.701	0.321
	Romania	28	4.82	1.765	0.334

Independent samples test

		Levene's test of equality for variances		t-test of equality for means	
		F	Sig.	t	df
Likely to Buy	Equal variances assumed	0.040	0.842	−1.388	54
	Equal variances not assumed			−1.388	53.926

Independent samples test

		t-test of equality for means		
		Sig. (2-tailed)	Mean difference	Std. error difference
Likely to Buy	Equal variances assumed	0.171	−0.643	0.463
	Equal variances not assumed	0.171	−0.643	0.463

Independent samples test

		t-test of equality for means	
		95% confidence interval of the difference	
		Lower	Upper
Likely to Buy	Equal variances assumed	−1.572	0.286
	Equal variances not assumed	−1.572	0.286

Table 5.35 Independent samples T-Test, investor evaluation of company transparency and country

Group statistics

	Country	N	Mean	Std. deviation	Std. error mean
Company_Transparent	Turkey	28	4.39	1.571	0.297
	Romania	28	4.29	1.487	0.281

Independent samples test

		Levene's test of equality for variances	
		F	Sig.
Company_Transparent	Equal variances assumed	0.106	0.746
	Equal variances not assumed		

Independent samples test

		t-test of equality for means		
		t	df	Sig. (2-tailed)
Company_Transparent	Equal variances assumed	0.262	54	0.794
	Equal variances not assumed	0.262	53.837	0.794

Independent samples test

		t-test of equality for means	
		Mean difference	Std. error difference
Company transparent	Equal variances assumed	0.107	0.409
	Equal variances not assumed	0.107	0.409

Independent samples test

		t-test of equality for means	
		95% confidence interval of the difference	
		Lower	Upper
Company_Transparent	Equal variances assumed	−0.713	0.927
	Equal variances not assumed	−0.713	0.927

References

Creswell JW (2009) Research design: qualitative, quantitative, and mixed methods approaches, 3rd edn. Sage, Thousand Oaks, CA

Chapter 6
Results Interpretation and Concepts Development

Accounting is a framework that, despite its high level of standardization, can be used and defined in flexible ways by different stakeholders (Dick and Missionier-Piera 2010). Accounting is not immune from clashes of interest. In contemporary times one of the big questions pertaining to the measurement and evaluation of accounting systems is how to weight and recognize the interests of different stakeholders within the tripartite discretionary, national, and international practice of accounting (Cline 2010). Romania and Turkey are particularly fascinating countries to study in this regard. Both Romania and Turkey are expanding rapidly; for some years past, the Romanian economy has grown faster than that of any other country within the EU, while in recent years Turkey's economic growth rates have only been exceeded by those of China (World Bank 2012). Turkey and Romania thus face significant incentives to measure and evaluate accounting practices in line with the potential of such practices to keep facilitating economic growth. At the same time, if these countries adopt principles of measurement and evaluation that reward overly aggressive accounting practices, then there is the risk of market backlash (and, in Romania's case, various other EU-mandated penalties that would come from undermining IFRS).

Five years after the Great Recession, the world continues to face an uncertain economic future. Economic growth continues in many parts of the world, whereas the older economic power centers—for example, the United States, Great Britain, and Japan—continue to languish. It is not yet clear whether global economic growth will slump again. Whatever takes place, there is an important role to be played by scholars and policy-makers who examine the role of accounting measurement and evaluation. How measurement and evaluation are applied will help to determine the financial stability of the world economic system, and within specific countries (Cline 2010). As such, it is of the highest interest to learn more about how measurement and evaluation are applied, especially by rapidly-growing economies such as Romania and Turkey.

Prior arguments point out that, even though, there are considerable benefits of accounting measurement theory, there are also criticisms argued regarding

I. Mert, *Assessment of Accounting Evaluation Practices*, Contributions to Finance and Accounting, https://doi.org/10.1007/978-3-030-98486-1_6

representational or illustrative measurement perspective. One fundamental point is to eliminate the wrong definitions in measurement in accounting and applying monetary values to the items of the financial statement of the company. Besides, continuation of qualitative early applications of accounting measurement theory that the points of the field are shown by random numbers, not by fixed numbers.

The value can be recognized basically an asset in motion. For this reason, it needs to be evaluated by utilizing different approaches. On the other hand, the value is measured in accounting by the one-type valued approach. This means that the accounting theory of measurement does not cover the principles created in the conditions of multi-valued logics, and if it is convenient, changeability of the recognized values of the asset can be termed by the other assets that the accounting science has not considered when measuring it.

Nowadays, accounting measurement theory of meaningfulness does not match with the meaningfulness with empirical importance as is demanded by outlined measurement. It needs to act like that to be regular with outlined measurement, if not, it should underline the terms of meaningfulness for accounting information.

It was discussed that value is not a clear concept that can believe any value in the discipline of monetary elements. Nevertheless, even though there is no an accepted definition, the accounting utilizes fixed forms to symbolize the value of a commodity. Therefore, it is needed to be clarified the reason that why in accounting measurement theory it is scholarly beneficial to change the continuity forms with fixed forms. Additionally, the accounting thought accept the equalizing figures of the empirical forms of the value to the elements of the empirical form that an unclear thoughts something like value is managed by the laws of feelings must be agreeable to the automorphism forms of monetary elements. For this reason, to imagine the agreeability, providing samples is needed.

Overall, the IFRS presentation offers a broad, but necessarily shallow, introduction to some of the issues inherent in the use of fair value accounting. The general impression to emerge from the presentation is that IFRS contains numerous processes, precedents, and forms of diligence that give companies guidance in terms of obtaining and recording accurate valuation for different kinds of assets. While there can be numerous complexities involved in the use of fair value, IFRS guidance combined with the experience of global accounting firms, past company practice, and the utilization of accurate valuation models can all help to ensure that fair value works as intended. Of course, if this point is granted, then the emphasis of fair value accounting lies in discovering best practices for valuation.

One of the purposes of this literature review was threefold: (a) To place the history of Turkey and Romania in context in a manner that would cast light on the evolution of the two countries' accounting systems, and on the larger historical and social forces that have influenced this evolution; (b) to offer an overview of U.S. and international financial standards and (c) to discuss how accounting practices can be assessed in each of the European Central Bank's (2006) ten criteria, namely (1) reliance on principles-based standards, (2) use of reliable and relevant values, (3) recognition of the allocation and magnitude of risks, (4) provision of comparable financial statements, (5) provision of clear and understandable financial statements,

(6) portrayal of the financial situation, (7) alignment of accounting rules and sound risk management practices, (8) promotion of a forward-looking recognition of risks, (9) avoidance of negative externalities and promotion of positive externalities, and (10) enhancement of market confidence and corporate governance. The overall conclusion of the chapter was that, according to the literature, there are numerous ways in which accounting practices and standards can be assessed, and that a holistic approach is the best way of assessment. In particular, the evaluation of an accounting system must be performed by examining the roles of government, law, business, IT, corporate governance, and other areas in determining the context of a given accounting system's adoption.

In performing any accounting evaluation of a standard, there are two layers of analysis. The first level of analysis is driven by the following question: (1) In what manner does a specific accounting standard (such as U.S. GAAP or IFRS) align with the generic requirements of accounting (for example, in the manner specified by the European Central Bank (2006) or another competent authority? The second level of analysis hinges on another question: (2) To what extent has a country adopted IFRS, or another accounting standard, taken steps—including legislative, legal, and private sector steps—to insure that the standard is not a dead letter, and that both its rules and principles are properly upheld? The literature review established a framework through which these questions could be asked. The purpose of the third chapter of the study is to present and defend a more specific methodology through which the second question can be asked. This methodology will prepare the way for the analysis of accounting evaluation in Turkey and Romania in chapter two.

The debate over the utilization of fair value and historic cost accounting is ongoing. Although fair value has been embedded into IFRS and on this basis is becoming an accepted global standard, there are many companies that continue to use historic cost accounting. It is also possible that, over time, there could be a backwards move towards the re-adoption of historic cost. The history of accounting standards does not necessarily exhibit linearity. However, even with this caveat, it appears to be the case that fair value accounting possesses a great deal of momentum. Since its appearance, fair value has continued to spread throughout the world, and the growing popularity of IFRS (which is mandated in many countries, and which can legitimately be acknowledged as the most important global accounting standard) means that fair value accounting will also continue to grow in usage and importance.

There are numerous ways in which to approach fair value accounting. To date, much of the literature has focused on fair value from theoretical points of view. To be sure, fair value has numerous theoretical advantages over historic cost, including the ability to capture value more accurately. However, the ultimate purpose of these theoretical advantages is to convey value to markets, and in particular to shareholders. The main importance of this study lay in its ability to identify the advantages of fair value accounting as reflected in various aspects of investor sentiment, particularly the following:

- Mean investor optimism was much higher for companies that used fair value ($M = 5.04$, $s = 1.503$) than for companies that did not use fair value ($M = 3.64$,

s = 1.471). This difference was statistically significant (p = 0.001). Chi-square analysis confirmed that investor optimism was unevenly distributed across companies that used fair value versus companies that did not use fair value (p = 0.006).
- Mean investor likelihood to buy more stock was higher for companies that used fair value (M = 5.25, s = 1.624) than for companies that did not use fair value (M = 3.75, s = 1.555). This difference was statistically significant (p = 0.001).
- Chi-square analysis confirmed that investor likelihood to buy more stock was unevenly distributed across companies that used fair value versus companies that did not use fair value (p = 0.002).

Although a company's location was not associated with any statistically significant differences in investor sentiment, the empirical study found that company locations were associated with some other important differences. In particular, it was found that:

- Mean revenue was higher for Turkish companies (M = $666.75 million, s = 1028.153) than for Romanian companies (M = $262.54 million, s = 121.191). This difference was statistically significant (p = 0.048). Turkish companies thus appear to generate more revenue than Romanian companies.
- Mean profit margin was higher for Turkish companies (M = 6.25, s = 3.758) than for Romanian companies (M = 3.61, s = 4.289). This difference was statistically significant (p = 0.017). Turkish companies thus appear to generate more profit margin than Romanian companies.
- Month-over-month stock price growth was higher for Turkish companies (M = 1.29, s = 2.070) than for Romanian companies (M = −0.14, s = 1.900). This difference was statistically significant (p = 0.009).

Thus, the main finding of the empirical study is that the use of fair value accounting is both recognized and rewarded by investors in the form of higher levels of optimism, higher likelihood of buying more stock, and better evaluations of company transparency.

The empirical literature on the advantages of fair value accounting remains in its infancy. Very little empirical work on this topic has been conducted, and the present study had a number of limitations that should be addressed by future scholars. In particular, future scholars should attempt to draw a larger and more diverse sample of investors, and utilize more control variables, in order to more accurately measure the relationship between the use of fair value accounting and investor sentiment.

This study contributed to an understanding of fair value in both Turkey and Romania, calling attention to some aspects of accounting in both countries that deserve further attention from scholars. It was found that IFRS adoption in Turkey has, in the technical sense, been relatively easy, since IFRS adoption coincides with the interests of large segments of the Turkish population and the stated policies of the Turkish government (Pope and Pope 2011). IFRS defines fair value as "*the amount for which an asset could be exchanged, a liability settled, or an equity instrument granted could be exchanged between knowledgeable, willing parties in an arm's length transaction*" (IFRS 2, Appendix A). As a nominal adherent of IFRS, Turkey employs this definition. The filings of Turkish companies tend to make extensive use of the fair value concept. For example, the Turkish Agricultural Bank (Ziraat Bankasi 2007) has an accounting policy in which fair value is used for all derivative transactions.

The main problems associated with IFRS adoption in Turkey have been related to corruption (Gregoriou 2009). Turkey has its own accounting standards board, which is actually part of a larger organization: The Market Oversight, Accounting, and Standards Compliance Division (Kamu Gozetimi, Muhasebe, ve Denetim Standartlari Kurumu, or KGK for short). Today, the KGK supports IFRS adoption in Turkey and publishes various documentation to assist Turkish companies to make the transition. However, KGK is a new organization, and it is not yet clear whether it can perpetuate a culture respect of IFRSs 8, 10, 11, and 12 in Turkey. KGK ought to be strengthened so that it can help to bring about the necessary changes in Turkish culture to generate organic support for these four IFRSs in particular.

The Romanian economy has undergone inflation and other economic problems in the years since 1989 (Hentea 2007). In Turkey, there arose a positive feedback loop in which the country's liberalization efforts (including the adoption of IFRS) helped lead to economic growth, which in turn solidified the country's commitment to liberalization. In Romania, no such virtuous circle has yet been established. The Romanian economy has improved in fits and starts, the project of full integration with Europe has been put off (as exemplified by the country's reluctance to adopt the Euro in 2007, and postponement of that decision until 2015 at the earliest), and Romania has also suffered because of the slow emergence of business interests and a civil society capable of counteracting the influence of decades of Communist role. All of these factors play a role in the evaluation of Romania's accounting system and the slow adoption of IFRS, which is handicapped not so much by an absence of will as by an absence of practical knowledge and experience. What Romanian accounting needs, therefore, is better education, training, and time.

Manea (2011) argued that, in contrast to Turkey, Romanian accounting has only recently become acquainted with the concept of fair value, largely after the country's accession to the EU. One of the problems faced by Romania in this regard is that the IFRS's lack of extensive guidance has made it difficult for Romanian accountants, who come from an accounting tradition in which the concept of fair value is absent, to quantify fair value (Manea). Irina and Sabina's (2010) meta-analysis of the Romanian accounting literature discovered that Romanian accounting scholars had not even reached a consensus on the definition of fair value.

In Romania, then, the problem is that scholars are still trying to conceptualize and quantify fair value, which indicates that there is not yet a national consensus on where to set the balance between reliability and relevance. In Turkey, on the other hand, there is a firmer tradition of using relevant as well as reliable numbers in the national accounting system, which in turn has facilitated the adoption of IFRS principles of relevance.

One of the problems with the Turkish accounting system in this regard is that it only recently began to abandon a rules-based accounting approach for the principle-based IFRS approach, and this transition has imposed a heavy burden on auditors, students, and businesses (OECD 2006). According to the OECD, Turkey's accounting system was adopted from older European models and was reliant on rules; however, during the process of Turkish candidacy to the European Union, the country adopted IFRS. Turkey's recent adoption of IFRS has resulted in a number of problems, including the failure of universities to graduate sufficient numbers of accounting trained in the new system and an over-reliance on foreign auditors (OECD). At the same time, Turkey's reliance on IFRS has been undermined by the somewhat capricious exercise of power by the government, which has imposed both fines and audits on political enemies. Thus, the best way to assess the Turkish accounting system vis-à-vis reliance on principles is as follows: The letter of the IFRS standard, as adopted in Turkey, is robust, but the environment in which auditing and enforcement take place is poor.

According to Vinals (2010), the Romanian accounting systems remains "heavily rules-based" (p. 21) despite the institutionalization of IFRS in the European Union, of which Romania is a member. Vinals pointed out that Romania has a dual accounting system, employing the principle-based IFRS in order to meet EU requirements (as in the case of public companies doing business in the EU) and retaining the rules-based Romanian system for domestic use. This dual system means that the Romanian accounting system should not be assessed as performing well on the European Central Bank (2006) criterion of reliance on performance-based standards.

According to the European Commission (2012, p. 5, 6), the general accounting principles followed in Romania are as follows:

- ***Going concern principle.*** *It is presumed that the entity is a going concern and will continue in operation without liquidating or curtailing materially the scale of its operations.*
- ***Consistency principle.*** *Measurement methods and accounting principles should be applied consistently from one accounting period to the next.*
- ***Prudence.*** *Assets and revenues should not be overstated, and liabilities and expenses should not be understated. However, the exercise of prudence does not allow, for example, the creation of excessive provisions, the deliberate understatement of assets or revenues, or the deliberate overstatement of liabilities or expenses.*
- ***Independence.*** *All revenues and expenses relating to the financial year should be taken into account, irrespective of the date of receipt or payment of such revenues or expenses.*
- ***Separation.*** *The components of asset and liability items should be measured separately.*
- ***Intangibility.*** *The opening balance sheet for each financial year should correspond to the closing balance sheet of the previous financial year.*
- ***Non-compensation of asset and liability items.*** *Asset and liability items or revenue and expense items should not be offset.*

- ***Substance over form.*** *Balance sheet and profit or loss items are presented taking into account the economic substance of the underlying transactions and not merely their legal form.*
- ***Materiality threshold.*** *Certain balance sheet and profit or loss items may be combined if: they are immaterial in amount; or such combination makes for greater clarity, provided that the items combined are presented separately in the notes to the financial statements.*

In terms of business and accounting, Turkey has taken a parallel path to many democratic European nations, and in this sense was a better candidate for IFRS adoption than the formerly-Communist nations of Eastern Europe. The end of the Ottoman Empire led to a period of state ownership of many important businesses. However, after 1950, the influence of private business interests in Turkey began to grow. By the 1980s, Turkish politicians were embracing many of the same policies of privatization and laissez-faire capitalism that were espoused by Ronald Reagan in the United States and Margaret Thatcher in the United Kingdom (Howard 2001). There has been an agreement between the most influential segments of the Turkish state (including supporters of Ataturk, the military, practicing Muslims, Kurds and ethnic minorities, and other) that business ought to have a more important role in Turkish life, and that the adoption of free and fair practices is an important step towards that goal (Pope and Pope 2011). While many other Muslim countries have seen the formation of businesses aligned closely with the interests of the state, and oftentimes in partnership with regime leaders, Turkey has long had a successful entrepreneurial class that has been able to thrive even without overt reliance on the country's political leaders (Pope and Pope).

For Turkey, the adoption of IFRS and fair value accounting has been driven by a number of interests. Initially, IFRS and fair value adoption were seen as a means of signaling that Turkey was ready to the join the European Union (EU), of which it has been a candidate member for several years. Lately, after many Turks began to despair of being admitted into the EU, IFRS adoption began to be seen as a boon to Turkish business interests in an era of globalization and liberalization. In recent years, Turkish economic growth has been extremely rapid, often second only to China (Pope and Pope 2011). In this environment, Turkish businesses have proven to be increasingly important investment opportunities for individuals and organizations from all over the world. Thus, the adoption of IFRS and fair value is a means of ensuring Turkish competitiveness in a global investment landscape, given that so many investors are already familiar with these approaches to accounting.

Investigation results have been the bases for this thesis together with the number of seven articles published in different journals, national and international.

As a conclusion, it is considered that this research has reached its target by providing some contributions for the utilization of appliers, experts, and theorizers. The discussions in this study between fair value and historical value can be utilized in applications of managerial accounting by the appliers for providing sensible, effective and improved information to the management as far as the company value is concerned.

References

Cline WR (2010) Financial globalization, economic growth, and the crisis of 2007–09. Peterson Institute, Washington, DC

Dick W, Missionier-Piera F (2010) Financial reporting under IFRS: A topic-based approach. Wiley, New York, NY

European Central Bank (2006) Assessment of accounting standards from a financial stability perspective. Retrieved from http://www.ecb.int/pub/pdf/other/assessmentaccountingstandards2006en.pdf

European Commission Retrieved from Romania (2012). http://ec.europa.eu/enterprise/policies/sme/business-environment/files/annexes_accounting_report_2011/romania_en.pdf

Gregoriou GN (2009) Emerging markets: performance, analysis, and innovation. CRC Press, Toronto

Hentea C (2007) Brief Romanian history. Scarecrow Press, New York, NY

Howard DA (2001) The history of Turkey. Greenwood Publishing History, Westport, CT

Irina AI, Sabina JA (2010) Does fair value represent a concern for Romanian researchers? Retrieved from http://anale.steconomiceuoradea.ro/volume/2010/n1/072.pdf

Manea M (2011) The fair value representation of the market value in accounting. CES Working Pap 3(2):277–292

Organization of Economic Cooperation Development (2006) Corporate governance in Turkey: a pilot study. OECD, London

Pope N, Pope H (2011) Turkey unveiled: a history of modern Turkey. Overlook Press, London

Vinals J (2010) Romania: financial sector stability assessment. International Monetary Fund, Washington, DC

World Bank (2012) Development indicators. Retrieved from http://data.worldbank.org

Ziraat Bankasi (2007) Unconsolidated financial statements together with review report. Retrieved from www.ziraat.com.tr/en/s/d/financials.doc

Chapter 7
Elements of Modern Accounting

Currently, the world is dominated by digital systems (Teru et al. 2019). E-accounting is a growing and developing concept in the discipline as well the research in accounting. There was a time when the companies got evaluated by the governmental accountability institutes, and the measures related to diminishing the account records, or the reports such as fire accidents burn the whole form was mentioned in the newspaper. The E-accounting practices encourage and emphasize digital and cloud-based record-keeping rather than recording details on paper. With the advancements in the digital world and information technology, many software has been developed to manage of accounting systems. Accounting is one of the most essential functions of an organization and is also called as 'mirror image of the company' (Teru et al. 2019). Traditional accounting practices are very conservative and time-consuming compared to modern accounting methods (Teru et al. 2019).

E-accounting involves using of various computer-based web tools, weblinks, cloud-based recording systems, data analysis tools, e-spread sheets, web-based databases of information and inventory, and other modern tools. Information technology has a significant impact on the ongoing businesses, the modern information technology tools have helped the growth of businesses by reducing the distance between the businesspersons and the consumer (Utami and Yulianto 2019). Information technology has also helped in cost reduction and adding flexibility to the business (Utami and Yulianto 2019). The online sales platform includes a menu for customer review and comments. The online customers give value to these comments and ratings about the product provided by previous users. This serves as an excellent tool for getting user's feedbacks. An online payment protocol has to be established for online sales, the convenience is offered to customers by allowing multiple payment sources such as direct bank transfer, payment using debit and credit card, Paypal, and other local money transfer methods. Online payments have initiated new ventures for accounting system management. There is a new growing field that includes the online database and inventory management. The training programs that online sales companies offer such as Amazon virtual assistant and other pieces of training have initiated pathways for online earning.

I. Mert, *Assessment of Accounting Evaluation Practices*, Contributions to Finance and Accounting, https://doi.org/10.1007/978-3-030-98486-1_7

Since today, many applications and advanced accounting software have been developed to provide the facility of the unified accounting system. With the development of E-accounting, recording and managing the details of the transaction has become easier. Accounting Softwares are also used for evaluating the financial conditions of the companies. The financial conditions refer to the estimation of viability, financial stability, and the revenue generation aspects of the company by calculating return on equity, return on assets, and parameters such as return on investment, the information for the previously mentioned parameters are taken from the accounting systems, and now software have been developed that automatically record and collect the financial information.

7.1 The Concept of Accounting Information System

An information system, in general, is the collection of computer-based tools that collect data, process it, transmit, store, convert, and prepared it by the usage of computer programs so that the process of decision-making can become easier (Jasim and Raewf 2020). The generalized accounting information system model has been presented below (Hall 2018) (Fig. 7.1).

The first phase or step in the Accounting Information system is the collection of the data. The system ensures the accurate and correct addition of the information in the software. The information is an asset as futuristic predictions depend on financial information. The process of data collection ensures efficiency and correctness. The software collects the data and stores it with proper nomenclature so that, the information can be accessed easily. The software can use multiple sources for the collection of data. When the collection is complete, the data is then stored in the

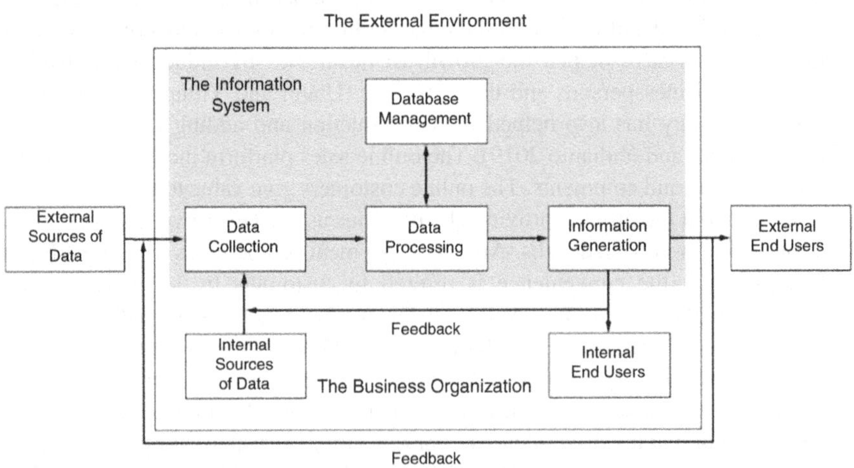

Fig. 7.1 Accounting Information System model steps (Image source: (Hall 2018))

relevant databases, some of the databases provide access to company employees only, while others are shared with the stakeholders and other institutes.

The next step is the analysis of the data. The analysis can be based on simple calculations but not confined to that, the analytical approach includes detailed statistical analysis, using custom-made algorithms, detailed accounting parameters evaluation, and the revenue allotment. The analysis further refines the already collected data into meaningful information that can be used directly for the decision-making process by the management. (Hall 2018).

The information then generated is transmitted, communicated, and shared with both internal and external users for different purposes. The outside sector users include the entities such as the beneficiaries, stakeholders, investment groups, suppliers, and local and international clients (Hall 2018). The internal users include all the administrative and managerial staff in the organization (Hall 2018). Feedback is then provided to the company for learning and implementation about the retention of information, resources, assets, and the other altering parameters.

The system is very smooth and automatic that increases efficiency. The tasks that required weeks are now finished in days. The approach is systematic, chances of error are minimal, and the information is not only secure but also accessible.

The data collection sources are critical elements of the information accounting system. The primary source of the data collection are the financial transactions that enter the accounting information system, these transactions can be done either from internal as well as the external sources. The main source of the data is external transactions. The data based on the transactions account for every financial activity irrespective of the magnitude. External financial transactions are the exchange of economic resources with other businesses and individuals from the outside. The primary examples are sales of products and services, inventory purchases, cash receipts, and disbursement (Jasim and Raewf 2020). Internal financial transactions involve the change or re-allocation of resources, budgets, and other resources (Jasim and Raewf 2020). Examples of internal financial transactions are the allocation of the raw material into the 'work in process '(WIP), the application of resources, labor transfer, up-gradation of WIP into inventory, and processing of purchase orders (Jasim and Raewf 2020). The internal bills, office consumption, and other internal costs required for running the company, and the purchase of equipment for the organization, hardware up-gradation, and purchase of software. It is necessary to maintain the details of all types of purchases, as the missing records create confusion and unaccounted resource allocation that can create problems in the financial reporting, errors in the estimation of the company's financial positions, and issues in the tax returns. The companies having detailed records of financial transactions either internal or external can very well assess their position and corrective measures can be taken. One of the main responsibilities of the accounting system is to report the financial situation of the company to the management in a presentable way such that management can decide on the measures that should be taken to either expand the business value or focus on the already existing projects.

There are different types of accounting information systems and the usage strongly depends on the nature of the company, size of the company, and the operational capacity. The types include un-automated systems that include traditional practices of recording the information using paper and pen. The traditional system of data recording and accounting practices requires manual data entry that is exhaustive and has great chances of human error. The growing businesses, infrastructure development, and other advances in the field of science and technology demand an advanced, fast, and efficient method of information recording and sharing. Therefore, a company relying on the older practices of information recording will have serious trouble with survival in the market.

In the Accounting information system framework, another method is the usage of a computer-based automatic transaction system. The fourth industrial revolution in which the advances in the field of the digital world, manufacturing, data analysis is so rapid, the resources and the transactions are required to occur at a faster pace and instantly. The advancements based on online transaction systems and banking have modified the banking sector as well. Any individual with a bank account and mobile-based application can transfer the money to any other person in few seconds. The bills can be paid online, the financial monthly statements can be generated using internet banking. E-commerce has resulted in the creation of online marketing and purchasing the domain. The success of Amazon and other online platforms has modified the business procedures. The evaluation and data recording procedures are also needed to be modified accordingly.

Another element of the information accounting system is the databases. The database systems have resulted in the removal of inefficiencies of the system and deal with the excess amount of the information, databases provide systematic storage of information, and availability is based on the relevancy. The accounting system is currently discarding the older methods of quantitative databases such as enterprise resource planning (ERP) (Jasim and Raewf 2020). The program interprets and processes the financial and non-financial information, and then finally stores it into databases (Jasim and Raewf 2020). The method involves the understanding of the marketing discipline other than accounting and develops the understanding of the user about the complete financial and economic situations (Jasim and Raewf 2020).

The system has also enabled the removal of the in-efficient practices related to the traditional accounting system, the procedures at the organizational level that result in loss of time and resources as well as the duplicate storage of information.

The average accounting speed and steps can be viewed in the figure presented below. The figure presents the four key stages of the account (Hall 2018) (Fig. 7.2).

As shown in the figure, the main accounting stages are the analysis of the financial transactions that are being carried out both internally and externally. The second step consists of analyzing the impact of transactions, either the transactions are contributing to the revenue and net capital is increased or the opposite is happening. The third step is to summarize the impact of the transactions in a presentable and precise form. The third step is further subdivided into two further steps. The last step is based on the preparation of the records, finalizing the entries, and closing the internal records. The steps should be considered as measures to be implemented in the software code.

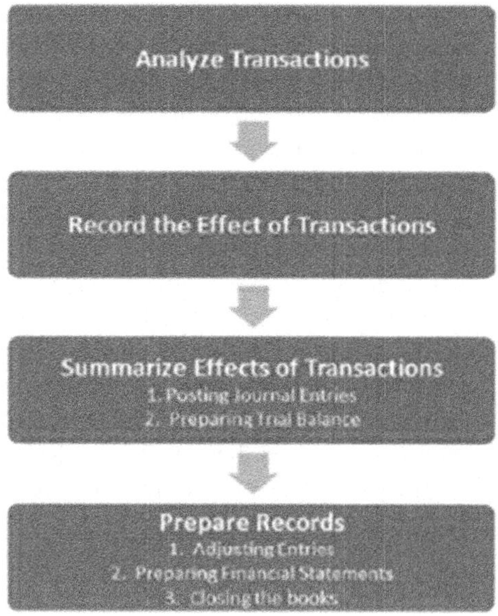

Fig. 7.2 Four key stages of the accounting are shown (Image Source: (Hall 2018))

7.2 Application of Artificial Intelligence in Accounting Practices

Artificial intelligence has modified the nature of decisions that are required. The application of artificial intelligence in accounting will be more intensive in upcoming years, and the incorporation of artificial intelligence approaches in the development of accounting will change the working frame drastically (Luo et al. 2018). Artificial intelligence can simply be defined as the technological development that allows the computer to have intelligence just like human beings to support intelligent working. Artificial intelligence is widely being used to develop intelligent devices, machines, programs, and robots to have better decision-making and thinking capability so that the true essence of automation can be developed. Artificial intelligent devices are designed by human beings, and special algorithms and methods are used for training the machine against specific information, popularly growing as machine learning.

In 2017 a Chinese government report included the term 'artificial intelligence, and then including the Ministry of Finance, 15 other departments collaborated and worked together to form one of the largest artificial intelligence centers (Luo et al. 2018). Deloitte Touche Tohmatsu that is one of the largest accounting firms in the world announced in 2016 the incorporation of artificial intelligence in the accounting, tax collection, and auditing sector (Luo et al. 2018). The incorporation of artificial intelligence in the field of accounting will significantly improve the working and operational efficiencies, and solve the problems of low value in the accounting disciplines (Luo et al. 2018).

- The methods, systems, framework, and algorithms through which accurate and reliable information and data is collected and converted into electronic data, it is self-controllable and adjustable as per the nature of the financial or organizational decision has to be made, and the decision is updated keeping in view the changing market trends, factors, and the variables. All the decisions and actions should be done by the software itself.
- The domain of the public is considered to be able to eliminate all the practices of conservative and conventional human behavior that is exhibited by taking the wrong decisions based on the limited understanding, exposure, and experience of the market trends, variables, and other associated processes. Artificial intelligence is based on providing all the content of human knowledge about the phenomena and events to the computer in such a way that the process is solely automated, Artificial Intelligence learns from the experiences already fed or collected by the program itself, and then predict the decisions, and the variable trends.
- It can gain and read information electronically in such a way that suits the protocols of information technology and the digital world, and the data and information are accessible, compared, editable, and transmissible to selected candidates.

  There have been many practical cases that demonstrated the success of artificial intelligence in making complex decisions in the most complicated scenarios.

7.3 E-Accounting Audit System

Accounting audit is the discipline of science-primarily dealing with the various variables and operational factors that the businesses and economic environment experience (Hamdan et al. 2021). There are many different applications of Artificial Intelligence, the artificial intelligence framework that can be used in the domain of accounting should comprise of the following points (Hamdan et al. 2021).

The E-accounting audit system is a structured and systematic approach that can provide sufficient evidence of traditional, electronic, and computer-based by using which the framework of an internal control system and financing is evaluated for the financial statement and the information and the estimation of achievement from its protection and truthfulness to full level confirmation to the data required by the users to ensure the authenticity and capability to be dependent upon the financial statement whether paper-based or digital (Hamdan et al. 2021).

There are two main objectives of the E-accounting audit system. The first objective is to review the computer-based work environment, evaluate the framework of the information systems, and identify its shortcomings (Hamdan et al. 2021).

Another goal of the E-accounting audit system is to analyze in detail the working of the company or business under evaluation, and compare the difference between the computer-based information and the traditional information and spot any differences between them, and to reach the point of agreeability to confirm the correctness and truth of the information using advanced artificial intelligence methods while performing intentional tasks (Hamdan et al. 2021).

The electronic auditing system is a complicated, continuous, modern, and updated approach used by modern companies in which the evaluator or auditor systematically provides evidence, proofs, means to respond and support the truthfulness of the information presented in the electronic financial report.

Electronic auditing is a complex task to evaluate the organizations' accounting credentials by using modern methods. The flow of information, the data storage, magnitude of the data, varying nature of the data, earning and revenues generated via online sales, and digital marketing are the aspects that make it impossible to conduct an audit of any company that utilizes modern business methods, using traditional accounting audit system. The traditional auditing system is slow and dependent upon the traditional evaluation methods. The modern valuation methods of evaluation of the true worth of the company are ignored by the traditional accounting systems.

There is a strong need for adopting modern systems and digital tools not only in management accounting but also in evaluation techniques as well. The most successful and innovative companies utilize the practices of the modern accounting system for recording the financial information and analysis of the financial position of the company.

Custom-made accounting software has been developed that collects the data from multiple sources and generates immediate reports about the outcomes of the transactions. The impacts of the transactions are mentioned by the computer program itself in terms of discrete mathematical values and calculations performed. The software also includes modern visualization tools, the graphs and charts are also displayed for the understanding of the trends, and also exhibit the stock exchange indexes, the rate of stock shares, and other relatable parameters. This software is also equipped with immediate reporting options in which the reports are automatically generated instantly, this feature enables the management to quickly attain the information required in the presentable form in critical situations. Modern tools and methods of accounting have resulted in the removal of challenges, delays, and other issues faced while using traditional accounting systems. Special training should be arranged for the staff and employees to equip them with the most relevant modern knowledge required to perform accounting operations in the modern world.

7.4 Modern Tools of Accounting

At the start of the nineteenth century, large firms started purchasing Enterprise Resource Planning System (ERP) software, and by the start of the twenty-first century, 90% of the large companies have already implemented the ERP system in their firms (Pervan and Dropulić 2019). Nowadays a large number of firms are using ERS systems, the highlighted software are SAP and ORACLE (Pervan and Dropulić 2019). However, a large number of firms also use global software programs that have a variety of new features and excellent integration approach such as Microsoft Dynamics (Pervan and Dropulić 2019). Microsoft reported in 2015 that there were more than 230,000 firms that were using Microsoft Dynamics. Four of the global leaders in the ER marketing domain as per the analysis are SAP, ORACLE, Microsoft Dynamics, and Infor. With the addition of advanced software features in ERP systems such as the inclusion of databases, connectivity with the customers, flexibility, real-time integration of information, field services, cloud-based services, and CRM based solutions, this will result in major changes in the working style and the framework of management accounting. One of the key benefits that ERP systems have offered is the integration of databases (Pervan and Dropulić 2019). The data collected from all the sources are stored in a central main repository (Pervan and Dropulić 2019). The creation of central databases allows the users to access any sort of information and data, and this access can only be limited if the user is not authorized to read and use such information. The permissive actions are added to encounter the challenges of cybersecurity and address the misuse, illegal and unauthorized use of information. With the usage of the ERP system, data is easily collected and analyzed, and this increases the efficiency of the accounting operations as well (Pervan and Dropulić 2019). The ERP system also reduces the time required for account closure and payroll processing (Pervan and Dropulić 2019). With the usage of modern tools, the reporting aspect of accounting is also modified, and it has changed the inter-organizational reporting methods (Pervan and Dropulić 2019). As the softwares have increased the magnitude of the data collection and reduced the time for working and analyzing the information, there now exists huge potentials for multivariate reporting and analysis.

The modern accounting system revolves around the concept of information gathering and approval of its authenticity. As the other aspects of accounting have been modified, further advancements include modern budgeting methods. Advance budgeting methods fuse the advantages of multiple budgeting concepts such as tolerance for the allowance of alterations and adjustments to budget format as the system of improvisation of budgeting to increase the ability to adapt to the changes in the external economic conditions and environment (Daryakin et al. 2019). The adaptability measures of the budget planning to the varying economic environment are normally achieved by shifting the attention and focus from the expenditure parameters of the budget towards the attainment of pre-planned indicator goals set and also consideration of the critical non-financial based indicators of the success in the adaptive budgeting system (Daryakin et al. 2019).

A critical advantage related to advanced budgeting methods is the chances of integration with the modern methods of cost accounting and analytical methods. It must be mentioned that the modern business and budgeting process should include tolerance for the variations and shifts in economic situations. The current era is an era where influencers, celebrities, and entrepreneur's comments on Twitter or media drastically increase the value of the stock share, their appreciation can increase and decrease the sales by a huge amount. It was recently observed that the value of Bitcoin crypto-currency has decreased by 12% after Elon Musk, the owner of Tesla and SpaceX Company said that Tesla will not accept Bitcoin as payment (Iyengar 2021).

Businesses and the industry overall have witnessed major changes since the advent of the fourth industrial revolution. Financial transactions, banking, modes of payments, and other aspects have also witnessed major changes. The accounting practices in the modern industrial age should also change to keep pace with the modern economics paradigm. The accounting departments of the companies that kept on relying on older methods of bookkeeping and assessing the financial information have suffered a lot. Modern accounting software should be used for the prediction of futuristic trends and the financial position of any firm. Moreover, the tools like artificial intelligence, text analytics, and machine learning should be used in auditing, budgeting, and taxation sectors to get to one of the best possible financial decisions independent of personal judgments, understanding, and experience. The staff of the institutes should be trained about the modern accounting system usage and the growing trends in the accounting sector. The challenges faced by the construction accounting industry can also be resolved easily by using modern accounting practices and methods. As the construction industry faces unique operational challenges that make it very difficult to increase revenues and net capital income. Similarly, construction accounting is also different from financial accounting.

The authors and the researchers have emphasized the use of proper accounting practices for the accurate, valid and update record keeping. The appropriate accounting practices enable the accountants and chartered accountants to accurately predict the reasons for low financial activities of the company. The trends of the businesses and marketing practices have been changed. The digital marketing approach has changed the methods of advertisements, and developed new methods for reaching a broad range of customers. The digital marketing tools have helped the businesses to grow and evolve in the modern world. The social media accounts of the companies are one of the key reflections of the company's products, schemes, discounts, and future planning. Nike and General Electric have used the techniques of digital marketing, unique user interaction approach and tried to tell stories associated with their products, and resulted in increased fan following on Instagram. Nike Instagram images inspire people to involve in healthy physical activities such as running, going to the gym, and beaches. Nike had 31.6 million followers on Instagram in 2015 (Baer 2015).

The banking sector has also seen massive changes. The banking activities are mostly performed by the account holders using the mobile application. The users can easily transfer funds at any time, and any day. Even in case of loss of credit cards or theft, the cards can be blocked instantly using the mobile application. The companies are given special incentives by the banks to open an account, and the lending operations are performed on soft terms. A prevailing trend in the banking system is the usage of Application Programming Interface (API) for making the propriety data accessible to anybody who has got access to it (Phaneuf 2021).

The modern economic challenges demand the modern approach for accounting to analyze the ongoing wealth transfer process and the management of accounts.

Modern accounting practices and the tools are required to record and analyze the ongoing transfer of wealth, constantly changing scenarios of global industries, valuation of companies, stock exchange trends, and the constantly changing trends. The budgeting and taxation reports should consider the modern methods and parameters that are more relevant to the variables used in modern accounting operations. The ERP systems have also been upgraded to provide multiple business evaluation and reporting options to business owners and users. The companies like Microsoft and Google are offering various workplace applications, add-ins, and the tools like machine learning for the analysis and reporting of the current economic trends of the market.

Reference

Baer J (2015) The importance of domain-specific expertise in creativity. Roeper Rev 37(3):165–178. https://doi.org/10.1080/02783193.2015.1047480, ISSN: 0278-3193 (Print) 1940-865X (Online). https://www.tandfonline.com/doi/pdf/10.1080/02783193.2015.1047480?needAccess=true

Daryakin A, Murtazin A, Valeev Y, Abdullaeva A, Dudochnikov A (2019) An integration of advanced budgeting, modern accounting methods and cost analysis. Int Trans J Eng Manage Appl Sci Technol 10(18). https://doi.org/10.14456/ITJEMAST.2019.257

Hall JA (2018) Accounting information systems, Peter E. Bennett Chair in Business and Economics Lehigh University, 7th ed., ISBN-13: 978-1-4390-7857-0, ISBN-10: 1-4390-7857-2. http://site.iugaza.edu.ps/hmadi/files/2014/11/JAMES-AIS_unprotected.pdf

Hamdan A, Hassanien A, Razzaque A, Alareeni B, Hamdan A, Hassanien A, Razzaque A, Alareeni B (2021) The fourth industrial revolution: implementation of artificial intelligence for growing business success. Springer, Cham

Iyengar R (2021) Bitcoin plunges 12% after Elon Musk tweets that Tesla will not accept it as payment. CNN. https://edition.cnn.com/2021/05/12/tech/elon-musk-tesla-bitcoin/index.html

Jasim Y, Raewf M (2020) Information technology's impact on the accounting system. Cihan Univ-Erbil J Human Soc Sci 4(1):50–57

Luo J, Meng Q, Cai Y (2018) Analysis of the impact of artificial intelligence application on the development of accounting industry. Open J Bus Manage 06(04):850–856

Pervan I, Dropulić I (2019) The impact of integrated information systems on management accounting. Management 24(1):21–38

Phaneuf A (2021) The future of retail, mobile, online & digital-only banking technology. Bus Insid. https://www.businessinsider.in/finance/news/the-future-of-retail-mobile-online-digital-only-banking-technology/articleshow/71945008.cms

Teru S, Idoko I, Bello L (2019) The impact of E-accounting in modern businesses. Int J Account Finance Rev 4(2):1–4

Utami N, Yulianto H (2019) Significant influence of information technology on the use of modern accounting software. IOP Conf Ser: Mater Sci Eng 662:022003

Legislations

*** Ordinul Ministrului Finanţelor Publice nr. 403 al din 22 aprilie 1999, pentru aprobarea Reglementărilor contabile armonizate cu Directiva a IV-a a Comunităţii Economice Europene şi cu Standardele de Contabilitate Internaţionale, publicat în Monitorul Oficial al României nr. 480 din 4 Octombrie 1999 (1999)
*** Ordinul Ministrului Finanţelor Publice nr. 1850 din 14.12.2004 privind registrele şi formularele financiar-contabile, publicat în Monitorul Oficial nr. 23 din 7.01.2005 (2005)
*** Ordinul Ministrului Finanţelor Publice nr. 1752 din 17/11/2005 pentru aprobarea reglementărilor contabile conforme cu directivele europene, publicat în Monitorul Oficial, Partea I, nr. 1080 din 30/11/2005 (2005)
*** Ordinul Ministrului Economiei şi Finanţelor nr. 2374/2007 publicat în Monitorul Oficial nr. 25/14.01.2008 privind modificarea şi completarea OMFP nr. 1752/2005 (2007)
*** Ordinul Ministrului Finanţelor Publice nr. 3055/2009 din 29 Octombrie 2009, pentru aprobarea Reglementărilor contabile conforme cu directivele europene, publicat în Monitorul Oficial al României nr. 766 din 10 Noiembrie 2009 (2009)

Scientific Studies Published in Journals or Volumes National and International (Studies, Articles, Thesis, Reports)

Aaharony J, Barniv R, Falk H (2010) The impact of mandatory IFRS adoption on equity valuation of accounting numbers for security investors in the EU. Eur Account Rev. `http://papers.ssrn.com/sol3/papers.cfm?abstract_id=1675485`
Abdel-khalik R (2008) The case fair value accounting. University of Illinois, CGA accounting conference, University of Ottawa, Canada on October 31, 2008 and at the Chinese accounting forum held at Nanjing University on December 6, 2008. `https://www.sec.gov/comments/4-573/4573-229.pdf`
Akgun M, Pehlivanli D, Gurunlu M (2011) A process design for auditing fair value. Maltepe University, Turkey. Int J Econ Finance 3(3). `http://www.ccsenet.org/journal/index.php/ijef/article/viewFile/11664/8299`
Al-Htaybat K, Hutaibat K, von Alberti-Alhtaybat L Global brain-reflective accounting practices. J Intell Capital 20(6):733–762

I. Mert, *Assessment of Accounting Evaluation Practices*, Contributions to Finance and Accounting, https://doi.org/10.1007/978-3-030-98486-1

Al-Khadash HA, Abdullatif M (2009) Consequences of fair value accounting for financial instruments in the developing countries: the case of the banking sector in Jordan. Jordan J Bus Admin 5(4). http://journals.ju.edu.jo/JJBA/article/viewFile/253/251

Antonescu M, Antonescu L (2009) The competences and the impact of evaluation categories on the fidelity of accounting information. Revista Tinerilor Economisti (The Young Economists Journal). Facultatea de Economie şi Administrarea Afacerilor 1(12):7–13. http://feaa.ucv.ro/RTE/012-01.pdf

Aslanertik BE (2009) Fair value considerations during the current financial crisis. Dokuz Eylul University, Turkey, paper presented at Econ Anadolu 2009: Anadolu international conference in economics, June 17–19, 2009, Eskisehir, Turkey. http://econ.anadolu.edu.tr/fullpapers/Aslanertik_econanadolu2009.pdf

Barth ME, Landsman WR (2010) How did financial reporting contribute to the financial crisis? Eur Account Rev 19(3):399–423. https://doi.org/10.1080/09638180.2010.498619. http://papers.ssrn.com/sol3/papers.cfm?abstract_id=1601519

Barth ME, Taylor DJ (2009) In defense of fair value: weighing the evidence on earnings management and asset securitizations. J Account Econ. http://papers.ssrn.com/sol3/papers.cfm?abstract_id=1478670

Barth, M.E., Landsman WR, Lang MH (1976) International accounting standards and accounting quality. Stanford University Graduate School of Business Research Paper No. 1976. http://papers.ssrn.com/sol3/papers.cfm?abstract_id=688041

Barth ME, Biscarri, J.G., Espinoza GL. Fair value accounting and firm valuation. http://pendientedemigracion.ucm.es/centros/cont/descargas/documento18505.pdf

Casta JF, Ramon O, Husson B, Philippe H (2009) Financial valuation and accounting are they finally reconciled? Round table conference, Conducted by Accuracy and Paris Dauphine University, 03 Dec 2009. http://www.accuracy.com/ideas/events/financial-valuation-and-accounting-are-they-finally-reconciled_40_event182.html

Cenar I (2011) Accounting policies and treatments of contingent assets and liabilities in public institutions. Annal Univ Apulensis Ser Oeconom 13(2). http://www.oeconomica.uab.ro/upload/lucrari/1320112/05.pdf

Christian L, Christian L (2009) The crisis of fair value accounting: making sense of the recent debate. Chicago Booth Research Paper No.33, Accounting, Organizations and Society 34. http://papers.ssrn.com/sol3/papers.cfm?abstract_id=1392645

Christian L, Christian L (2010) Did fair-value accounting contribute to the financial crisis? J Econ Perspect. http://fic.wharton.upenn.edu/fic/papers/09/0940.pdf

Cioara NM, Tudor AT (2010) The model of historical cost and fair value in the context of national and international regulations. EuroEconomica 24(1). http://journals.univ-danubius.ro/index.php/euroeconomica/article/view/270/253

Damian S (2011) Evolutia contabilitatii in perioada de tranzitie a economiei Romanesti, Teza de doctorat, Universitatea "Babes-Bolyai" Cluj-Napoca. http://doctorat.ubbcluj.ro/sustinerea_publica/rezumate/2011/contabilitate/Damian%20Sorin_RO.pdf

Damodaran A Musing on valuation: fair value accounting. ERP and the dark side of valuation. http://people.stern.nyu.edu/adamodar/pdfiles/country/SFDayOne.pdf

Daryakin A, Murtazin A, Valeev Y, Abdullaeva A, Dudochnikov A (2019) An integration of advanced budgeting, modern accounting methods and cost analysis. Int Trans J Eng Manage Appl Sci Technol 10(18)

Deaconu A (2009) Solutions for measuring the fair value of the workforce. http://steconomice.uoradea.ro/anale/volume/2009/v3-finances-banks-and-accountancy/150.pdf

Deaconu A, Buiga A (2011a) Accounting and the environmental factors – an empirical investigation in post-Communist Romania. Account Manage Inf Syst 10(2):135–168. ftp://ftp.repec.org/opt/ReDIF/RePEc/ami/articles/10_2_3.pdf
Deaconu A, Buiga A (2011b) Accounting and the environmental factors - an empirical investigation in post-communist Romania. J Account Manage Inf Syst 10(2):135–168. http://econpapers.repec.org/article/amijournl/v_3a10_3ay_3a2011_3ai_3a2_3ap_3a135-168.htm
Deaconu A, Bonaci C, Popa I (2008) Valuation of inventories considering the fair value options. Babes-Bolyai University, Faculty of Economics and Business Administration. http://steconomice.uoradea.ro/anale/volume/2008/v3-finances-banks-accountancy/1003.pdf
Deaconu A, Silvia C, Filip C (2009a) Legitimacy to develop fair value measurement standards: the case of the IVSC Discussion Paper-Determination of fair value of intangible assets for IFRS reporting purposes. MPRA Paper No. 16850, posted on 18 August 2009. http://mpra.ub.uni-muenchen.de/16850/1/MPRA_paper_16850.pdf
Deaconu A, Popa I, Fulop M (2009b) Aspecte conceptuale si tehnice privind viitoare reglementari contabile pentru IMM-uri in Europa. MPRA Paper No. 14778. Posted at 23 April 2009. http://mpra.ub.uni-muenchen.de/14778/1/IMM2009TAE.pdf
Deaconu A, Buiga A, Nistor CS (2010) The value relevance of fair value, evidence for tangible assets on the Romanian market. Transit Stud Rev. 10.1007/S11300-010-0131-9, South Eastern European studies, published online by Springer Verlag at 9 April 2010. http://link.springer.com/article/10.1007%2Fs11300-010-0131-9#
Deaconu A, Cristina N, Dan C (n.d.) Considerations on the fair value of revenues recognized in financial statements. http://steconomice.uoradea.ro/anale/volume/2009/v3-finances-banks-and-accountancy/149.pdf
Demski JS (2005) Accounting and economics. University of Florida, Aug 2005. http://fisher.osu.edu/~young.53/Demski_Accounting_and_Economics.pdf
Dumay J (2016) A critical reflection on the future of intellectual capital: from reporting to disclosure. J Intellect Cap 17(1):168–184
Dumay J, Guthrie J, Rooney J (2020) Being critical about intellectual capital accounting in 2020: an overview. Crit Perspect Account 70:102185
Eastman H (2010) International financial reporting standards. Mensuracao de Valor Justo, November 2010. www.cpc.org.br/pdf/HilaryEastman.ppt
Gaffikin M (2005) Creating a science of accounting: accounting theory to 1970. University of Wollongong. http://ro.uow.edu.au/cgi/viewcontent.cgi?article=1048&context=accfinwp
Gao P (2012) A two-step representation of accounting measurement. The University of Chicago Booth School of Business. http://faculty.chicagobooth.edu/pingyang.gao/research/papers/AH2012.pdf
Georgescu I, Budugan D (2008) Use of the cost/volume/profit analysis to estimate earnings. Anelele Stiintifice Ale Universitatii “Alexandru Ioan Cuza” din Iasi, Tomul LV. http://anale.feaa.uaic.ro/anale/resurse/01_C01_Budugan_IGeogescu.pdf
Georgescu I, Budugan D (2010) The role of internal assignment prices in the evaluation of the transactions between profit centers. Anelele Stiintifice ale Universitatii “Alexandru Ioan Cuza” din Iasi, Numar special. http://anale.feaa.uaic.ro/anale/resurse/ctb2budugan.pdf
Georgescu I, Budugan D, Cretu L (2010) Estimating the cost-value relationship using instruments of managements of accountancy. Ann "Stefan cel Mare" University of Suceava. Fascicle of The Faculty of Economics and Public Administration 10(2, 12), 242–247. http://www.seap.usv.ro/annals/ojs/index.php/annals/article/viewFile/305/312
Georgescu I, Betianu L, Macovei C. The role of the management accounting in financial auditing quality enhancement. http://www.researchgate.net/publication/228229468_The_Role_of_the_Management_Accounting_in_Financial_Auditing_Quality_Enhancement

Georgescu I, Cretu L, Georgescu M. Management accounting between monist and dualist accounting systems. http://www.conferencedevelopments.com/files/Georgescu-Cretu-Georgescux.pdf

Gogan L, Artene A, Sarca I, Draghici A (2016) The impact of intellectual capital on organizational performance. Procedia Soc Behav Sci 221:194–202

Goncharoc I, Triest SV (2011) Do fair value adjustments influence dividend policy? Account Bus Res 42(1). http://papers.ssrn.com/sol3/papers.cfm?abstract_id=1348264

Guse GR, Dascalu C, Caraiani C, Lungu CI. New approaches to costing models in Romania: the recognition of externalities. http://www.fse.tibiscus.ro/anale/Lucrari2011/147.pdf

Hassan MS, Percy M, Stewart J (2006) The value relevance of fair value disclosures in Australia firms in the extractive industries. Asian Acad Manage J Account Finance 2(1):4–61. http://web.usm.my/journal/aamjaf/vol%202-1/2-1-3.pdf

Hellstrom K (2005) The value relevance of financial accounting information in a transitional economy: the case of the Czech Republic. Centre for Financial Analyses in Accounting Stockholm School of Economics, SSE/EFI Working Paper Series in Business Administration, 10. http://swoba.hhs.se/hastba/papers/hastba2005_010.pdf

IFRS (2012) Fair value measurement for assets. Joint World Bank and IFRS foundation "train the trainers" workshop hosted by the ECCB, 30 April to 4 May 2012

Jasim Y, Raewf M (2020) Information Technology's impact on the accounting system. Cihan Univ-Erbil J Human Soc Sci 4(1):50–57

Kothari SP, Ramanna K, Skinner DJ (2010) Implications for GAAP from an analysis of positive research in accounting. J Account Econ (JAE), Harvard Business School, Accounting and Management Unit Working Paper, No. 09-137, University of Chicago – Booth School of Business Working Paper No. 09-22, September 2010. http://papers.ssrn.com/sol3/papers.cfm?abstract_id=1413775

Loyarte E, Garcia-Olaizola I, Marcos G, Moral M, Gurrutxaga N, Florez-Esnal J, Azua I (2018) Model for calculating the intellectual capital of research centres. J Intellect Cap 19(4):787–813

Luo J, Meng Q, Cai Y (2018) Analysis of the impact of artificial intelligence application on the development of accounting industry. Open J Bus Manage 06(04):850–856

Man M, Rvas B, Gadau L (2011) Historic cost versus fair value, Polish J Manage Stud 4. http://www.pjms.zim.pcz.pl/PDF/PJMS4/HISTORIC%20COST%20VERSUS%20FAIR%20VALUE.pdf

Martin B (2009) Accounting for goodwill. J Account Finance Bus Stud 45(3):379–389. https://doi.org/10.1111/j.1467-6281.2009.00295.x/abstract

Matis D, Bonaci C. Raportarea Financiara si Invataminte in Vremuri de Criza. Universitatea Babes-Bolyai, PPT presentation

Michailesco C, Karine F (2010) From learning to rationalization: the roles of accounting in the management of Parisian great exhibitions from 1853 to 1902. Account Bus Financ Hist 20(1): 67–90 http://basepub.dauphine.fr/bitstream/handle/123456789/2427/fabre.pdf?sequence=2

Mihcailesco C (1999) Une étude empirique des déterminants de la qualité de l'information diffusée par les entreprises françaises au cours de la période 1991-1995. CNRS: UMR7088 – Université Paris IX - Paris Dauphine, Comptabilité Contrôle Audit 5(1):83–108. http://halshs.archives-ouvertes.fr/halshs-00540576

Mihcailesco C (2000) Perspectives pour la recherché sur les déterminants de l'offre d'information des enterprises. CNRS: UMR7088 – Université Paris IX - Paris Dauphine, Comptabilité Contrôle Audit numéro spécial, pp 83–94, décembre. http://halshs.archives-ouvertes.fr/halshs-00540575

Mihcailesco C (2007) *Contrôle de gestion de projet au 19ème siècle,* CNRS: UMR7088 – Université Paris IX - Paris Dauphine, Comptabilité, Contrôle, Audit 13(2):31–52. http://halshs.archives-ouvertes.fr/halshs-00338976

Muller KA III, Riedl EJ, Sellhorn T (2008) Consequences of voluntary and mandatory fair value accounting: evidence surrounding IFRS adoption in the EU real estate industry. Harvard Business School, 09-033. http://www.stieykpn.ac.id/images/artikel/Consequences%20of%20Voluntary%20and%20Mandatory%20Fair%20Value%20Accounting-Evidence%20Surrounding%20IFRS%20Adoption.pdf
Mustata RV, Matis D (2004) From historical cost to fair value. Volumul, Audit si convergenta contabila, Editura: Sincorn / Cluj Napoca, ISBN: 973–9234-53-4
Mustata RV, Bonaci CG, Matis D (2010) Strategies in optimizing the output of financial reporting: project for a national perspective. Ann Univ Apulensis Ser Oeconom 12(1). http://oeconomica.uab.ro/upload/lucrari/1220101/14.pdf
Mustata RV, Bonaci CG, Strouhal J (2013) Fair value developments and professionals' perceptions. Wseas Trans Bus Econ 10(3). E-ISSN: 2224-2899, July 2013. http://www.wseas.org/multimedia/journals/economics/2013/085707-104.pdf
Musyoto SW (2011) Implications of the homomorphism definition of measurement on accounting measurement theory. The 2011 Maui international academic conference, Maui, Hawai. http://conferences.cluteonline.com/index.php/IAC/2011HI/paper/viewFile/77/75
Nita MM (2009) Aspecte Nationala si Internationale Privind Utilizarea Tehniilor de Evaluare in Contabilitate,RFPC nr.1/. http://discutii.mfinante.ro/static/10/Mfp/revista_nou/2009/200901_art.pdf
Orten R (2006) Development of accounting and accounting profession in Turkey in the second half of 20th century. Gazi University, Turkey, 11th world congress of accounting historians, Nantes, July 19–22, 2006. http://journal.mufad.org.tr/attachments/article/206/a8-development_of_acoounting_in_the_first.pdf
Patricia A (2009) Global financial crisis: the challenge to accounting research. Account Org Soc 34(6). http://www.deepdyve.com/lp/elsevier/global-financial-crisis-the-challenge-to-accounting-research-ZACBerY1qg
PriceWaterhouseCoopers (2007) Guide to fair value measurement. www.nacubo.org/documents/.../PWC2007_FairValueGuide_Final07.pdf
Richardson AJ, Eberlein B (2011) Legitimating transnational standard-setting: the case of the international accounting standards board. J Bus Ethics 98(2):217–245 http://link.springer.com/article/10.1007%2Fs10551-010-0543-9#
Solas C, Ayhan S (2008) The historical evolution of accounting in China (Novissima Sinica): effects of Cultura (2nd part). Spanish J Account Hist 8. http://www.decomputis.org/dc/articulos_doctrinales/solas_ayhan8.pdf
Stephen C (2007) Discussion of 'standard-setting measurement issues and the relevance of research'. Account Bus Res 37(Suppl 1). http://www.tandfonline.com/doi/abs/10.1080/00014788.2007.9730080
Sumner DA (2009) Recent commodity price movements in historical perspective. Am J Agric Econ 91(5):1250–1256. http://www.aae.wisc.edu/events/papers/DeptSem/2009/sumner.10.09.pdf
Tabara N, Rusu A (2011) Considerations concerning the impact of creative accounting on the quality of the information presented in the annual financial statements. http://www.bursedoctorale.ro/public/documente/articole/1331713123_Articol_rev_Rusu_AF_FEAA_Octombrie2011.pdf
Teru S, Idoko I, Bello L (2019) The impact of E - accounting in modern businesses. Int J Account Finance Rev 4(2):1–4
Thibierge C (1997) Contribution A L'Etude Des Determinants De La Comptabilisation Des Investissements Immateriels, Thesis, Universite Paris IX-Dauphine, UFR Sciences Des Organisations. https://intranet.escpeurope.eu/~bmt/thib/publi/THESE_CT.pdf
Turel A (2009) The value relevance of IFRS: the case of Turkey, Istanbul University, Pressed by Acta Universitatis Danubius. Oeconomica 5(1). http://journals.univ-danubius.ro/index.php/oeconomica/article/view/81

Utami N, Yulianto H (2019) Significant influence of information technology on the use of modern accounting software. IOP Conference Series: Materials Science and Engineering 662:022003
Vyas D (2010) The timeliness of accounting write-downs by U.S. financial institutions during the financial crisis of 2007-2008. J Account Res December 6. http://papers.ssrn.com/sol3/papers.cfm?abstract_id=1491017
Wallison PJ (2009) Fixing fair value accounting. OECD J Gudgetting 2. ISSN: 1608-7143. http://www.oecd.org/gov/budgeting/45362933.pdf
Whittington G, Saporta V, Singh A (1997) The effects of hyper-inflation on accounting ratios: financing corporate growth in industrial economies, vol 23. The World Bank, Washington, DC. http://forecasturkey.com/Articles/Multilateral%20Agencies/international%20agencies/IFC/IFC%20inflation%20accounting.pdf

Other Sources (Internet Sites, Legislations)

ACM Digital Library, Failure of measurement system? Some lesson from fall of Enron Corp. http://dl.acm.org/citation.cfm?id=1865390
Baer D (2015) How Nike conquered Instagram. Bus Insid. https://www.businessinsider.com/how-nike-conquered-instagram-2015-12
Balanced Scorecard Institute. http://www.balancedscorecard.org/
Balanced Scorecard in Romania. http://www.balancedscorecardinromania.ro/
Bank of International Settlements, BIS Annual Reports 1931 to 1996 http://www.bis.org/publ/arpdf/archive/
Chartered Institute of Management Accountants (C1MA), Better Budgeting – A report on the Better Budgeting forum from CIMA and ICAEW, July 2004, http://www.cimaglobal.com/documents/importeddocuments/betterbudgeting_techrpt_2004.pdf
EconPapers, on-line Economics working papers, journal articles and software. http://econpapers.repec.org/
Econbiz, Virtual Library for Economics and Business Studies. http://www.econbiz.de
Eur-Lex, Access to European Union Law, Authentic electronic Official Journal. http://eur-lex.europa.eu/en/index.htm
http://en.wikipedia.org/wiki/International_Financial_Reporting_Standards
http://en.wikipedia.org/wiki/Inflation_accounting
http://en.wikipedia.org/wiki/Historical_cost
http://hbr.org/2013/03/why-fair-value-is-the-rule/ar/1
Iyengar R (2021) Bitcoin plunges 12% after Elon Musk tweets that Tesla will not accept it as payment. CNN. https://edition.cnn.com/2021/05/12/tech/elon-musk-tesla-bitcoin/index.html
Phaneuf A (2021) The future of retail, mobile, online & digital-only banking technology. Bus Insid. https://www.businessinsider.in/finance/news/the-future-of-retail-mobile-online-digital-only-banking-technology/articleshow/71945008.cms
Perseus Digital Library. http://www.perseus.tufts.edu/hopper/
Pervan I, Dropulić I (2019) The impact of integrated information systems on management accounting. Management 24(1):21–38
Raportul studiului Balanced Scorecard in Romania 2010. http://www.indicatorideperformanta.ro/premium/rapoarte/raportul-studiului-balanced-scorecard-in-romania-2010-8.html
Value Based Management, Product Portfolio Management: Summary of the BCG Model. http://www.valuebasedmanagement.net/methods_bcgmatrix.html
Online information Platform. http://www.ebalancedscorecard.ro

The manufacturer's authorised representative in the EU is Springer Nature Customer Service Centre GmbH, Europaplatz 3, 69115 Heidelberg, Germany. If you have any concerns regarding our products, please contact ProductSafety@springernature.com

Printed and bound by CPI Group (UK) Ltd, Croydon, CR0 4YY
30/09/2026
02225309-0020